A PRIVATE TREASON

INGRID GREENBURGER

A PRIVATE TREASON

A GERMAN MEMOIR

LITTLE, BROWN AND COMPANY
BOSTON–TORONTO

SECOND PRINTING
T 10/73

Library of Congress Cataloging in Publication Data

Greenburger, Ingrid, 1913–
  A private treason.

  1. Greenburger, Ingrid, 1913–
I. Title.
PT3919.G7Z52   838'.9'1209 [B]   73-10046
ISBN 0-316-32666-6

Published simultaneously in Canada
by Little, Brown & Company (Canada) Limited

*To my sons, André and Francis,
and to my grandsons,
Michael and Holaran*

A PRIVATE TREASON

"Hurry!" Ljuba called from the barnyard. The horses were hitched.

"Coming!" I flew down the stairs and out the back door, climbed onto the runabout seat, and off we were in a rattle, Ljuba shouting to hasten the horses on. They tore down the rough forest road, neighing, making the buggy careen and bounce in the air. Ljuba sat, feet planted wide apart, counteracting the tossing and swerving with her arms and open hands, which loosely held the reins. "Raaaah . . . !" she sang out. A rich plume of summer dust trailed from the rear wheels.

We clattered full speed through Dravograd. Every head turned; Ljuba laughed. And then we were on the road that followed the course of the Drava River. The road was deserted, and only few and far between did houses show among the fields. The chain of green hills on the other side of the river made a hedgerow shielding the Yugoslav meadows from an Austria where Nazis now marched.

Ljuba finally pulled the buggy to a halt. She tethered the horses to a roadside tree and led the way through grass grown high, through sorghum, timothy and dandelion. We stepped across railroad tracks. Cows were grazing there.

We went up a rise to get a better view of the tracks, which now and then disappeared among the trees or behind a hillock. Squinting, we determined the spot where the train would make its first appearance, the Austrian

train that transited through Yugoslav territory, its doors
sealed.

I glanced at Ljuba, wondering whether the conductor
might not have changed his mind. He risked a lot, and
she hadn't promised him a reward. She did not believe
in bribes.

A week before, Ljuba had taken that same train in
order to talk the Austrian conductor into tampering with
one of the door seals so the fleeing man could jump
off. A week gave him ample time to reconsider the risk
he ran. "What if the conductor won't do it?" I asked.

A smile crinkled the corners of Ljuba's eyes. That
was all. Not the trace of a doubt. If only the man coming on the train could see her. As we waited, the stranger's fear sat in my throat.

"Now," Ljuba said, pointing at dark puffs of smoke
welling up from between distant trees and leaving a
growing dark ridge over them, like loose dirt tossed up
by a digging mole. We heard the train hoot, then it came
into sight. At once Ljuba was on her feet, shouting:
"There're flags on the engine! The gall! How dare they
fly their flag on Yugoslav soil!" The flags on each side
of the engine were as yet unrecognizable as such, they
looked more like a snail's feelers, but I, too, knew what
they were.

Ljuba stood uncertain, biting her lip. Her gaze moved
to the cows and suddenly she laughed. "You watch for
our man. As soon as you see him jump, get to him. The
password is 'Ljuba.' Run for the buggy and untie the
horses. If they come after him, take off, straight on.
Turn in at the first dirt road and stop at the farm there.
They know me."

"And you?"

Ljuba was off down the incline. What did I know

about handling horses? I ran after her, called out, but she would not listen. Arms waving, she yelled at the cows: "Yaaah, yaaah, yaaah . . ."

"Ljuuuu . . . baaa!"

The train's thunder was upon me. Its whistle shrieked. Red swastika flags filled my eyes, clutched at my stomach for a nauseating eternity. The click-click of wheels exploded in a fracas of braking, of hissing steam. The next moment, nothing. Then Ljuba's voice soothing the cows in Slovenian. Just as I caught a glimpse of all the cows only a few yards in front of the engine, I saw a man drop into the grass. I ran to him, said: "Ljuba."

"Ljuba," he responded and fell in with me. He was a poor runner, and when I reached for his hand, I saw how gray he was, an old man, certainly fifty. By the time we reached the buggy, he was flushed and out of breath. Why ask him whether he knew how to handle horses?

So far nobody was after him. The train stood knee-deep in the tall grass, as if a whole summer had passed in these minutes and the grass had closed in on it. A waving brakeman was shouting at the cows, but they stood motionless, on wooden legs.

"The woman!" my companion gasped. "There — on top the locomotive!"

Ljuba! A tiny jockey on a huge beast. Hunched over, she now crawled backwards and then disappeared from sight. She reappeared at the engine's wheels and calmly proceeded toward us. After some ten steps she stopped to look back at the brakeman yelling German orders at the Yugoslav cows. Ljuba watched. Was she laughing? And then I heard her call to the cows in Slovenian: "Go home, dear friends . . . go home, and thank you . . . go home, my dears." All the cow heads turned her way. "Go home . . . go home . . ." With some delay her words penetrated. The lead cow slowly turned around, and in the leisurely manner of cattle, the others fell in line. But they took their sweet time about leaving the tracks.

"That's Ljuba," I said to the refugee. She was coming through the high grass, so innocent-looking in her summer dress.

"I'm Ljuba," she said and reached up to shake hands with him. And as he bent toward her, he suddenly seemed much younger.

Ljuba handed him one of the captured Nazi flags. "One for you, one for me," she said. They tore them up and scattered the red bits in the grass. They looked like poppies. And somebody, passing through after us, may have added "poppies" that never were to the sum of his memories, to the landscape of his world. The error would scarcely have mattered. Of what man sees, of light and shadow and all the colors falling into his soul, he selects what to retain, and determines what to call it. He gathers only that with which he can prove that the world is as he sees it. And from the warp and woof of life he picks a thread here, another there, and weaves himself a dream. Yet, this world of his is true, for by creating it, he made it be.

My story tells of the warp and woof of one such dream cloth.

Is this fiction? Nonfiction? It seems people have to know. The publisher will ask, the booksellers and the librarians will ask. The reader will want to know.

The weaver cannot tell. The cloth is real to her. But then she isn't sure whether she herself is. She might be Man created in God's image, trying her own hand at creating. She might be but a second's ephemeral smile on God's grave lips, a brief pause in His eternal, irremediable loneliness. Or if He were a faceless cloud of hydrogen drifting through the darkness, would that make her something real, nonfiction, a tiny bang in the silence of space?

I have neither mother tongue nor fatherland. I lost both. I do not want them any more.

Once my mother tongue was like a tree outside my window, rustling in all my days and all my nights, teaching me to wonder, telling me to search.

The tree lies dead, hoodlums felled it and cut themselves clubs to kill with. The branches are brittle sticks on the ground. The dead leaves rattle. The rattling evokes the stamp of booted marchers and their rallying call to murder. I have no use for my haunted mother tongue.

The loss has crippled me. Writing in another language, I am a mountain climber with a peg leg. Yet the mountain calls, and fool that I am, I set out.

I do not miss the country I lost. When I hear *"Vaterland"* or *"Heimat,"* my heart draws a blank. That cruel winter killed my roots.

Long since, the Thousand Years' Reich has disappeared and so have its deadly divisions. Swastika banners are faded remains of a fall long gone, but within me the murderous flags will not fade, the sound of marching columns will not die. It is as though it was only yesterday that they pulled on their boots and armbands, smashed shop windows, and flung books on flaming pyres; only yesterday that with eyes burning with the hunger for national greatness they demanded fratricide, and a cowardly people responded with roars of *"Heil!"*

They had been my playmates, then my schoolmates. Of a summer day we had romped on the Wannsee beach, paddled our canoe under the hanging branches of old willow trees along the shore, and in the mysterious shade there, we wondered about life and kissed.

They tightened leather straps on bellicose chins. They sharpened switchblades and sang: "When Jewish blood drips from our knives . . ." Their faces pale and strained with ecstasy, their arms raised like swords toward the wind-whipped forest of screaming flags, they vowed to subjugate the world.

Nobody lit a peace candle. Germans poured into the night-dark streets to watch Nazi torchlight parades. The eerie light of the flames danced across the houses, reddened windowpanes — a preview of the hellfires to come. Wisps of smoke drifted across the sea of faces like lines of sooty writing, Satan's very own handwritten invitation to the *Götterdämmerung*. And for an RSVP thousands of throats burst into song: "We will march on after everything has gone to pieces . . ."

Run! Run! The blood they will spill will stain my own hands. Look at their faces, they lust after death. Don't waste time asking questions, don't reason, run! Run before it is too late. I know that suddenly it will be too late. I can't explain, but I sense it. I sense it, and that's all. Run, for God's sake, run!

What spared me having to live with a guilt I could not expiate?

Berlin . . . I had loved her sandy lands, her sparsely set, long-legged pines which, tall and straight, forever pointed at her unassuming skies, at wandering clouds that gave mysterious answers to the questions of my childhood years.

Berlin, my mother, died. She left her pale skies in my eyes, her lively pulse in my step, her ready laughter in my throat. And not altogether did she perish in the brown-shirted morass, for I, her child, escaped.

I loved her countless lakes, lakes that forever anew open into other lakes. Water everywhere, as if someone had spilled a sackful of silver coins. Berlin was flocks of white sails before the wind, peals of laughter from bobbing canoes. Berlin was weeping willows along the water's edge like the bowed heads of kneeling women, their long hair dipping in the wavelets.

In winter mysterious white mists veiled the frozen lakes. Shrieking and laughing, we children warily skated close to the shore. Once I let the lonesome, gray lake dare me and, undaunted by the loud crackling of the living ice, I skated on and on into the ever-deepening winter stillness, when all of a sudden I was seized by a profound terror, by a sense of the limitlessness of the universe. An angel set a slim silhouette on the ice not too far from me, a skater performing a serene ballet, tracing loops into the white air.

Berlin's streets, which I knew like the back of my hand, I have forgotten. Uhlandstrasse, Bayerischer Platz, Tauentzienstrasse . . . they won't take shape before my mind's eye. I must have wanted to forget Berlin, Berlin my love who betrayed me.

I found new *Heimaten*. Vienna, for one. Except that the zithers in Vienna's vineyards were already playing her swan song. Five years with Jan, new friends — just a day and a night, so it seemed, and it was all over. German bombers circled low above the roofs, warning the city to do as it was told. Storm troopers goose-stepped.

The rap-tap . . . rap-tap . . . of marching columns
was everywhere, all day long, all night long. And the
roars of *"Heil!"* And drunken rowdies storming houses,
herding their victims. Jews, kneeling in Vienna's Kärnt-
nerstrasse in sudsy water, scrubbed the pavement and
laughing SA men goaded them on.
"Heu-te . . . ge-hört . . . uns . . . Deutsch-land
. . . mor-gen . . . die . . . gan-ze . . . Welt." Rap-
tap . . . rap-tap . . . and the unrelenting rumbling of
Big Brother's planes.

Next a Dalmation island was *Heimat* for me, donkey
trails heavily scented with myrtle and thyme, white stone
walls hot from the sun, arid land washed by blue waters.

Home was a whitewashed room in the house of the
widows Ruška and Milića, half an hour's walk from the
small harbor town. At day's end I liked to go a way up
on one of the hillsides. There, I had a view of the flat
shoreland and the gentle sea below, and of the moun-
tainous mainland across the water. I would watch the
hues of sunset bewitch its barren rock, make it seem
weightless and translucent as if of glass, pink glass fading to yellow, then cooling to a limpid blue.

Dusk made the coast stone again, tragic stone, which
the swiftly falling night covered with velvety darkness.
And the mountain silhouette looked like a huge body
then, sleeping.

The island also covered itself with a cape of blackness, humbly effaced itself, allowing the star-silvered
Adriatic to engage in its nightly dialogue with the great
mother sea above. Stepping softly, I made my way downhill past pale stones, through warm darkness scented

with laurel. All around the air throbbed with the war-
bling of countless nightingales and over the flat shoreland lay the breath of the sea.

Someone moved along the path up ahead. Likely
Branko, going fishing. When the indistinct figure reached
my landladies' terrace, it was swallowed by the darkness
under the vine-hung pergola. If it was Branko, he would
now reach up to snatch a grape in passing. Ruška and
Milića in their bedchamber would hear his soft footfall
and the rustling of the vine. And visualizing the man's
hand that reached into their solitary life, their grave
eyes would smile.

The window of my upstairs room looked across this
leafy roof over the sun-parched, stony land unable to
slake its thirst with the clear, blue waters that licked its
shoreline. Many an afternoon I would see Branko in the
tiny lot that held his fig tree. I would see him bend down
and straighten up to place stone after stone on the rock
wall. Later, he passed by the house for a glass of water,
and Ruška and Milića would hand him a glass of wine.
His sun-furrowed face sweaty, he would sit under the
pergola.

Why did he slave in the hot sun, in the harsh glare,
for so little in return? Why not move to the rich fields
of Croatia?

Branko, squinting into the glare, laughed. He was
wedded to the island. She was given to him, for better,
for worse, for richer, for poorer.

"And you love her, don't you?"

Love her? How was he to tell? He could not quite
say where he himself ended and she began. Her sun-
hot stones under the soles of his feet every day, her
dusty stones in the palms of his hands have made them

one. If he folds his arm across his face to rest for a moment, he finds her scent emanating from his skin, her laurel, her thyme. Why dream of the rich fields of Croatia? His innermost being is bound up in his island, in the newborn light of her mornings, in the heat of her sultry days, in the translucency of her evenings, in the sway of her liquid skirt. Why ask why he carries her stony cross?

Branko laughed out loud to save face. Didn't the sea feed him? In long, breezy nights didn't she carpet his dory with silvery fish? Cool his hands? Soothe his strained eyes? And spreading about him her limitlessness, didn't she make him a free man? "Ay!"

On his return in the morning he would spill the sea's gifts next to the sink, casually, as if this, his daily bread, were a trinket found at play. Man's work was what he did later in the day, when with love in his heart, and obstinance, he defied the scorching sun, when, salty sweat on his lip, he toiled to make the stone bear fruit.

From afar, from another small lot on the rockwall-checkered hills, comes singing. Branko listens and then he shouts in the islanders' mournful way to that distant voice. "Draaa . . . go . . . miiiiiirr!" He sings out the other man's name in minor key, draws out the last syllable on a long, rising tone, and lets it finally fall off like a wail.

The islanders' strident, melancholy shouts that drag across the island at the end of the day have a ring of tragedy. Until I became used to them, they alarmed me. But in time I learned what the messages they made carry across the stony miles were saying. "Draaa . . . go . . . miiiiir . . . weeee . . . haaaave . . . ca . . . la . . . maaa . . . ry . . . for . . . din . . . nerrrr . . . you . . . are . . . wellll . . . coooome."

"I'll . . . beeeee . . . oooo . . . verrrr . . . Braaan
. . . kooooo . . ."
"Un . . . tiiiiil . . . laaaa . . . terrrr . . . Draaa
. . . go . . . miiiiir . . ."
"Un . . . tiiiiil . . . laaaa . . . terrrr . . . Braaan
. . . kooooo . . ."
And the distant voice would pick up the song once
again: *"Duni vetre malo se Neretve, pa rasteraj tamu
od Mostara da ja vidim moju milu malu . . ."* ("Wind
blow a little from Neretve and scatter the clouds over
Mostar so I can see my little darling . . ."

Morning brought a knock on my door: Ruška and
Milića, black kerchiefs wrapped tightly around their
heads. They showed me the empty marketing basket to
tell me they were going to town, and their grave eyes
asked: do you need anything?

I drew a fish on a piece of paper and a wine bottle.
I drew a tomato and wrote "4" beside it. I drew a loaf
of bread. The kerchiefed heads nodded. Ruška, the
tall, angular one, put her hand flat on the paper and
quickly lifted it to ask whether that was all. I nodded:
yes. She folded the sheet and slipped it into the pocket
of her loose, black cotton skirt.

I watched them go down the narrow, white path,
their backs straight, their black skirts swaying. Their
eloquent hands were busy again, accompanying their
ceaseless, husky-voiced chatter, which they had interrupted for a moment because I, poor stranger, didn't
understand their language. If I did not know their
words, I understood the language of their eyes. And I
knew that it meant they liked me when their brown
parchment hands presented me with an artichoke dripping with olive oil.

I reached for my canvas sack, checked its contents: pencils, eraser, watercolor box, water flask, brushes, rag. I added a chunk of bread and a bit of red wine. Somewhere among the stone walls I would sketch fig trees, or women leading donkeys.

Before noon I would make my way to the harbor town, to the pier beside the massive ramparts. Islanders and tourists alike, and the town's dogs and children, gathered there at noon to watch the southbound steamship moor and to scrutinize the new batch of tourists. The northbound came at four o'clock, but hardly anyone bothered to go, except those seeing somebody off. The noon gathering was a social event and one was sure to find anybody one was looking for. Once the steamer sailed on, everybody would drift to the Café Corso's sidewalk tables. Herr Schmidt would be in the noon crowd, nod greetings, say a word to this one and that one. He knew everybody. But at the café, he would sit alone, for he had no friends. Herr Schmidt was a Nazi agent.

Schmidt roamed the island like a stray cat, and on my walks I would inevitably encounter him. In the presence of others he was friendly to me and the other refugees. But when he happened upon us on a lonely path, he delighted in displaying the notebook in which I featured as a traitor to the *Vaterland* and to the "master race" I was born to. He would wave his book in my face and allude to coming victories.

We could not go to the local police and denounce him. In the eyes of the jittery authorities all of us were suspected of spying. We had to tread softly in order not to jeopardize the precarious hospitality extended to us.

Insecurity made us fearful, and our fears clouded our common sense. It didn't occur to us that it was unlikely that Wilhelmstrasse had a Herr Schmidt on its payroll solely to spy on one renegade German and a handful of escaped Jews. Then we heard rumors about secret fortifications or submarine bases in the rocky cliffs of the mainland coast, and we began to wonder whether Herr Schmidt was not spying on something of far greater consequence.

One morning we noticed Schmidt lolling in a rowboat midway between the island and the mainland, his field glasses trained on the empty rock. Was Yugoslavia earmarked for Austria's fate?

Periodically Schmidt boarded the four o'clock northbound, and would be gone for a couple of days. Instead of his faded cotton slacks, he wore an inexpensive, ill-fitting suit and a nondescript tie. From one such trip he did not return. Rumor had it that he had vanished from the boat en route, that he had been slipped overboard. Alexis, the owner of the Café Corso, insinuated that others of his kind had met with the same fate. Also from Alexis we learned that nobody had claimed Schmidt's belongings, and that they were so few that when Schmidt's landlord packed them to hand them over to the authorities, a single carton held everything.

Had Schmidt's notebook drowned with him?

Our small group of refugees stayed cautiously aloof from newcomers. Yet, watchful as we were, we didn't detect a new Schmidt, and we began to doubt that he had been a Nazi agent at all. This hungry-looking, poorly clad man might have been only a psychopath. And, embarrassed at our melodrama, we no longer talked about him.

I was at the fishermen's harbor looking over that morning's catch when someone grabbed me by the arm. "Quick," Erich Gold gasped. "He's come."

In long strides he led me to the end of the pier and, refraining from lifting his hand, he said: "Out there." Midway between the island and the mainland a man lolled in a rowboat, field glasses trained on the empty rock. A fishing rod was propped against the bow, but the man didn't check the line.

We sat on the pier wall waiting for the man to head for shore. We would intercept him to see who he was.

The sun beat down on us, the glittering water blinded us. One hour . . . two hours . . . In the distance a speck took shape. It was a northbound tanker moving very slowly. Another half hour went by before the ship came abreast of the island. Slowly she glided past, obliterating the rowboat. When she had cleared our view, the rowboat and the man were gone. Unbelieving, we scanned the water. Then the tanker was too far off for us to see what flag she was flying. It seemed she was making way much faster now.

At the Café Corso we tried to wash down with slivovitz the notion that we were sitting ducks in Yugoslavia. But where could we go? For a refugee the map of Europe held only closed frontiers.

When we could no longer bear the look in each other's eyes, we separated. I went to Mirko. His mother was as always downstairs cooking. In her black cotton dress and black kerchief she stood at the black stove in the half-light of the shuttered room. When she turned her proud, silent face, I greeted her: *"Dobra veča, gospodina,"* and hurried up the narrow wooden stairs. Mirko was in his small monastic room, reading. His faun's face welcomed me with an amused smile. Two blond curls stood up like small horns. "Listen," he said and picked up the volume of French poetry. I took the other chair and listened to him read verses by Rimbaud and Verlaine. My French was poor, and his had a strong Slavic accent, but I rested in the rhythm of the lines, watched his lips strain to pronounce the French "u," a sound foreign to his tongue.

The summer season ended. Mirko packed his frayed volumes of poetry, and together with the last tourists, he boarded the four o'clock northbound to teach in Zagreb. The sidewalk tables of the Café Corso stood deserted. Only the few refugees, who had no home to go home to, gathered there now to speak of those they had called friends for a season — "Crazy Boy" from Chicago, the three "Irish Kids," the cynical Köhlers from Cologne, Dr. Mihailovič, "Utrecht," Mirko. . . . "Let's keep in touch" . . . "Be sure to write" . . . "And should you happen to come to Belgrade, to Paris, to New York . . ."

Sirocco. Leaden clouds rolled low overhead, low across a sea that was a herd of black beasts with tattered, brilliantly white manes. The hotel on the bay had battened its windows and doors, piled brown sandbags around the empty white terraces. A group of kerchiefed women stood rooted to the pier, their ample black skirts fluttering in the wind as they stared at the evil sea for sign of their husbands' fishing vessel.

Sirocco's restlessness had driven me from the house. Its oppressiveness weighed on my chest like sorrow. The streets looked desolate. The Corso's sidewalk tables had disappeared. I braced against the airless wind sweeping the wet, battered shore road.

For a while I gazed at small, distant boats anchored offshore, bobbing wildly. When I could no longer bear the sultry wind, the gloomy sea, the lonesome boats, I scrambled uphill through brush and over stone walls. Then I turned inland along the road, walked head bowed into the wind and the dust it carried, strode out with determination as though I had a goal, as though there were a way out of my dead-end existence.

The inland hamlet, as though long deserted, seemed to be inhabited only by the wind. Lifeless windows reduced the small houses to stone belonging to the stony ground.

An ache in my chest, I sat on the church step in the relentless wind, wishing for tears, for release. Of a sudden I was on my feet, shouting into the wind, and arms wild, I jumped crazily among the dead abodes.

A door opened, an old woman beckoned. Her wilted hand drew me into the kitchen, poured a water glass brimful with warm, freshly distilled *rakja*. "*Živili,*" I said, raising the glass and downing all of it, a glassful of liquid fire. Had she called me in because she knew me? Her age-dimmed eyes did not speak. Nor could I find among the wrinkles a hint of pity for the dancing dervish she had invited. "I'll better be on my way," I said in German, translating with gestures, and adding: "*Dobra veča, gospodina,*" good night.

Gravely, she pointed at each of my eyes with a trembling, crooked finger.

What did she mean? Her stare unsettled me.

The withered lips moved soundlessly. The shaky hand made the sign of the cross over my face, and then it rustled over my hair like paper tissue. I kissed her and was out of the house, running down the road with tear-filled eyes. And when she could no longer see me I sat on a rock and wept.

Fall. St. Martin's Day children disguised as devils and witches leaped over crackling bonfires lit along the shore road, along the pier. The patter of their running feet haunted the empty streets. Whisk brooms and death masks demanded my small coins.

I turned homeward, leaving the goblins behind. The villas alongside were dark, and the voices from their waterfront terraces were only the memory of past summer nights.

Leaves rustled underfoot. Lines by Rilke came to my mind:

> *Wer jetzt kein Haus hat, baut sich keines mehr.*
> *Wer jetzt allein ist, wird es lange bleiben,*
> *wird wachen, lesen, lange Briefe schreiben*
> *und wird in den Alleen hin und her*
> *unruhig wandern, wenn die Blätter treiben.**

Where might I be come winter? Not on this summer island, I felt, but where?

The widows' dark house rose up, suddenly. Stepping on the smooth terrace, after the trek across rocky ground, was like coming into the stillness of a sheltered marina after a day out in rough weather. On my table I found a plate — tender, freshly dried figs with a sprinkling of almonds on a bed of grape leaves, a St. Martin's Day plate. Why could I not stay here? Why did I have to consider Hitler's next move? Why was my life determined by visas, residence permits, by the paranoia of Ministries of the Interior, by nervous officials? I wasn't

---

* Who has no house now, won't build one any more.
  Who is alone now, will long remain so,
  Will sit up late, read, write long letters,
  And will restlessly wander up and down the paths,
  When the leaves blow about.

a Trotsky, just a girl. All I asked for was that I might live under Ruška's and Milića's roof. The world was playing with me, letting the arsonist douse its cities with gasoline. It was that smell in my nose that made me take the four o'clock northbound, and from Susak the night train to Zagreb, even though I didn't know where I would go from there.

Zagreb's station was coppery in the glow of the rising sun, and Mirko had come to meet me. We drifted into the city's park, which at this early hour belonged to the leaf-strewn paths and to the silent pond. We sat on a bench and watched swans soundlessly gliding by.

"Where will you go?" Mirko asked. The hand stroking mine belonged to a fearful schoolteacher, not to the lightfooted Pan of that summer island. "France," I said, off the top of my head.

Go where?

I wandered down Preradovičeva all the way to the railroad station. I climbed worn, wooden steps, and from the narrow pedestrian overpass I looked into the station, at the travel-dusty Orient Express headed for Paris.

The locomotive, billowing white steam from under its wheels, had the mien of a preening peacock. Newspaper boys shouting headlines burst onto the platform. Their frenzied voices seemed to announce the end of the world, an earthquake, war.

The locomotive shrieked. Metal doors were shut in a wave of bangings. A hush fell, and the train stood with bated breath. Hands fluttered out the windows. Then car after car glided from the station twilight into the sun outside, and the Orient Express was off, off to France, leaving me at the iron railing of the overpass.

France . . . As though fate had dropped a seed into my mind. France . . .

Fate has ways and means to overcome obstacles, open border gates, provide an unattainable visa. But it takes its own good time, and first I was to be on a milk train that crawled from stop to stop to Ljuba's farm in the Slovenian mountains. She met me with the runabout and, horses neighing, we raced across the autumn valley. "France?" she mused. "We'll find a way." A smile crinkled the corner of her eyes, and she shouted to the horses: "Raaaah . . . raaaah . . .!"

March 1939. Czechoslovakia was falling to the Nazi invaders as the Orient Express brought me to France, to a Paris in mourning. Rain was beating her streets, was running down her buildings, dripping from her trees. An ominous sky cast a light of doom. Clusters of flags, the flags of the Entente Cordiale, were fastened everywhere. Although rain-soaked, their colors were strangely bright, glowing like bouquets of late-summer flowers. Sudden gusts churned the flags against cornices and ornaments, then pulled them loose again, making the wet cloth snap hard, like a volley of shots. Whistling gusts rippled the sheets of water on the pavement, beat the rain in my face. The tears of France blended with my own merely for the first time.

War strained to break out. Paris fitted its citizens with gas masks, ordered thousands of refugees to leave Paris. Foreign tourists, sunning themselves on the Côte d'Azur, left in droves, and distraught *hôteliers* were given penny-pinching refugees in exchange.

Once again, I was on a train. As the night express sped south, I peered into the darkness to catch bits of

France — a fence . . . a field . . . a row of poplars
. . . a road crossing . . . a kitchen garden. . . . Bleak
stations evoked long-gone geography classes, homework
hastily copied from a classmate's notebook — Dijon
. . . Mâcon . . . Lyon . . . Valence. . . . Weariness took me on a seesaw ride, dipping me into sleep,
bouncing me up again. Another gray station, empty plat-
forms: Avignon. *Sur le pont d'Avignon l'on y danse,
l'on y danse.* . . . The train moved on. Suddenly drow-
siness fell from me, and I peered into Provence's moon-
white night with a feeling of homesickness, as though I
had already lived through the years still to come, as if
yesterday and tomorrow were interchangeable, as if the
dry fields, the solemn stones, the silvery mist of its olive
trees already symbolized that which was yet to be given
to me, and I was irretrievably to lose. If it was fate that
whispered into my ear on the overpass at Zagreb's station, then it had me now where it could heap on me
the enchantments reserved for a heart in love, and then
take me into the soundless night of loss.

Had fate tried to tell me that my lot would inter-
weave with that of France when it made my birthday
July fourteenth, Bastille Day?

Perhaps a French fairy godmother stepped to my
cradle and endowed me with the spirit of *liberté, égalité,
fraternité*. Perhaps she whispered in my infant ear to
come to France when my *Vaterland* let me down. Did
she foretell that my fellow countrymen would riddle
André with bullets, and that I would be carrying his
child, never to lose either him or France altogether?

However, the Bastille Day on which such a fairy godmother might have stepped to my cradle was in 1913,

and World War I was to come first, the war to end all wars.

World War I was an old-fashioned war that took place at the front. I was spared the terror of howling sirens, of crowded cellars reeking of fear, of familiar streets smashed into rubble. And my father, rather than being a stranger on a photograph, came home to me every night. He was a newspaperman working in Berlin.

World War I lasted long enough for me to know that there was a war on. If I was too young to grasp its full meaning, I was able to observe that it made grown people weep. The war lasted long enough for me to enrich my vocabulary with "the enemy," "the front," "field of honor," "victory," weighty words veiled with mystery. War was Papa grumbling over sawdust bread, over *Affenfett*, Mama lamenting over rotten potatoes. War to me was one-legged men on crutches begging at street corners. The *Vaterland* had given them an iron cross for the leg they had lost in the *Schützengraben*, the trench. When Mama chatted with a neighbor or with women at the store, I would hear them say "our boys in the trenches," and my young mind made itself a picture of a weedy ditch somewhere in nowhere filled with the legs the one-legged men had lost there. Just as often the women mentioned the *Erbfeind*, the hereditary enemy. His name was *der Franzose*. They would pronounce the "z" with a sharp, contemptuous hiss, for *der Franzose* was cowardly, underhanded, unwashed, and promiscuous. If such adjectives were over my head, the women's tone of voice made it clear that *der Franzose* was a despicable breed.

Der Franzose was somewhere far away, no threat to me. What made my heart leap into my mouth were the black women, women wrapped in black from head to toe, faces concealed by black veils. When one drifted into the store, the shoppers' chatter stopped cold, and I grabbed Mama's hand even though Mama herself was in dread of the faceless apparition. The shopkeeper would hurriedly gather up what the wraith wanted, to make her leave as quickly as possible. Once she was out the door, the other women would take a deep breath, as if once again a great danger had passed. On one occasion I asked Mama what the black woman might do to us, but Mama only responded with a distressed *"Ach, child . . ."* and I did not dare pursue it.

World War I killed Uncle Ludwig, Mama's brother. I remember the day when he came home on furlough. That was early in the war, and I was not yet two. Yet that moment when Grandmama transferred me from her arm to Uncle Ludwig's open hands, hands reaching for me and gathering me to him, is a vivid picture etched into the very fiber of my heart.

The next time Uncle Ludwig was home on furlough, he sat motionless on a chair in his room, wouldn't look up or speak a word. It must have been in the hope that we little ones, whom he loved so much, would revive his shocked heart that we were taken to him. His deep-set gray eyes, however, didn't see us. They remained fixed on a picture only he could see and whose horror held him captive.

Nobody knew how to help Uncle Ludwig. It was a war too early for psychotherapy. Since his wound did not bleed, he received orders to report back to the front, to Verdun.

Verdun kept Uncle Ludwig to fertilize its battered fields with his rare talent and his visions; and with time its fields began to bloom with white crosses for miles on end. But wooden crosses do not bend in the summer breeze.

Uncle Ludwig was a sculptor, but he had to pursue his calling in secret. Grandpapa, who would not have it that a son of his became a "starving artist," had ordered Ludwig to channel his talent into architecture. Ludwig let his father believe that he was attending the university while in fact he spent his days at a sculptor's studio shaping lumps of clay into eloquent human faces.

After Ludwig had fallen on the "field of honor," Grandmama secretly went to see those Ludwig had been close to. She visited Ludwig's mentor, and she engraved in her mind the studio where Ludwig had been allowed to be the man he was. She went to see the young woman who was grieving for Ludwig as I was to grieve for André one war later. Grandmama brought some of Ludwig's sculptures home but had to set them up in the attic room where Grandpapa never set foot. He refused to be confronted with the proof of his son's disobedience. But Grandpapa commissioned a marble bust of the son he had loved and lost, of Ludwig as he wished to remember him.

The work was not entrusted to the sculptor who had only to glance at the now empty potter's wheel to see before him Ludwig's fine head, but to a stranger who had to rely on photographs. The sculptor of Grandpapa's choice must have studied the photos with much care, for he chiseled into the features of the marble head Ludwig's sensitive soul vulnerably exposed. And Grandpapa received the son he had failed.

The marble head was mounted on a pedestal and given the window corner of the dining room, whence it would look upon the family gathered around the table on Sundays. His glance turned inward, a forgiving smile on his lips, Ludwig endured our strained holiday meals.

I would steal into the dining room when nobody else was about to gaze at Uncle Ludwig, or to cry near him when I was unhappy. Heathen that I was, I directed my prayers to him, and it was Uncle Ludwig who answered them throughout my childhood.

When I was fourteen, I attended a boarding school that instilled in us a spirit of *Völkerverbrüderung,* the brotherhood of nations. While Hitler began to form his storm troops, we strapped blankets and tents to bulging knapsacks and traveled to Verdun to hike across the Meuse-Argonne battlefields. The gently rolling land there held neither farmhouse nor tilled field, only ruins and stumps of burned trees, and, amidst summer-dry grass, white crosses as far as the eye could reach.

As I made my way through the sea of crosses, I hoped against hope to come upon Uncle Ludwig's grave. Lagging behind the others, I read each name, French, English, German names, designations of German infantry divisions . . . U.S. First Army . . . U.S. Second Army . . . French Fourth Army . . . French Sixth Army. . . .

The sun scorched my head as it must have scorched the lips of the soldiers who had lain dying there. The grass rustled, insects buzzed, and I lost count of time, of crosses.

My eye caught a scattering of black — the others waiting for me, sprawled in the grass. Behind their black school berets stretched more fields of white crosses unending.

We proceeded to Fort Douaumont — a small grassy hill that had eyes, eyes through which human eyes had seen death come. We filed through the casemates. We gazed at what had been a trench, a shell hole. Mother Earth had spread a blanket of whispering grass and wild flowers over the blood-soaked ground.

We boarded a ramshackle bus and for yet more miles and miles we rolled across land cross-stitched in white. Blurred crosses swam in my tears, dropped upon my hands, and I fervently vowed: WAR NEVER AGAIN!

Hitler crushed my vow under his heel. German tanks, invading Czechoslovakia and Poland, mangled it. And German divisions ground it into France's soil. My heart was still heavy with the countless crosses of Verdun when I had to ask it to beat for World War II. Let it pound with distress, but it had now to beat for the peoples whose men and women were fighting and dying so that my murderous *Vaterland* might be checkmated.

France, as if she knew my heart, brought me one of her vanquished soldiers to love and protect until the day she had to ask me to give him back to her, because the price she was asked to pay for her liberation included his life. That day came on June 6, 1944, the day of Operation Overlord, the day when the U.S. First Division, the U.S. Fourth Division, the U.S. Twenty-ninth Division, the British Third Division, the British Fiftieth Division, the Canadian Third Division, the British Sixth Airborne, and the U.S. Eighty-second Airborne put the name Normandy, the names Utah Beach, Omaha Beach, Gold Beach, Juno Beach, Sword Beach with a branding iron on history.

André, under orders to lie low and wait for the time when experienced officers would be needed to harass the

Germans, was called to report to Vercors maquis headquarters.

He carefully checked the tires of his bicycle to make
sure that they would hold out on the rough roads of the
Vercors mountains. I made an inconscipuous roll of the
few things André was to take along: one shirt; one
change of underwear and socks; a cube of soap the size
of a die, our monthly ration; a small box containing a
supply of hand-rolled cigarettes; a pad of notepaper; an
apple.

How little man needs on his way to death. The
smaller his bundle of earthly possessions, the easier for
him to forget that what he might have to give up is the
whole world: the rustling of trees, the sound of voices,
looking into another's eyes, laughing, walking in the
wind, drinking water; and all he ever dreamed about;
all he meant to do; his being a man on planet Earth; his
striving to become Man.

War demanded that André think only of the bicycle's
tires; and that I make an inconspicuous bundle without
wondering whether one shirt would suffice. War demanded that our minds turn to liberation, away from
death.

Both of us on the same bicycle, we rode through the
meadows to the village for the last time. My seat was
the baggage carrier, and my hands were on André's hips.

We stopped at the tiny post office. Madame Giraux
dropped the postal window's bars to press André to her
heart. André took the motherly face between his hands
and kissed his *Résistance* comrade.

Across the street, at the *mairie,* Mademoiselle Anne
blessed André, her grave eyes responding to his exhilaration.

Two houses farther on, we were ushered into a small

living room, and under the gentle eyes of a white-gowned Jesus, the eyes of the Holy Mary and of four walls of saints, André promised a mother that he would look after her teen-age daughter, who had already left to join the Vercors maquis. But this young girl, too, was among the several thousand French youths who were soon to die on the Vercors.

We left the village on foot. We walked slowly, André guiding the bicycle with one hand. The sky was blue, the fields were in bloom, and the tremendous cliffs of the Vercors, rising from the Isère valley, were bathed in the sun. The land seemed to know that liberation was close at hand.

But when we reached the intersection with the *route nationale* and turned to each other, I knew with a sharp, irrefutable clarity that of all the last good-byes this was the final one. He gave me a puzzled look and took me in his arms. "But the war is over, Grenouille! The Nazis are finished."

I must not waste precious seconds, seconds that had to take the place of an entire life. I needed them to engrave the beloved face in my heart, his radiant, finely chiseled face with its volatile lines of sadness.

A last hug. André mounted the bicycle: Exuberantly he shouted to the fields: *"Nous les aurons!"* and he took off to his death.

He glanced over his shoulder again and again, waved. His arm stretched high, he jiggled his hand. He tilted his head back, and I knew he was laughing with the joy of life. He moved away farther and farther, waving once again. Then he kept his eyes on the Vercors mountain where they were to bury him.

By the time the U.S. Seventh Army reached the Dauphiné, André lay dead. The Vercors maquisards

lay dead, all except for a few. The villages and the ham-
lets of the high plateau were charred ruins, La Mure,
La Chapelle-en-Vercors, Saint-Martin, Vassieux-en-Vercors, the town of Saint-Nizier. . . . Their people had
been shot for giving milk and eggs to the maquisards.
In one village the Germans drove the women and children into the church, nailed up the doors, doused the
foundations with gasoline, and burned all to death. The
men hung from seesaw gallows or lay gunned down, as
the villagers of My Lai were by the sons of our liberators.

Mother Earth has covered the blood-soaked heaths
of the Vercors with a blanket of whispering grass and
field flowers. On the slopes where the maquisards died,
Olympic slalom skiers now gracefully trace lines in the
snow. Someday, perhaps, my son André will visit Saint-
Nizier to search among the rows of white crosses for
the one that bears his father's name, the father he never
knew, who was gunned down by his mother's people.

A killer's face does not bear the mark of Cain. Did
God see no need to provide for it? Was the God who
created man in His image a destructive God, a God of
devastation and wrath? Did He mean to create a killer
who, given time to learn, would blast the earth to smith-
ereens?

Why then would God have planted into man's soul
this longing for the beauteous path?

Those who seek to free themselves of the burden
of endlessly searching die within. They lose their sense
of direction, and their wanderings lead nowhere. They
walk on simply because they are on a road. But the first
fork will disconcert them. They will try to reason which
way to go; and not to feel so lost, they will pack to-

gether and declare that the majority vote is proof their
conclusions are correct. Walking on, they will shout and
sing loudly to keep their indefinable fear at bay. And
whosoever voices doubt, they will kill for the good of
all.

White crosses do not divulge whether beneath them
lies a killer or one who died searching for the beauteous
path. The crosses speak only of suffering and of the
mirages that fool man. Wind will stroke the grass.

World War I, the war that was to end all wars, ended
on a gray November day among the plank-and-sawhorse
counters of our neighborhood open-air market. Berliners, looking through baskets of yellow turnips and rot-
ting potatoes, straightened up as the word was passed.
Defeat! The kaiser in flight! They stared at each other.

"Kommt, Kinder," Mama said, reaching for Dalla
and me. She sat the oilcloth marketing bag on top the
baby carriage and made us hurry.

A woman caught her by the coat sleeve. "Revolution,"
she said. Mama shook free, and lips resolutely set, her
perky nose cutting the air like the sharp bow of a ship,
she steered a straight course for home.

Neighbors were gathered in front of our apartment
house — a flock of shaken birds. "Spartacists have bar-
ricaded a street over at the Hubertusallee." The word
"Spartacists" was new to me, but the wide-eyed woman's tone of voice insinuated that Spartacists were something bad, like *der Franzose*. Mama picked up Müsi,
our baby brother, and fled into the house.

Grandmama came. Mama made coffee. They huddled
on the sofa whispering breathlessly, and I overheard
Grandmama say that Spartacists ate little children. I
must have caught words out of context.

I don't know what compelled me to have a look at the Spartacists, but it is unlikely that curiosity got the better of my fear. All I remember is a sense of urgency, and that I went there with determination. To establish what? The fact that I took my Sunday coat indicates it was a mission of importance.

I sneaked away, softly pulled the front door closed, and tiptoed down the stairs. Once outside, I ran until I was around the corner and out of sight.

There was no way of avoiding the Waldpark. My heart in my mouth, I peered into the square block of winter-dead playland — gray, sandy ground, tall, straight-growing pines, their tops veiled in mystery by the November afternoon. Behind the bleak columns of tree trunks stood the spooky, boarded-up merry-go-round. With ghosts at my heels I flew toward the Hubertusallee. And there I lingered at the intersection to size up the two Spartacists at the barricade across the street. Wondering what?

I went over, looked up at the pale faces above pea-soup-colored mufflers, the kind German women had knitted at patriotic Kaffeeklatsches for "our boys in the trenches." The Spartacists wore soldiers' uniforms, but where the insignias of rank and unit had been, the cloth looked new, darker than the rest of the battle-worn, rain-bleached *Feldgrau*. They were sharing a cigarette, handing it back and forth. They inhaled deeply and, engrossed in it, their glances passed over me.

Is it possible that I remember the faces of the two Spartacists to this day? Was the memory kept alive because in the next war I was to see many faces like theirs, drawn, chilled, and with eyes sitting in shadowed orbits? These two happened to be called Spartacists, but their faces were the face of man enduring life.

When their cigarette was reduced to the butt, they stuck it on a pin and smoked it to the last shred of tobacco that way. Only then did they give me a glance, and one of them asked me whether I lived on the closed-off street. Intimidated by the gruff sound of his voice, I clutched the clay marbles that happened to be in my pocket, and suddenly my hand was up and the marbles on my open palm.

"For us?" asked the Spartacist with the raspy voice.

I nodded yes.

"What do you know!" he exclaimed. And his cold fingertips, gathering the marbles, scurried across my hand like mice feet. "Well, thanks ever so much," he said and gave one of the marbles to his companion.

I took off in a joyous dash. And skipping with gladness, I retraced my steps alongside the wooded Waldpark. That gladness kept the ghosts at bay, made me triumphantly glance at the boarded-up merry-go-round. Glad about what? I wish I knew, all I remember is the feeling.

Twenty years later I gave the Spartacists' pin trick a try. By then I was a refugee in France, and World War II had made cigarettes scarce. The pin trick didn't work. The cigarette the Spartacists had shared must have been a real one. The sorry butt of my hand-rolled cigarette held no last shreds of tobacco, only nicotine-stained, soggy paper. Even if rolled with care, such cigarettes thinned out toward the ends. The tobacco was dry crumbs, would not spread evenly, and tended to trickle out. It required know-how not to draw bits of tobacco with every puff. The tobacco was secondhand, retrieved from old butts. And when all we had was two butts, the cigarette we rolled was very thin, thin as a straw.

The original butts from genuine, manufactured cigarettes we carefully saved, and every smoker carried a
small box in his pocket, the *mégot* box. *Stummel* was the
Berliner's word for cigarette butt, and what a lowly
thing a *Stummel* had been. By the time I became acquainted with the French word *mégot,* it meant a precious possession. To offer a friend a couple of *mégots*
was to be generous. In war, squeamishness goes out the
window. We would pick up *mégots* from the street, or
from under the sidewalk-café tables. In those years, the
streets of France were not littered with *mégots,* so luck
was with us if we happened upon a couple of black mar-
keteers who did their wheeling-dealing at our Café
Littoral. They smoked real cigarettes and carelessly
dropped the butts under the table. We would occupy the
tables around such happy smokers, hail passing friends
to increase our force and help bar outsiders from getting
a wedge in. Sipping Vichy water, we counted the butts
falling to the floor, and as soon as the smokers left, we
descended on the harvest like a flock of voracious birds.

Why not quit smoking?

We were hungry. A cigarette pacified our empty
stomachs. We feared the landlady because we chronically owed rent, and a smoke gave us the courage to pass
her door. A smoke gave us the courage to face the
grocer, to ask him once again to give us our oil ration
on credit. And when we tapped the town's electric lines
because ours were temporarily disconnected, we needed
a cigarette to steady our nerves while dinner cooked on
a hot plate heated with borrowed current. We needed a
cigarette to endure the uncertainties of our refugee
existence, and to keep alive the sweet illusion that the
Allied invasion was imminent.

When we had no *mégots,* we smoked rose leaves, corn

silk, linden blossoms, kitchen herbs. All tasted ghastly. And when we got hold of a real cigarette, we would share it with our best friend or friends, pass the cigarette around as the Spartacists had done.

The winter of the Spartacists also brought me face to face with *der Franzose*. This shapeless boogeyman was heralded by a powerful wind that tore through our living room and Papa's study, leaving chaos. Papa and Mama and our old nurse Wawa ran this way and that, grabbed pieces of furniture, heaved, pushed the sofa up-ended into another room. The dining table was moved, Papa's leather chair. Rugs were rolled up and unrolled. The pieces of a bed were carried into Papa's study and reassembled there. And a chest of drawers took the place Papa's desk had vacated. Wawa washed the curtains and pressed them. Mama came hurrying with an armful of bedding. Papa took down pictures and hung up others. Wawa lined drawers with fresh paper. Mama polished a mirror, spread a fringed table throw, moved a vase from this spot to that, plumped cushions. Then she stepped back and gravely evaluated the room requisitioned by the Armistice Commission for *der Franzose*. I can't recall whether I was curious or apprehensive.

Dalla and I made our curtsies to a slight Capitaine Reveault and his wife, the most astonishing-looking wife I had ever seen. German wives had an air of authority. They proudly balanced a mass of hair waved with hot curling irons. The diminutive wife of *der Franzose* clung to a puppy dog, and her terrified eyes tried to hide behind the bangs of her dark pageboy bob. Since only children wore short hair, I stared at Madame Reveault in utter amazement.

Perhaps she had been told that Germans ate French-women, for she would never leave their room while the Capitaine was away. She slept until noon, and then we would hear her talk in rapid French to her puppy.

The Capitaine brought their provisions home, and Wawa cooked for them. Even though they had their dinner late, when we children were already in bed, the delicious smells from the kitchen kept us awake, and we counted the recurrences of Wawa's busy footfall to and from the Reveaults' room — hors d'oeuvres . . . soup . . . main course . . . dessert . . . coffee. . . . Finally Wawa would be at our door, whispering into the dark room: "Are you asleep?" As though catapulted out of our beds, we dashed to the kitchen, nighties flying, to fall over a morsel of pâté de foie gras, a slice of roast, a lick of Hollandaise sauce, and our three fingers competed to wipe up what was left of a foamy lemon pudding. We did not have to go to bed hungry, as French children would in the next war, but since our wartime fare then consisted mainly of cabbage, yellow turnips and gray potatoes, we feasted on the flavors clinging to the Reveaults' bowls and platters.

And then Christmas neared. Each day we opened one of the small windows on our Advent calendar. The Sunday windows were larger than the weekday windows and instead of a transparent red backing they had a picture of a pine branch with a burning candle. We could scarcely wait to reach the last window, the largest of all, the Christmas window, which would hold a picture of the manger and of the kings bringing presents to the infant Jesus.

German Christmas is celebrated on Christmas Eve, and the twenty-fourth of December was for us children the longest day of the year. Wawa was busy in the kitchen, from which we were barred that day. And our mother would stay behind the closed doors of the Christmas room. Secretly she decorated the tree, filled Christmas plates with spice cookies, nuts, and apples rubbed to a high polish. Rather than wrapping our presents, she arranged them on tables amidst pine branches, goodies and candles.

We, who were never at a loss for things to do, suffered through that unending day, languishing at the window, peering at the gray winter sky. We breathed on the cold panes, cleared little peepholes, and stared and stared, wishing that darkness had already come. Finally we heard our father come home, but on this day we were not allowed to rush to the foyer to greet him. Straining in the doorway we called him with high-pitched voices, but his footfall and a rustling of paper moved toward the living room.

Wawa, her face flushed from the heat of the oven, hurried us to the bathroom, washed us, brushed our heads, laid out fresh underwear, our Christmas dresses and Müsi's white sailor suit. My glance strayed to the window filled with the dark of night and for a breathtaking second I saw the face of Santa Claus.

The Christmas bell tinkled. Suddenly shy, we filed into the light of flickering candles, into Christmas scents — fresh pine, apples, cinnamon and cloves, vanilla and anise, candied peel and ginger. The glittering tree made me catch my breath. Mama, at the piano, played *"O du fröhliche, o du selige, gnadenbringende Weihnachtszeit,"* and we gathered around her to sing Christmas carols. Singing with trembling lips, I fastened moist eyes upon the doll longing for my arms.

Later there was a soft knock on the door — Capitaine Reveault. He put into each child's hands a bar of chocolate and an orange. *"Fröhlike Weihnakten,"* he said, and at his funny pronunciation we burst into happy giggles. He blushed, we blushed, and we curtsied, and he stroked our heads, wiping away notions that *der Franzose* is bad.

Grandpapa as well was getting a *Franzose* of his own. When the Armistice Commission requisitioned one room in his spacious villa, he behaved as though he were being dethroned. The war had been enough of a dilemma to him. It had forced him to call the nation of Voltaire enemy, to ban French wines from his table, to bury his admiration for French enlightened thought six feet under patriotism, to bear the loss of a son. He had done all that, done his duty, done enough. It was adding insult to injury to ask him to expose himself to the vexing experience of billeting a Frenchman who might not be his sort of Frenchman, might possibly lack refinement, not know his Molière, his Montaigne, his Madame de Staël, might not be cut of the cloth of a Voltaire.

We arrived at the usual Sunday dinner burning with curiosity about Grandpapa's *Franzose,* but we had barely come through the door when Grandmama hushed us with fluttering hands. "Not a word about *der Franzose, Kinder.* There *is* no *Franzose* in the house. You understand, there *is* no *Franzose* in the house."

We understood. We were used to Grandpapa's incomprehensible decrees. And it scarcely puzzled us when Grandmama added with as much emphasis that we were to curtsy respectfully should we encounter the gentleman, greet him by addressing him by his rank and name, and if spoken to answer politely.

In the course of the day we observed secretive signals

exchanged between our grandparents, no more than an intangible something in their glances, which would have gone unnoticed had we not been cautioned. It was clear to us that Grandmama stepped into the hall to ascertain whether Grandpapa might safely go upstairs or across the hall to his architectural office. We froze each time in the effort to appear ignorant of these maneuvers. Had our faces betrayed us, Grandpapa would have ridiculed all of us, would have denied everything. Had he said as much as one word regarding the Frenchman? Of course he hadn't, Grandmama had. Had she perhaps failed to convey to us his wish that we show the stranger every courtesy? No, she had conveyed that. So?

We knew better, but that was immaterial. He ruled us, a fickle king whose word was law. He was the all-powerful puppeteer who manipulated us according to his momentary fancy. Nobody ever dared to challenge him. What mattered was to make it through Sunday by alertly avoiding the traps he set. It was a great strain.

I should have felt free and at ease Monday through Saturday, but so strong a personality was he that he was present even when he was not on the scene. He could be miles away and I would feel his disapproving stare between my shoulder blades. And since I felt it most of the time, I was burdened by a perpetual bad conscience.

Perhaps my strength had elements of his, for I took revenge, challenged him by taking liberties, though preferably in his absence. What pleasure to hold my fork improperly, knowing that it would thoroughly shock him could he see me. I got even with him by turning the pages of a book carelessly, by running down the street shrieking, by saying "what?" instead of "I beg your pardon." Such minor infractions gave me a sense of delicious triumph over him, made me feel free of him, made me feel as if I had showed him, the high and mighty, that he could rule me on the unavoidable Sunday only, when all of us, children and grown-ups alike, had to kowtow, reduced to puppets he made tiptoe across the stage of his whims.

Of my rebellion, he made naught. He forced his rules of conduct upon me insidiously, and one day, years later, I was to realize that the criteria I called mine were in fact his. I have modernized them, but they are still his. My book of etiquette is a relaxed one. But when I am exposed to graceless manners, Grandpapa within me will jump like a Jack-in-the-box.

He was a tall, trim man who moved with studied grace and who gestured with restraint. Although he had considerable charm, he was reluctant to display it, as though we were not worthy of the full extent of it. His refined demeanor would remain unimpaired even at his nastiest. He would not raise his voice in anger, nor deviate from his impeccable language while he smote us with his disdain.

He read much. When he was kindly inclined he would impart to us the beauty of a prose line, or a well-formulated thought. He was a sensual man who would touch a sculpture to feel a curve, who would run a carefully manicured finger along the lines of a drawing. His enlightened mind was a searching one. He was, I believe now, a man longing for the beauteous path, but was caught in a web of conflict within himself. What a strain it must have been on him to find a *modus vivendi* for the contradictions he harbored.

He was a Freemason. We knew which trunk in the attic held mysterious Freemason whateveritmightbe, but we didn't peek or ask Grandpapa what Freemasonry stood for. That subject was taboo, too sacred to be talked about with anyone.

His social attitudes were Victorian. His mind's companions were Goethe and Voltaire. To what point he agreed with them I can't say, for what he said to us for educational reasons and what he believed were not necessarily one and the same. He was haughtily individualistic. He kept what he held true an untouchably private matter. He accounted to no one. Of God he did not speak.

Since I felt besieged by my grandfather throughout my childhood, I kept him under close observation to forestall, to be prepared. In time, my alertness for his next move, his next switch of mood, turned into searching for what lay hidden. And what I detected in his face at an unguarded moment left me wondering. It seemed that my devil-ridden grandfather struggled to measure up to some high ideal. Perhaps the goal he had set himself was unattainable, the flesh too weak to keep pace with the yearning spirit. As he was too proud a man to lower his harsh demands, he suffered. Perhaps the pressure of his frustrations and his dissatisfaction with himself vented themselves in the volatile moods and tyrannical whims that were the cross of his loved ones. As characteristic as they were of him, they stood in flagrant contradiction to the man who was otherwise so extraordinarily disciplined, in his work, in his habits, in his contacts with outsiders, in his physical demeanor, his every gesture, his poses, his gait. And never, not ever would he show or mention that he didn't feel well. Was his moodiness really lack of self-control or was he, imprisoned in his conflicts, begging us to come to his aid? At times I wondered whether Grandpapa, my adversary, wished, but could not bring himself to say, that he loved us.

As a young child I saw only the waves that tossed me. I bitterly resented that he held a license for being delightful now and obnoxious a moment later. I rebelled at being denied any resort, at having to submit in utter helplessness. And to see even the grown-ups submit to him, allow him to cut off their conversation if the turn it took displeased him, made my own helplessness take on unbearable proportions.

I choked with the urge to rebel. But any expression of it, if only politely voiced disagreement, was unthinkable, and the slightest sign of it was instantaneously snuffed. For putting me in my place, Grandpapa had a fiendishly effective line: "Poor, stupid little Ini." He smote me with "poor, stupid little Ini," burned it as with a branding iron into my heart.

I can't believe that he intended to stigmatize me, to cut me down so small that I should harbor for life the nagging ache of my worthlessness, to the point that I would never ask myself to accomplish anything.

Was he convinced that I could take it? That the tears he made me shed were good for me, would nourish my strength? They did, Grandpapa, but you played a dangerous game. You did not cut me down, did not make me turn aimlessly in neurotic circles, but you slashed deep, deep, and to this day the old scar hurts when strained. If I grew strong fighting you, credit for it I claim for myself. Pushed down by you, I stood up again countless times.

I faced Sundays with dread. I entered my grandfather's house with a bright battle flag in my heart, but more often than not also with wet panties. My mother wouldn't think of setting out without taking changes along both for Müsi and me. Dalla's apprehension produced nosebleeds. Once she bled so profusely halfway between Grunewald and Lichterfelde West that Mama had to make her stretch out on the sidewalk to protect the Sunday dress from the bloody flood.

Grandmama received us, worry-eyed. A pretty band was slipped over Dalla's and my head to keep our hair in good order. My whole being revolted against that silk ribbon as though I were put in chains, and shackled I was, for the ribbon symbolized all the rules of conduct I had best heed. I loved to run fast, light-footedly, to skip, leap, tumble, but here I was not permitted to rejoice. I was to be a pleasure to Grandpapa's eyes.

It remained a mystery to me how he, behind the closed door of his study, could know when we were finally neat enough to be greeted by him. No signal was given. But at that exact moment the door opened and there he was, tall, impeccable, viewing us benevolently, a lopsided smile on his full lips, a smile of superiority, of reluctant kindness, of resignation that once again we should fall short of his expectations. The ritual demanded that one child after the other rush to him joyfully and lovingly reach up to kiss the cheek he lowered in such a manner that it almost remained out of our reach. And with the kiss we had to twitter: "Good day, dear Grandpapa."

Of course I rushed, and reached, and kissed, but the "dear" would sometimes simply not come to my lips. Hurrying through the greeting, I hoped he would not notice that one word was missing. He always noticed. He would remain stiffly inanimate until I repeated the prescribed phrase, the "dear" included. When his victory was won, he would give me a pitying glance and say: "Poor, stupid little Ini." Helpless before him, I would grin sheepishly, but inside I burned. I ached to scream into his face that I was not poor, not stupid, not stupid at all, but that he was simply not *dear* to me. But speaking up was inconceivable. No matter what he did or said, our response had to be: "Yes, dear Grandpapa." And when he reduced me to nothing, I had to smile politely. No one contested his right to rule us as he pleased.

I might have rammed my fists into him one day had it not been for the swing in the backyard. The swing, my magic swing, helped me endure Grandpapa. I would run for it as a hurt child runs for its mother. Sobbing hard, I would sadly rock to and fro, and the screech . . . screech . . . of the swing's iron rings would be companion to my weeping. To and fro . . . to and fro . . . surrounded only by trees and bushes. From the tear-blurred branches peace flowed into me, and soon my yearning for the feel of freedom would get the better of my anger and pain, and I would grip the ropes and push off hard, work the swing higher and higher, give it all I had until I seemed to be flying into the tree crown, into the white clouds. Wind in my hair and the damn ribbon to the devil, I would sing loudly, sing away oppression. And then I would sing sweetly, make believe I was a famous singer facing an auditorium with a breathless audience. And when, eyes moist with emotion, they burst into a roar of applause, I had Grandpapa licked.

After I had withstood my most powerful grandfather Sunday after Sunday throughout all my childhood years, I was an old hand at holding my own when the all-powerful Herr Hitler appeared on the scene. His branding me "traitor to my country" ran off me like water off a duck's back. Coming from his mouth, the words never took on any meaning. As to what I owed my country, I had my own ideas: to stand up to be counted as one of the Germans who would not say yes to Hitler. "Traitor to my country" was savorless ersatz for "poor, stupid little Ini." "Stupid," Herr Hitler, "stupid" was my Achilles' heel.

Even for that word he came too late. My grandfather had hardened me to it. I don't thank him for that, since I do not know what motivated him, and the price I paid was high. But I have forgiven Grandpapa because he is no longer here to explain.

I do thank Grandpapa for having instilled in me a sense of *noblesse oblige:* I could not join the hunters of the defenseless. I thank him for having been an example of proud independence; had I fearfully run with the crowd, shouted what they shouted, my mind would have been haunted by Grandpapa's sneers. I thank him for having been such a stickler for manners and conduct; it is impossible to murder with propriety. I thank him for having given us a clear picture of a civilized human being, according to which Hitler was a foaming hyena, ridiculous rather than awe-inspiring. His speeches, which sounded like the lowly ravings of an *agent provocateur,* could not capture me. What a German under the Nazis was asked to do or acquiesce to, Grandpapa had labeled indecent. This undramatic word sufficed him to mark for us anything immoral, unethical, ignoble, unthinkable. And no measure of rebellion against him would have let me risk giving him cause to call me indecent.

The day I went to see my grandfather for the last time was an ordinary weekday, for by next Sunday I was to be far from Berlin. As I approached his house I again and again felt the need to take a deep breath.

How was I to tell him that I was leaving Germany for good? How was I to make him understand? He won't even hear me out. He will raise one eyebrow, twitch his jaw muscle, his signal for telling me that he did not wish to hear any more about a matter. Or he might cut me off with a small, inpatient flick of his hand, or totally ignore my words, put on a Mozart record and force me to listen in respectful silence. Surely, he will not allow me to say what I came to say. To him it was poppycock. "The Nazis?" he might say as if he had not heard correctly. And then haughtily: "I don't concern myself with scum."

If I was to find him in a mellow mood, my words might elicit a smile, that condescending smile involving only half of his mouth. He might ask me with that cutting tone of voice what exactly I meant by "leaving Germany." And he would give me that pitying look, pitying me for my stupidity.

But I have to tell him, I have to.

Maybe I should explain all of it in a letter. And have him remember me as a coward?

Grandmama received me, her eyes, as usual, puddles of worriment begging for a clue to the crisis she needed to prepare herself for. Grandmama lived a life of anticipating crises. I did not have the heart to tell her of what magnitude the crisis of this afternoon would be. I avoided her eyes, ashamed to let her down.

Grandpapa greeted me warmly. To see him so pleased over my coming unnerved me.

Even though he was in his eighties, he carried himself erect, and his step was as light and decisive as it had always been. Yet he looked suddenly aged. Was it a certain weariness in his haughty eye? The strong, willful features seemed delicate, strangely serene. Was it the afternoon light? Had the wing of death already brushed his brow and wiped away the scorn of a lifetime? His gentle tone pained me.

Grandmama served tea. I was grateful for the minutes of small talk that allowed me to rehearse the opening sentence I had prepared.

Grandmama removed the dishes, and as soon as we were alone, Grandpapa's eyes bluntly challenged me to come out with what I had come to say. His forthright stare cut into me and made my voice unsteady. "Tomorrow I'm going to Vienna, Grandpapa."

The gray bristles of his eyebrow arched. "You are matriculated, the universities are in session, yet you are home and talking about traveling? What is your explanation for so much erraticism?"

"I'm leaving Germany."

"To study at the University of Vienna? You can't. Monetary restrictions prohibit the transfer of monies to foreign countries."

"I know. I won't be able to continue my studies. But I'm leaving. . . . I leave Germany for good."

"Are you." His tone was caustic, his eyes like hard pebbles. "I don't recall any such plan having been discussed."

"The decision was mine."

He laughed. "Fortunately you have parents and grandparents who will see to it that you stay where you belong."

"At first I felt it would be running away, but now I know there's nothing anybody can do against the Nazis and —"

"Spare me your childish political views."

What did he know of my views? I had never dared to speak to him about them, and at present I no longer knew what my views were. Too many of my questions remained unanswered, leaving me troubled. And he would be the last to try seriously to help me understand the world.

"The Nazis will force me to join up. Because of my looks. . . . I'm a living Nazi poster, Grandpapa."

He winced, barked: "You're speaking to your grandfather!" After collecting himself he said: "At the university you kept company with Communist students. Are they leaving the sinking ship like rats? Is it they who now make decisions for you?"

"No. They consider it cowardly to leave." They still believed that they could fight the Nazis with leaflets and by painting slogans on walls. Some went into the woods at night with amateur radio transmitters and broadcast speeches against the Nazis.

"Many don't consider it cowardly to exchange the red shirt for a brown shirt," he said. "Surely you have seen the stands the Nazis have set up in the streets, the posters and streamers inviting the Communists to sign up for the storm troops and all will be forgiven. Birds of a feather flock together. Have you noticed how long the lines are?"

I had. Long lines of grim-faced, shamed men, shuffling toward the stand with hanging heads. When their turn came, they signed up and received their brown shirt and their pair of boots, and food rations for their family. They had been on welfare for years, living in garden huts. "They do it for the food, Grandpapa, for their children," I said from the need to give the turncoats a measure of justice. "They're beyond caring, Grandpapa."

He shot a quick glance at me. Furious? Or puzzled what to say to someone as stupid as I was? "I sympa-

thize with what you feel," he said softly, "but your
conclusions are wrong. It requires much knowledge to
understand matters of politics and economics. For you to
even try is preposterous. You have everything you need.
You will go back to your school and study. That, and
nothing else, is your duty to yourself and to society.
Isn't that so, Ini?"

That kindly spoken plea made me burst into tears,
and stammeringly the truth poured out of me. But what
I really felt was too vague, too emotional to be to my
grandfather reason for leaving Germany. "I feel like
I'm in a nightmare, except it isn't a nightmare, it's real.
Something has me by the throat all the time. I feel that
something horrible is closing in on me. I don't know
what, but sometimes I think I could touch it if I put my
hand out. I'm filled with such dread. I can't sleep. At
night I see in my mind's eye streets littered with dead
people, dead people everywhere."

"We must not allow dread to get the better of us.
We are aghast at this hoodlum regime, but we must let
reason prevail."

"I feel that if I listened to reason I'd be trapped.
Something is warning me, urging me to leave before it
is too late." Grandpapa peered at me as if he might
find in my face what I was unable to formulate. "Grandpapa, they're killers, they're insane, the way they march,
the way they speak, their eyes, they'll do anything he
tells them to do. All day long they march. That awful
sound . . . it's wherever you go. I hate to leave the
house, and if I have to, I run in dread of meeting another column of marching storm troopers. And then I
hear them and know there's no escaping them, they're
everywhere, marching, marching. And everybody is
frightened, nobody dares not to salute them, but I won't,

I won't do it. I'd feel as though I was surrendering to them. Last night our street was full of SS running in and out of houses, cellars, hunting someone. They were shouting like drunkards. They were blowing whistles. They had dogs. I can't bear it, Grandpapa. And it isn't a matter of politics, it is not. It is something awful. I won't be trapped here."

"Ten marks is all you're allowed to take out. You don't know what it means to be penniless, alone. You are not prepared for that, it will crush you."

"Their flags and their loudspeakers and their faces crush me. I'm sick to my heart and sick to my stomach. And I'm also terrified. They force people to inform on others. They beat people to death to make them tell what they know. I don't know what I would do, I'm frightened, I don't want to die, Grandpapa."

He sat with bowed head, as if all alone. I wiped my wet cheeks, relieved at admitting my fears. Of course, I was unable to name what I sensed. How could I have envisioned what was to stagger the imagination of mankind? I was a field mouse on the ground who sensed the falcon circling.

Grandpapa's voice came softly. "If I were younger," he said, "I might leave with you." A sharp ache clutched my throat. And as if with that everything was said, we sat in silence. Dusk settled in the room. Grandpapa's hair gleamed white. Our hands were on the table, two pairs of strong hands, his gouty, the joints knobby, but strong nevertheless, mine young, still slender, but stronger than a girl's hands are as a rule. Then he spoke. What he said was both familiar and new, new because of his effort to convey to me, at this very last opportunity, what mattered most to him. Time was short. He could give me only the essence of what he had gathered in a lifetime. And I listened, aware that sentence by concise sentence, he was handing me my inheritance.

"Promise," he said then, as I stood before him like a young knight before his king, "that you will uncompromisingly defend what you hold dear. Always. Whether the course you take is deemed foolish or wise by others, never be deterred from that road which is uniquely yours." I promised.

"You are the one I am proudest of," he said and locked me in his arms. All my growing years I had craved for so much less. Now I could not rejoice; pain at having to give him up tore through me. But when I said "Farewell, dear Grandpapa," the obligatory "dear" for once came to my lips of its own accord.

Poor Grandmama was no match for Grandpapa. She was his foremost victim. I pitied her, but often my pity yielded to exasperation. And since much of my energy went toward defending myself, I had not much to spare for her, who gave up long ago. As a child, it didn't occur to me that she might not always have been a victim par excellence, that the now-tired eyes might have shed many bitter and angry tears.

A picture of my grandparents, taken in the early years of their married life, shows her as a well-put-together young woman. She is sitting up straight on a chair, her girlish hands a bit unsure on her legs. He is standing beside her, very self-assured. Her sweet face has a generous mouth and a good chin, but it is the face of a girl, not that of a young woman. On her lips lingers a touchingly innocent smile, and her round eyes under delicate, arched brows are utterly guileless. She radiates such an air of virginity that one must assume she slept through her husband's caresses, perhaps dreaming of holding kittens in her lap. In the picture she wears a high-collared, long-sleeved dark wool dress that is almost puritanically demure. But two rows of small buttons underline the curve of her shapely bosom, and the rich folds of bold plaid swelling over a *cul de Paris* bring the viewer to speculate on the young lady's behind. The smart plaid tail must have been a concession to Grandpapa, for Grandmama's hairdo indicates that she was neither fashion-minded nor vain. Her finely textured hair, parted in the middle, modestly brushed upward all around and pinned in a neat flat bun, reminds one of a collapsed soufflé. Downy fuzz makes the hairline indistinct and contributes to her air of innocence. Surely, she was totally unsuspecting of what lurked in the strong-minded young man who came to ask for her hand. And what an awakening once she found out that he was a temper-ridden child, who rather than guiding and protecting her, taunted and intimidated her into the role of a caught, harassed mother. I was not to see any more the guileless eyes that must have liked to laugh. By my time they had taken on a hunted look, her dreamy lips had withered, and her gentle hands fluttered restlessly.

She was not the kind of grandmother I wished for, one who would cuddle us. Besides, her puritanical sense of duty demanded that she instill in us what she found so disastrously lacking: humility, renunciation, modesty, frugality. Her teachings failed to win me. Her sorry example was a warning of where her philosophy would get me. Also, she had little occasion to do her duty by us since she was always preoccupied with Grandpapa, always apprehending the next mood, the next command, the next sign of his disapproval of her. Her brows worriedly arched, she scurried about like a lost soul. She had put her head on the sacrificial altar of her marriage long ago and allowed her husband to harass her as though she were atoning for a grievous sin. His inventiveness knew no bounds, and since his architectural offices were in a wing of their house, he harassed her all day long. Housecleaning had to be done invisibly. At the sound of his footfall, Grandmama had to make the maid and her cleaning paraphernalia vanish from sight, for Grandpapa wished not to be bothered by the thought that the hands that served him at dinner had scrubbed floors, dusted, polished brass knobs.

In the game Grandpapa played, Grandmama was a lady of leisure. As if it were an indulgence to make her feel needed, he had designated to her tender care certain small tasks. Whatever she was doing she had to have her ear cocked for his call, and when she hurried to him, neither her attire nor her appearance was allowed to betray that she had been busy with household tasks. She was his, and he wished not to know that she had any purpose in life other than doing him small favors. He contended that she alone knew how to adjust the blinds just right, how far to open the windows so that his blueprints were not blown about. Only she was allowed to sharpen his pencils because she did it with tenderness. Only she was mindful enough to place a stamp on an envelope with an eye to the well-balanced arrangement of address, stamp and margins. Since he abhorred the clatter of typewriters, they were banned from his office. His exquisitely handwritten letters were multiplied on an old-fashioned copy press, and it was Grandmama who had to do it because she handled his letters lovingly, not in the matter-of-fact manner of his assistant. When she came in answer to his call he smiled magnanimously and praised her as one would a half-witted child.

Even greater demands were put on her when the telephone company installed dial telephones. Grandpapa raged. How dare the telephone company interfere in his way of life, rob him of the operators' voices, which had brought to his days a touch of mystery. He had given names to those disembodied females, even had a favorite, Helena. And before lifting the receiver he always made a quick guess whether it would be her voice saying: "Your number, please." Deprived of them, Grandpapa refused to dial. He sulked for several days. Then Grandmama was elected to do the dialing for him. "Julie . . ." He did not have to shout. If his voice did not carry to where she was, she would sense that he called and rush to him. She had to run often now, for Grandpapa was an active man. And he would watch her dial, an amused smile on his lips. The new game began to compensate him for the loss. Her duty done, Grandmama would run from the study to yield to the choking that increasingly plagued her. Yet Grandmama tended the rampant vine that was suffocating her, just as the Germans passively looked on at Hitler amassing the horrendous guilt that would be loaded on their shoulders.

When Grandmama's hair turned white, Grandpapa forbade her to get old. He insisted she have her hair cut short and waved in the latest fashion. The quiet dresses she had worn were banned, and so were the lace jabots and the high lace collars with their fishbone stays. She was told to wear fashionable prints, and the neckline had to be scooped to show off her still-youthful shoulders. To disguise her wrinkling throat she was permitted a velvet band round the neck. She chose black velvet and was reprimanded, for black was old. He presented her with ribbons of soft pastel colors, delicately adorned with stones or sequins, as if the bands were to draw attention to an area of perfection rather than to hide a fault. Grandmama's choking, which had been relatively inconspicuous behind the lacy collars and jabots, made the ribbons twitch and their adornments glitter. Did he sense that this unladylike affliction was his docile wife's revenge for all he made her swallow? "Your ribbon, Julie!" he would harshly call her to order. The family round the Sunday dinner table would freeze, stare at the plates not to see the tears in Grandmama's eyes, not to watch her humbly suffocating. I burned to call out: "Smash your plate, Grandmama! Fling your napkin in his face! Run out and bang the door!" But I knew she would not make use of my support.

Grandpapa sulked if she wore the elastic stockings the doctor had prescribed for her tired ankles. He showed annoyance if her aging, brittle fingernails broke, or if her thinning voice quavered. He acted as if her aging were a display of poor manners, meant to offend him. Or did he need her to look youthful to quiet his own rather unfounded fears of aging?

Duty required Grandmama to stay alive long enough so that she would be there to close his eyes and escort him to his resting place, that she be the one who would suffer the loss and weep, she the one to choose a tombstone and have flowers planted on the grave, the flowers he had liked.

When all that which Grandmama could still do for him was done, she finally sat back to rest her tired feet and her weary heart. How free she felt at first. She said so to my mother. But freedom had come too late, she could no longer adjust to it. Her mind, conditioned to harassment, felt at a loss and grew confused, inventing the hardship she now lacked. Thus, only death set her free.

May he be free now, too. And should Grandmama be running for him from one end of infinity to the other, God in His mercy will have provided her with wings.

My father was quite the opposite of Grandpapa. He was ready to do almost anything for the sake of peace at home. To shield himself from the restless sea he lived in, he wore a protective shell. He scarcely ever opened it enough for us to see him really, but his was a well-shaped, softly colored, pleasant shell, dear to us. As water must constantly flow through a shell for it to live so did love constantly flow from the narrow opening of my father's shell. Loving, touching with gentle hands, giving, was his form of speaking. For that which mattered, he could not find words. But I loved my remote and unknowable father.

We did not see much of him. He left the house at a very early hour to be at his office for the "making up" of the noon paper. And night conferences frequently kept him late. But no matter how late it was, he would bend over our beds to bring a sweet moment into our dreams with his kiss.

The little time he had with us he asked to be left unburdened. He did not want to hear about our trespasses, be told about complaints from school or neighbors. A half hour of quiet loving, showing us an interesting gadget, touching fingers, saying just a few words, that was his and our happiness. Our upbringing he left altogether to our mother. My guess is that he chose to keep out of it since differences of opinion would have resulted only in more of Mama's stormy retreats to her bedroom, which he dreaded as much as we did.

I liked to be awakened by the sound of Papa's morning bath water, or by the marvelous aroma of his breakfast coffee. Cuddling my pillow, I listened to his soft footfall, his going from here to there, getting dressed. In the deep early-morning stillness sounds carried clearly. I would hear him speak to our dachshund Dina. She kept him company during breakfast, sitting on a chair he drew close to his, and I knew when Dina snatched a piece of bread from his plate, because Papa would burst into happy laughter. Mama objected to the liberties Papa granted Dina, but Mama was not around that early to curtail what was perhaps Papa's happiest hour. My love for him was very much bound up in the lightness of his voice and laughter when, alone with his dog, he was free to let down his guard. During these magic moments I knew him, and a great joy over feeling him so near would come over me.

Papa and we had a morning ritual that he would never skip. When I heard him come, I would quickly shut my eyes and pretend to be asleep, as if finding me awake might embarrass him. He would tiptoe to our beds and slip between our lips a small square of white bread heaped with his very special jelly, which our mouths readily accepted even if we were still asleep. Mama objected to these treats since they left our pillowcases sticky, but Papa would not be deprived of this mute expression of his tenderness for us.

My mother ought to have been manager of a huge plant or coordinator of something of scope. A household with three children was too small a realm to satisfy her. She had a keen intelligence, inventiveness, a passion for organizing, and she had Grandpapa's tireless energy and drive. But as he was her father, the only career she was allowed to consider was marriage. By the time other women of her generation wedged into the male world, she was already caught in a rut of misusing her energies and talents. Project after project, conceived with great ardor, evaporated, to leave her drifting in a gray mist of frustration. She suffered with vigor and our childhood was washed by the incoming and outgoing tides of her despair.

Her mood, rather than switching with the fickle unpredictability of Grandpapa's, changed with all the signs of a brewing storm. Fearful of the undeterrable outcome we would watch the landscape of her face darken. The most insignificant vexation might start it: milk boiling over, or being mistaken in the day the egg man came. *"Ach,* terrible, terrible," she would wail, and distress would shatter her features. She would feed the initial annoyance with bits she picked up along her way as a small snowslide picks up stones and snow on its way down a slope to become an avalanche of devastating power. Once Mama's emotional avalanche had reached the size to make her burst into excruciating sobs, she would let it sweep her into her bedroom. The door would fall shut with a bang, blinds would come down in a furious clatter. Her face drawn, her hand weak, she would lie in the dimmed bedroom for several days. And tears trickling down her face she would dream of a private sanitarium where solicitous nurses and devoted physicians shirked no effort to coax a smile to her pale lips. To atone for such an indulgence she would deny herself treats offered, take only some weak tea and strained oatmeal. Poor Mama. She could not see that her dungeon's door was locked from the inside. But she made it to the luxury sanitarium. And when she returned from the rest cure in the Bavarian Alps, her radiant beauty made me stare at her with mute adoration. She was suntanned, her eyes were bright, her step was light, her voice gay. She sat with us through our children's supper, entertaining us with descriptions of the sumptuous establishment, of the deep carpets, her luxurious room, her private terrace, the delicious meals. Her eyes twinkled mischievously as she told us that she and patients she had befriended sneaked outside by night to play hide-and-seek in the moonlit meadows, jump pasture fences, and race each other. She had outrun them all. The "dear doctor," she explained, had left it entirely up to her when to rest and when to be up and about. She said he realized that she knew best what her nerves needed. When he found her up late, the belle of the ball, he danced with her until dawn. He took her to her room and tucked her in and kissed her good-night. Eyelids fluttering, she added: "Just in fun, of course." And next morning with her breakfast tray came a whole forest of roses.

The doctor's roses still glowing under her skin, and invigorated from jumping pasture fences, she played the piano for hours on end without tiring. She played very well. She also made plans to sew dresses for us, to take us on excursions, and to have the apartment redecorated.

It was during these days of euphoria that she burst into our nursery with an armful of parcels, materials for sessions of arts and crafts, which, she said, she would hold with us regularly twice a week. Out of the bags tumbled shiny, colored paper, scissors, glue, tinted raffia, sealing wax, pieces of linoleum and cutting tools, embroidery cards and wool, clay, beads, balsa wood, and precut leather for bookmarkers and for eyeglass holders. Mama was as excited as we were. She dropped hat and coat on the nearest chair and set about to organize. While she gave each material and each tool a place on the table, which they were to keep forever, she spoke of the joys of creating. In a brand-new, lined notebook she wrote out the schedule of arts and crafts sessions for the next weeks and, our cheeks glowing, we finally started out on session number one. We watched her magic hands transform a few strands of raffia into a doll, crochet a small red skirt, and give the doll shoes of softened sealing wax. Then it was our turn. Dalla's doll came out perfect. Mine was a spidery thing. And Müsi's was mostly done by Mama. They were to become historical monuments, for the second session of arts and crafts never took place. The afterglow of the doctor's roses faded, and Mama mourned them in the seclusion of her dimmed room. When we reminded her of the program upon her reemergence, she sighed: *"Ach,* children . . ." And her pained face, her faint voice, made Dalla turn to her drawing board, Müsi and me to our dolls and teddy bears.

The reasons for my mother's distress were beyond my grasp. I frequently believed that something I did had unleashed the latest crisis, so that through the days of her confinement I carried the burden of my awful guilt. Müsi's unconditional love helped me over these rough spots. Dalla was angered by our mother's states, but she would not voice what her eyes accused Mama of. Papa took flight to night conferences. And Wawa, who knew the ins and outs of people's hearts, but kept her insight a secret, tried to give to everyone according to his need. She kept running to the sickroom, and then to us to cuddle us, to make us laugh. And she prepared our favorite dish, farina sprinkled with sugar and cinnamon

and browned butter. Wawa dispersed the shadows cast
by Mama's eclipses.

Wawa had come to my grandparents as a nurse at the
time when their four children were small. Since they
were unable to pronounce their nurse's difficult name,
they changed it to Wawa. They surely had reasons
deeper than phonetics for giving her a name so close in
sound to Mama.

Wawa had come by her understanding for children
the hard way. She had been orphaned when she was six.
A Pomeranian farmer took her in, but he demanded that
she do a full day's work at the house and at the stables
for her keep. Only in Grimm's fairy tales are orphans
treated as cruelly as she was. Her masters gave her no
tenderness. They were generous only with strict demands and harsh rebukes, and refused to let her attend
elementary school. While the family was eating, she was
made to stand behind her mistress's chair, stand straight
and motionless, for these farmers, not used to being
served, fell upon the bowls without her help. At the end
of the meal, Wawa was permitted to scrape into a bowl
whatever was left, which was a matter of luck, and like
Cinderella she had to take her dish to the pile of wood
beside the stove.

One day, when she was a teen-age girl, she was called
to the *Gute Stube,* the parlor. A farmer, whom she had
seen arriving with a horse-drawn wagon, wordlessly
looked her over. He fingered her muscles, had a look at
her teeth, finally nodded. Her mistress told her that she
was to go with this man and marry him. And the fiancé
counted out a number of bills, which her foster parents
pocketed.

Her few belongings in a kerchief, she climbed on the wagon. In silence they drove through fields to the parson's house, where she was married to the stranger.

He was a widower with a great many children, the oldest of whom was near Wawa's age. Since she knew what it was like to be deprived of a mother's comforting arms, she gave his children all the tenderness she had been unable to give to anyone else. The man, more than twice her age, whose bed she shared, remained in her eyes her stern employer. She submitted to his needs like another chore, and he never let her know that such nights might be sweetened with loving caresses.

Then the man died, leaving her just the roof over her head, his many children and an infant son of her own. To provide for the children now dependent on her, Wawa took in laundry and washed and ironed day and night. But between the loads of wash she found time to caress and console, to patch trousers, sew on buttons, and brush the many heads until their hair shone.

My grandfather, visiting with a Pomeranian client, heard about this diligent woman. He pulled up in front of Wawa's house in a dogcart and asked her to become nursemaid to his children. Wawa accepted. The older of the widower's children were on their own by then and with the generous wages Grandpapa offered, she would be able to pay apprenticeship bonds for the younger ones. She took pride in seeing to it that each child learned a respectable trade that would give him a standing in the community.

When my mother, her sister, and her two brothers started school in close succession, Wawa took her mending to the table where the children did their homework. Her black eyes would leap from the darning mushroom to a child's finger moving along the line of a primer, and her ear would strain to catch the murmured syllables. She bought herself a lined notebook such as the children had, and in bed at night she practiced upstrokes and downstrokes, then the beautiful letters of the alphabet, and then entire words, filling a whole page with each. Her happiness made up for lost sleep. Once she knew how to read, she borrowed books from Grandpapa's library and until late into the night she read Goethe, Heine, Shakespeare, Zola, Dickens, read avidly about the world of which she had seen so little yet knew so well because she knew man's heart.

Once all the widower's children could stand on their own feet, Wawa opened a savings account to provide for a dowry for the widower's daughters. But before it was time for buying sheets and towels, her savings came in handy for rescuing her employer. I do not know what brought my grandfather to a major financial crisis. Had he lived too lavishly? His custom-made suits and custom-made shoes? The barber coming each morning to the house to shave him and keep his hair in perfect trim? Whatever, merchants were coming to the door with bills and had to be turned away. Nor could he pay Wawa's wages, but she was not one to run when the chips were down. She went to the bank every other day and secretly paid pressing bills so that the family could eat and their good name remain untarnished.

Wawa was essential even when the children had outgrown the age for a nanny. And when my mother got married she took Wawa along. Dalla was born, and soon after I came. Wawa went to Uncle Reinhold when his first child was born, and then she returned to us for Müsi. Her absences from our house must have been short, for all my memories see Wawa on the scene. Surely, we needed her most.

When I came into this world, Wawa's hair was already white. But she was by no means an old woman. Her black eyes were fiery, her lips full, her flesh firm. And way into her old age her healthy skin was to retain its lively color. She was a small, compact person, bosomy and short waisted, and of proud carriage. In all humility, Wawa was vain. She would not have it any other way than to look, at all times, as though she had just bathed, just brushed her hair, just changed into a freshly starched, freshly pressed white cotton blouse. She wore always the same kind of Gibson girl outfit: a black skirt of crisp cheviot, snugly fitted to her definite waist and her perky hips, and starched, white cotton blouses buttoned up to the neck. And always she wore the exquisite gold brooch, a token of my grandfather's gratitude.

I loved Wawa. She was my safe burrow. No urgent chore ever prevented her from gathering the child in need of comforting in her arms. And nothing was as comforting as weeping on Wawa's firm bosom, in the fresh scent of her body, in the crispness of her starched blouses. She would never sigh when we made demands on her during an already taxing day, nor did our sibling fights ruffle her. She settled them astutely by calming each of us and blaming none. Nobody had to tell us to respect Wawa. Her unconditional devotion to all of us was obvious even to a child, and so was her self-control in the face of Mama's despair and Grandpapa's chicaneries. Fickle demands and moodiness she met with calm magnanimity. And injustice she stared into the ground with unflinching, glowing black eyes. Wawa, who proudly walked through a difficult life, was a queen to me.

Her queenliness had failed to rub off on the one stepdaughter we knew, because she lived in Berlin. Frieda

Müller was stout and had massive arms that gave evidence of her indulgence in pork chops and sausages. She also had a wart on her face, sprouting several hairs, uncurbed. And Grandpapa would have been aghast over Frieda's manners. She gestured without restraint, laughed loudly, wiped her mouth with the back of her hand, and quite frequently Wawa saw cause to interrupt Frieda's lively chatter and admonish her: "Not in front of the children, Frieda!"

Frieda fascinated me, and so did the mysterious world in which she and her husband Erwin lived — their quaint apartment house, the odd smell that had permeated its corridors. Was it cabbage? The tread-worn, uncarpeted stairs thrilled me, the dark hallways with their rows of badly scuffed doors, the Müllers' doorbell, whose yellowed button, sluggish with age, no longer protruded from the nondescript metal facing.

The Müllers' front door opened directly into the kitchen, where sausages hung in the window above clay pots with parsley and chives. This kitchen was the landscape of the Müllers' life, and all the action took place at the small table with its thumbtacked oilcloth. Countless were the onions that Frieda had chopped there through the years, the salamis she had sliced. There they received their guests, read the evening paper, had their marital fights. There they laughed, wept, sulked at each other, and built their dream castles. Perhaps the erosion of the oilcloth roses testified to how much had taken place here, for whenever I sat at that kitchen table I had the peculiar feeling of being hot on the trail of the elusive thing the grown-ups called life, a secret carefully kept under lock and key in the world I grew up in. I was even convinced that a certain whiff my nose discerned in all the rich smells within this small kitchen was the very scent of life. It was carried by the aroma of pieces of plum cake and crumb cake heaped high on a platter; by Frieda's coffee, a mixture of coffee beans and roasted barley with a pinch of chicory for body. The coffee was served in a big, mottled enamel pot, and sugar and cream were already added to it. Gloating, I visualized my grandfather at this oilcloth-topped table, his glance fleeing from the enamel coffeepot only to be waylaid by the window hung with salamis. In Frieda's kitchen, the very antipode of his polished world, he held no power, and that made me feel gloriously at ease.

When we could eat no more, Frieda handed us the "rummage box," a carton filled with odds and ends she had collected for visiting children. It contained empty yarn spools, some glass marbles, bottle corks, wool thread, belt buckles, a three-legged papier-mâché dog, a bashed-in Celluloid bathtub duck, old theater ticket stubs, and yellowed postcards with faded greetings.

We carried the box to the *Gute Stube,* the adjoining parlor, which the Müllers used only on special occasions. Ecru lace curtains, depicting Greek urns with overflowing grapes, covered the two small windows and kept the room in mysterious dimness. On the hard, red plush sofa we went through the contents of the rummage box, dividing the items among us with relentless justice. But if my eye watched closely the dealing of theater stubs, my ear strained not to miss a word of what was said in the kitchen, Frieda bringing Wawa up to date on what had occurred since her last visit. Wawa now and then hushed Frieda to curb her uninhibited reporting, and a sentence would drown in a swish of whispering as if being rinsed down the drain. But for Frieda's spellbinding revelations, I would have had to assume that adult life was the worst of doldrums, for my parents failed to discuss their affairs in our presence, and Sundays at our grandparents' house, the topics of conversation were culture, travel, history (avoiding all controversy), family background (reverently). How were we to know whether anything of interest ever happened in our elders' life? Frieda, on the contrary, elaborated on her husband Erwin's piles. And that I was left to wonder what piles might be did not in the least lessen the breathtaking picture Frieda conjured of the Müllers' evenings: Frieda at the kitchen table darning Erwin's socks. Erwin on the floor, his bared behind in an enamel basin, his hairy legs anchored in felt slippers, the evening paper between his white knees. Slowly and gravely he would read to the darning Frieda everything from the news to the job offers. And struggling to decipher a difficult word, he would add a bubbling fart. The scene taking shape before my mind's eye, rather than making me laugh, struck me as being astonishing, fascinatingly interesting.

Next, Frieda proceeded to tell about old Frau Schreiber, second floor rear. Her son and daughter-in-law had talked her into going to a nursing home, and of a Sunday afternoon the couple came to move her. Frau Schreiber was already in hat and coat when she learned that she could not take along her old cat. When she protested, her children grabbed her. She scratched and clawed, and in a split second she was out of the coat, tearing off her clothes. In knitted midriff and cotton flannel bloomers she ran into the hallway, screaming for help. Tenants burst from their apartments on all the floors, and at the sight of the frail old woman in her underwear, struggling with the hefty couple dolled up for the trip to the nursing home, no one saw need to ask for explanations. Shouts and raised fists drove son and daughter-in-law from the house.

The victory called for a celebration. The tenants on Frau Schreiber's floor dragged tables and chairs into the hallway and helped Frau Schreiber into her best dress. Some men took off to get beer and *Bockwurst,* and Frieda and her next-door neighbor hurried to the bakery for plum cake and crumb cake.

Listening to the story, I had visions of coffee and beer flowing, of men in T-shirts and women in aprons laughing, shouting, and chewing wurst. This was life! Yes! And somehow I sensed that life was both glorious and sad. I swallowed the lump in my throat and added to my vision of the hallway feast the earsplitting sounds of a brass band. How could Grandpapa's stilted celebrations ever measure up to anything like this?

We lived on a short, quiet street in Grunewald, a Berlin suburb. Just before the war imposed restrictions, a builder had erected on one side of the street three stately apartment houses of light sandstone with neoclassic touches. And he fitted the houses only with the best. A strip of green ran out front, bordered by a low, extraordinarily solid stone wall topped with wrought iron, emphatically marking what was private. From the green strip within, each ground-floor apartment was given a few feet of front yard: a spot of lawn, a bit of gravel path, and a small, flowering tree. The ground-floor apartment of our house belonged to the Schwarzes, and their golden laburnum tree dropped its blossoms into the sandbox set up for baby Beate. The sandbox was of a size sufficient for a toddler, but whenever Frau Schwarz's stare did not keep us at bay, we older ones would descend upon it to play "bakery." Frau Schwarz was blissfully unaware that we let little brothers, practically equipped by nature, moisten the white sand to give it the proper adhesion for shaping patties. The only child deprived of the sandbox was ten-year-old Karl-Titus Schwarz, whom we could see sitting behind the window, cramming Latin. If he stole a longing glance at us, he instantaneously received a slap from his vigilant mother.

The windows of our houses looked over Herr Krüger's flower nursery. His neat rows of flowers ran all the way into the narrow apex of the triangular lot — golden daffodils in spring, gladiolas, zinnias and glowing red dahlias in summer, and asters pink and purple in fall. Even on the grayest winter day, old Herr Krüger would be moving about, stacks of red clay pots in his arms. Bordering the nursery behind Herr Krüger's shack and hothouse lay the "goat garden," which extended to the other end of our street. Collectively, our parents rented this property to give us children a protected playground. Two goats tethered there led us to give the garden its name. It was a place where we were free to shout and shriek, as there were no houses alongside. Under the garden's acacia trees we dressed and undressed our dolls. In the open field we played catch. On the former tennis court we jumped rope and drove our hoops and held scooter races. And heart in mouth we bicycled on the roof of the shed next to it. Children somewhat older than I climbed from there into the branches of a tree. They had formed a secret club and, hidden in the foliage, they smoked to lend weight to their oaths. It was very difficult for them to snitch the needed cigarettes, and when I solved that problem, I was awarded membership despite my insufficient age. My father's silver-lidded glass boxes were always filled to the brim, and they looked just as full after I had taken out a handful of cigarettes. The gang swore me in and I signed the stat-

utes with a preschool scribble. I smoked my first cigarette, pledging to keep the gang's activities a secret. The
activities limited themselves to smoking and to taking
oaths.

At that time, my favorite doll was Rosa. When I
happened to hear the name Rosa Luxemburg, I extended my doll's name to that. I liked the way it sounded,
it had rhythm, pum-pum pum-pum-pum . . .

Dalla sneered. "Rosa Luxemburg? Hahaha!"

Why hahaha? Wrinkling my nose, I aped Dalla:
"Bababa!" And I stuck out my tongue.

"Luxemburg!" Dalla huffed as if Luxemburg were a
dirty word.

I screamed: "Stupid! Stupid!" I would not give up
such a beautiful name. Turning my back on Dalla, I huddled with Müsi. To protect Rosa from Dalla's derision
we resolved to call her only by her first name and to add
Luxemburg in an inaudible whisper. However, worse
was to happen to Rosa.

One day when I was alone in the goat garden, the
Rettloff boys showed up. They were big boys, twelve
and thirteen. They ambled over to where I was sitting
in the grass with Rosa and grinned down at me. Clutching Rosa, I jumped up, but they barred the way and
said they would let me go only if I told them the secrets
of my gang. How could I? I had given an oath!

They lit a cigarette and blew the smoke in my eyes.
They brought the glowing end so close to my arm that
the heat made me wince. The acacias were in bloom and
white blossoms dropped silently to the sunny ground,
and through the feathery foliage I could see my house,
but nobody came to my aid.

"Tell us!" the Rettloff boys shouted.

They pulled Rosa from my arms and with the cigarette they burned a hole in her Celluloid hand. Howling, I threw myself upon them. They laughed. I pleaded with them to let go of Rosa, and finally they consented to take it out on me. They tied my ankles and tied my hands. They knotted a rope around my waist and dragged me across the rough ground of the goat garden. My crying only heightened their merriment.

"Have you had enough? Will you tell?"

I would not, I was too desperate.

That suited them fine. Giggling their heads off, they dragged me on until they tired. They warned me not to tell on them or they would get hold of Rosa, tear off her wig, push in her eyes, and chop off her hands and feet.

I ran from their laughter, my dress ripped, and with scratches all over. The closer I came to home, the harder were my sobs and the greater my longing for comforting arms. My aghast mother pressed me to tell what had happened, and since I could not tell, I said I had saved the *Vaterland*. I felt that this was somehow true.

In the days of the Rettloff boys, Hitler was only a paperhanger, and Eichmann still in school. Many years had to pass before they would set up Auschwitz, but the Rettloff boys needed no Auschwitz for inspiration. They returned to the goat garden for another day of fun. They snatched little Simon Fischbein from the group of small children at play. They roped him to a tree and spat on him. And they forbade us ever again to play with him because he was a dirty, cowardly Jew, they said.

We sobbed loudly. Little Simon wept soundlessly, without hope. Although he himself had not known ghettos or pogroms, this first exposure to wanton cru-

elty and humiliation awakened the collective memory
of his people, so it seems, and told him of the loneliness
of the Jew.

We could not help Simon, for all of us were little
and the Rettloff boys were big. But perhaps, as I stood
helpless, it was determined that I would not side with
the man hunters later on.

The Rettloff boys, sticking their heads together, whispered and giggled. They untied little Simon to lead
him away, and they told us that he should die were we
to tell a soul of what had taken place. Simon between
them, they took off toward Hohenzollerndamm. We ran
from the goat garden to our street, where we hung
around listlessly. Frau Fischbein appeared, asked where
Simon was, and fearing for his life, we shrugged. Frau
Fischbein glanced down the street in both directions,
and her eyes asked: but wasn't he playing with you?

We ran to tell our mothers that little Simon had disappeared, and they came to help Frau Fischbein think
where he might have gone. My disappearances were
mentioned and that children do take off, driven by a
sudden longing for adventure.

"Not Simon," Frau Fischbein said.

Our mothers were at a loss what to say, they didn't
know Frau Fischbein too well. She never dallied for a
chat. It was said that Frau Fischbein wore a wig, which
I would not believe because it seemed too silly for words.
But I gave her a covert look. Perhaps it was true? Perhaps she always wore a hat to prevent the wig from
flying off? Even now she wore a hat although she was
not going anywhere, had stepped outside only to call
Simon. The hat gave the distraught mother an even
more tragic air.

"Does Simon have a scooter?" one of the mothers

asked, and suggested that he might have gone to the asphalt-paved streets beyond Hohenzollerndamm. We liked to go there with our scooters and roller skates because the pavement was smooth, and hardly a car passed through on weekdays. These streets ran through the *Schrebergärten,* a block of tiny garden lots where the Berliner grew his beans and tomatoes. The owners came only on weekends, when they would weed and water the vegetables while coffee simmered on their Primus cookers.

It was in one of the small sheds of the *Schrebergärten* that Simon was found late that night. To punish him for his Jewishness, the Rettloff boys had nailed boards across the door so that he would have to stay among shovels, rakes and hoes until the weekend.

Little Simon did not tell on the Rettloff boys, unless he confided in his parents, who chose to keep the knowledge locked in their hearts.

The Rettloff boys grew up and, for all I know, it might have been they who herded an entire French village into the church and nailed boards across the door and doused the foundation with gasoline and set the church on fire.

Little Simon was merely the first Jew I saw being led away. When the time came for thousands to be led away, I was no longer a child, and not quite as helpless. To some I could offer a night in safety. Others I could help to make it to the train that would take them to another country. There they would have a chance to survive if a friend lent a hand, if luck was with them, if faith in Hitler's defeat gave them the strength to live with adversity. For many, luck ran out. For many it proved not enough to have faith. And some lost faith.

I myself was a refugee among them when the biggest

Jew hunt I was to witness took place in conquered France in August 1942.

Many hundred thousand Jews had made their way into France, German Jews, Austrians, Czechs, Poles. And when the Nazi armies penetrated France, these Jews joined the stream of terrified French civilians making their way to the south. For a while they felt safe in the unoccupied half of France, the *zone libre,* but when all foreign Jews were ordered to register, they knew far ahead of time that the day they were hunted down and loaded on cattle cars was in the making.

Only a few dared not to follow the order. They had been granted asylum precisely because they were Jews, and the evidence of it ran through the texts of their official dossiers. All they could do was keep informed of the preparations made behind the walls of police headquarters. Some, who had means, bribed officials to pass word to them once the date for the hunt was set. The others had to rely on the grapevine bulletins. Every rumor was discussed. All their lives depended on not dismissing the one shred of news that would be the warning to run and hide. Run where? Hide where? They did not know. They hoped that once that moment came, Frenchmen might open their doors.

The French were preoccupied with their own sorry fate. They were dispirited by their defeat, and by hunger. Resistance in mind and action was still just beginning, had roused from torpor just a small minority. Besides, many Frenchmen considered the refugees foreign idlers, rich tourists who basked in France's sun while France lay bleeding. A few knew better, knew that the refugees' expensive-looking clothes were all they had left from better times, that they did not have a franc to

their name, owed rent, owed the grocer, could not pay
their electric bills. They knew that the refugees sitting
on the beaches and in the cafés were neither wealthy nor
lazy, but were not allowed to take a job. But such Frenchmen would simply not believe that anyone granted asylum in France might be handed over to Hitler's hench-
men. Even André, who through me knew so much of the
refugee lot and the fears of the Jewish refugees, felt
offended when I suggested that they might be deported.
Hurt in his national pride, he laughed into my face:
"Mais alors, non! Ne soyons pas ridicules!" It was un-
fathomable to him.

Aside from the dangers involved in harboring a fugitive, aside from the inconvenience of having a stranger
in the house, that fugitive would have no ration tickets.
How could he be fed when his hosts had not enough for
themselves? The Jews were not unreasonable in having
grave doubts about the help they could expect. Yet the
only chance for escaping capture hinged on that faint
hope.

Months went by and the pending threat took on a
quality of permanence. The preoccupation with it seemed
less and less justified, more and more the invention of
paranoid minds, or the self-importance assumed by people who had nothing to do all day while out there, somewhere, the huge, terrible war went on.

I was at the house of my French friends, Raimond
and Elaine, young designers who, caught by the deadline
for commissioned comic strips, had asked me to help
them. All day the three of us had bent over the drawings.
Finally we stopped for a plate of tomato salad into
which we dipped the day's bread ration. Then we worked
on. We would have to give most of the night to it.

Raimond turned on the radio for the late French-language news from London, and we drew close to catch the words behind the barrage of screechings and howlings from the German jamming. *"Ici Londres, ici Londres, des français parlent aux français. . . ."* With bated breath we listened to the *messages personnels,* cryptic phrases that were vital information to someone of the French underground somewhere in France. "The house needs repair . . . the house needs repair. . . . Jean loves Ninette . . . Jean loves Ninette. . . . The cat spilled the milk . . . the cat spilled the milk. . . . Come now, my friend . . . come now, my friend. . . . The fog lifts at eight . . . the fog lifts at eight. . . ."

Like a shipwrecked man on a deserted island, waiting day after day for a ship to come and seeing sails or smoke in the far distance, so did we, fallen to the wayside of the war, wait for the Allied landings. That hope carried us from one day to the next, through years. Almost anything was to us a sign of the nearness of the invasion. Every bomber squadron rumbling high overhead. And the words of the *messages personnels,* even though we knew they were coded messages, turned into heralds of the invasion each time their meaning gave the slightest hint. "Come now, my friend" to us meant NOW, now the invasion. "The fog lifts at eight": what could it mean to our longing hearts but that it conveyed the time of the coming of the British fleet. And when on the morrow our hopes were disappointed, we nourished new hopes and saw new signs. Tomorrow, and tomorrow, and tomorrow, through years and years.

"Ici Londres, ici Londres. . . . Attention, Lyon! Attention, Lyon!" The urgency in the announcer's voice gave us a jolt and, our knees crowding, we listened to the warning. A mass arrest of foreign Jews was sched-

uled for this night for the area of Lyons. And the Frenchman in London appealed to his compatriots in France to
give aid and shelter to the persecuted, to leave doors unlocked, not raise alarm if they heard hurried footfalls
and a rustling in their gardens. And the announcer appealed to Lyons's clergy.

"Fat chance," Elaine said bitterly. "I doubt the
bishop of Lyons is in the habit of listening to the BBC."

He was, though. And the fisherman of souls ordered
the gates of his compound opened. When by morning he
viewed his weighty catch, he donned the shepherd's
shirt and wrote a pastoral letter to the priests of France
to do as he had done. And the hundreds of envelopes
bearing his message made it to their destination in spite
of the vigilant German controls, perhaps through faith.
Many French priests, white-frocked Benedictine monks,
brown-frocked Franciscans, whom the *Résistance* was to
number among its most valiant men, made their first step
in response to the bishop's call, the crucial step not to
give Caesar what was Caesar's. And inevitably it set
them on their way to the ranks of the underground.

When the BBC signed off, we remained seated close to
the silent radio, with visions of what was to take place
in Lyons this very night. Then it occurred to us that it
might not be limited to Lyons. If it were, Jews elsewhere
would be forewarned.

It was past curfew, and the dark, narrow streets were
patrolled by gendarmes. We would have to exercise
great caution to reach the Jews of our town. We would
need luck, too.

We put out the lights before opening the door, for
blackouts were strictly enforced. The house stood in an
orange grove low on the hillside, and the dark shadows
of the trees shielded us. At the gate, Elaine turned left

toward the lower road. Raimond and I went uphill, up the Montée Guillaume, up the long steps paved with round, slippery stones. Above us, the dark clump of the old town proper, its medieval houses crowding the top of the hill, was silhouetted against the star-strewn sky.

Although the sky was clear, the night was dark. Raimond, shod like me in rope-soled espadrilles, proceeded soundlessly at a cautious pace. I followed, leaving a couple of yards between us so that I could hide should he walk into the arms of a gendarme. At the ancient, asymmetrical arch that marked the entrance to the old town, Raimond stopped me, and for a minute we stood listening for the sound of a gendarme's slow footfalls, or for sand crunching, or for a cough. Then we moved into the narrow passageway up the uneven steps. Among the houses it was so dark that we had to grope our way, and we advanced with a wall-ward list to be able to flatten out against a house at a moment's notice, or slip into the blackness of a doorway. I was seized by a childish fear that my hands might suddenly touch something awful, like the unidentifiable things in an amusement park's "tunnel of horror," and I moved along, clenched fists pressed to my chest.

The row of houses at our right ended. We were on the top of the hill, coming to the vast plaza. Ahead loomed the outline of the massive medieval fortress which, centuries ago, had defended the town against Saracen invaders.

Raimond signaled that he would now separate from me. We did not dare even whisper. I saw him skirt the fortress ramp before he became one with the darkness.

All alone I was frightened, even though nothing more could have happened to me than to be arrested and spend the night at the *commissariat de police*. I was not

Jewish. But I might have to answer a lot of questions. If I was not Jewish why was I a refugee? If I was not Jewish was I not a traitor to my country? Or a spy? No, a coward, that's what I was, a coward frightened of the dark, frightened of the stillness.

I kept close to the fortress wall, looked about, listened before passing the church. The only sound came from the trickle of water falling from the ancient fountain as it had year in, year out for centuries, to run from the stone basin down the neatly stone-faced gutter of the Montée des Sarrazins. A hundred feet from where I stood, the few stores in the old town sat one next to the other: Hippolyte Napoleon's grocery, Fifi's bakery, Innocente's tiny shop carrying whitewash, some screws and nails, rope and kerosene. Next door was the narrow-chested Hôtel de la Goulu, and Café Paul Cézanne, and across the street Mario's bistro. Beyond, the *montée* continued its steep descent — a silken sash falling down the hill's dark shirt.

We had decided to send our Jews to the vineyards surrounding the town. But where would we put them then?

I peered down the *montée* to make sure that a gendarme was not sitting on the steps to the stores. A cat made me jump and I pressed myself into blooming vines that cascaded down a wall.

Still shaking, I noticed how glaringly white my old grayed espadrilles shone in the night, and dashed down a narrow flight of steps all the way to Laszlo's door. "You . . ." he said, visibly relieved. He was fully dressed and from his shoulder hung a bulging musette bag. He had heard the broadcast and was about to leave.

"Where to?" I asked.

He shrugged. "The vineyards. Then I'll see."

"Ange's vineyard," I told him. He nodded and was on his way.

I wished I had asked him the time. It seemed I had been out for hours. What time of the night do they pick for raids?

I ran on, flew down the next flight of steps to Peter and Else's gate. It creaked. Dry leaves rustled under-foot as I crossed the small square of paved courtyard. Else opened the door sleepy-eyed, hair tousled, clutching her flowered cotton gown. "Tonight?" she asked.

"Then you know?"

"Why else would you come in the middle of the night?"

"Ange's vineyard. You know how to find it?"

"Oh, God," she gasped and her hand flew to her mouth.

"Hurry, Else, will you."

"Oh, God!"

Peter appeared behind her and I ran off, on to the next, and the next, and the next.

Four would not run to save themselves. The history of their people, the people chosen by God and abandoned by God, had conditioned them to being victims. They had no faith in vineyards, no faith that a door might open to them, that a Gentile's hand might offer protection; and none of my words put hope into their hopeless hearts. Then I had to leave them because there were still others I had to rouse.

After the last one, I went to meet Raimond and Elaine under the dark arcades behind the church as agreed, to make sure that each of us had been able to complete his mission. Together we returned to those who had refused to run.

We found Rosen's door slightly ajar, and stood uncertain whether to be relieved or alarmed. Raimond put his finger to his lips, listened, and gave the door a push. In the middle of the dark room Rosen was sitting on a chair, a suitcase beside him. Like a man on a bench at a rural bus stop, he was waiting for them to come and take him away. He kept sitting there like that as we talked and he bore our words as if they were falling rain he had to put up with since the bus had not yet come into sight.

Finally, nothing accomplished, we could only leave to see the other three once again. Raimond gently touched Rosen's shoulder. "You'll not be foolish, *mon vieux*. At Ange's vineyard you'll find the others."

"Merci," Rosen said with a kindly nod for the well-meaning innocents who could not comprehend what it meant to be a Jew.

We found Anna and her teen-age daughter Natasha and Natasha's girl friend Tamara seated one beside the other on the threadbare sofa, white kid-gloved hands in their laps, and on their heads little black straw hats that had been fashionable some years back. Tears were trickling down their faces and their lips were quivering. They wept soundlessly, without hope, as little Simon Fischbein had. Was he sitting somewhere beside a packed suitcase, because he remembered that we hadn't made a move when the Rettloff boys led him away? Or was he running, hoping for help, because what had engraved itself into his memory was the anguish he saw in our eyes?

"Vineyards!" Anna said in a burst of scorn, and softening her tone, she added: "My dears, I'm weary." Natasha slipped her kid-gloved hand into her mother's, and Tamara, her dark eyes flashing pride, said that she would not let her best friend go to the ovens alone. As we pleaded with them, Tamara's eyes filled with all the Jewish heartbreak and tragedy of a thousand years and then an impenetrable curtain dropped over them, shutting us out from a world where we had dared to trespass. Silenced, Raimond stared at the floor.

As he led us outside, he glanced back hissing: "Anna, the Nazis won't have to take Natasha and Tamara to Auschwitz, since you are doing it for them." And filing through the dark alley back to the *montée* I heard Raimond behind me sob.

On the *montée* we sat down on the nearest doorstep, spent. The town sat under a bell jar of stillness. Perhaps it would wake up to a day like all others, and we would shake off a nightmare. All the running and stir looked suddenly foolish. The thin stream of water running down the gutter gurgled softly. No other sound anywhere. None of us had even come across the gendarme on duty. Likely he stayed at the station house, playing belote with the others. Not even a cat in sight.

"I'll go to Hanna now," I said.

Raimond nodded his hanging head.

It was just a hundred feet down the *montée*. Hanna and I were next-door neighbors. Our houses were built against the hillside, and what was upper story toward the *montée* was on ground level in the back. A flight of crooked stone steps rose from the street, then forked. One branch, curving off in a haphazard fashion, led to Hanna's door and the other branch led up to a terrace. On the right side of the terrace was the door to my apartment. Against the left sat a small one-story house where a carpenter and his wife lived. They were refugees from Alsace, and had come only recently. The bay window of Hanna's one-room apartment was a full story above the *montée,* but nobody lived below her. Behind what looked like a high, windowless stone foundation was a wine cellar whose back wall was the hill. The cellar was empty except for a few large wine barrels in which André had hidden stacks of underground newspapers, and another time four rifles, carried there in an old mattress in broad daylight.

Hanna let me in and scurried back to bed. Drawing the blanket up to her chin she said she would not go, that she did not believe that the dreaded moment had come. As if with her disbelief she could sway fate. The more I talked to her the deeper she slipped under the covers, a little animal fearfully trusting in its burrow.

"Go away," she said. "I don't want to hear another word about it. I won't open if they come. Now go, go."

Not open? One good kick with a boot would make that door give.

"Go," she said, "Please go, go to bed, leave me alone!"

Angry and hurt, I left. I helped Hanna to get out of Austria, had borrowed Ljuba's Yugoslav passport, on which she made it into Switzerland, helped to get her into France, and then saw her through many months, for she was penniless. And now she refused my help. All would have been for nothing because of her childish wish to make what she feared disappear.

From the steps I glanced up at her kitchen window, a small black square. Because of her own incomprehensible decision, Hanna was sitting in a trap.

I went to my apartment to watch the *montée* from my window. If they came, if they pried her out of her burrow, I could not help her. All I could do then was run

outside not to let her be all alone. I could call to her:
Hanna, survive it, don't ever give up! And perhaps my
words would stay with her.

The *montée* remained deserted. I drew the shutters
closed, opened the slats, and stretched out on my bed to
listen for the sound of footfalls. But all I heard was the
rivulet's whispering, and the chant of countless frogs at
the cisterns in the distant vineyards.

I couldn't grasp right away what had happened and
how I came to be standing in the middle of the room.
The drumming, I believed, was my racing heart, but
then I realized that it came from Hanna's door. Even
though I had rushed to forewarn everybody of this, now
that it was really here, it seemed unbelievable. Shaking,
as if it were my door they were banging on, I clamped
my hands over my ears. Don't listen, Hanna! Don't
open! Don't open! Don't open! Don't open!

I peered through the shutter slats but from my window I could see only the bay window. Don't open, Hanna! Outside your door is Auschwitz!

Stop banging, you numskulls! Don't you realize she
isn't home! You hear me, she isn't home!

Then I could no longer bear it. Heedlessly I burst
outside and ran down the steps, almost falling over a
gendarme who sat there.

"Are you the lady from that place?" he asked, pointing to Hanna's apartment.

"No, I . . . I live here," I stammered. "I heard the
noise . . . I thought . . . what . . . what's going
on?" My incoherent babbling fit the occasion. "She isn't
home. She went to Antibes, I think. Yesterday. She mentioned something about staying with friends for a while.

What happened? Why are you . . . I heard the noise . . ."

The two gendarmes left. From behind my shutters I watched them go up the *montée,* dissolve in the darkness. Out again, down the steps, up Hanna's, I rapped at her door, called. No answer. I rapped a light rhythmic pattern, put my lips against the edge of the door. No response. I ran down the steps and called from under her bay window, called louder, ran back to her door, rapped, called. "Hanna, open up, every minute is precious. Hanna, it's me, please!" I peered into the keyhole. The key was in it. Had they seen that? Wouldn't that be the first thing they looked for? Did they follow orders perfunctorily, not that eager to catch anyone? Or stupidly? Would they be back? "Hanna, for God's sake open up!"

The key was being turned. Just that. I waited, puzzled, then I pushed the door open. She stood there in her thin nightgown like an apparition, motionless, mute. "To my place, quickly!" She did not stir. I reached for her hand. "Come, Hanna!" Then I realized that she couldn't move, that fright had paralyzed her. I picked her up, carried her down the steps. She was a great deal smaller than I, but short of my landing I had to put her on her feet and somehow she made it up. The carpenter's door opened, and he stepped out fully dressed despite the hour of night.

"May I help?"

I told him what was happening.

"Bon Dieu," he breathed. "Poor France! My poor France!"

"I'm taking her to my apartment. She is in no condition to make it to the vineyards. But she isn't safe with me. The gendarmes have seen me dart outside, and everybody knows we are close friends. They might come to search my apartment. Would you take Hanna just for tonight?"

He shook his head. "You see . . . my wife and I, we're leaving. Right now. We're going underground. I've received orders to report for active duty in the German army. You see, the *boches* have declared us Alsatians Germans. I don't speak a word of German, but that doesn't faze them. They could come for me at any moment. Technically I'm a German deserter." He shrugged, and the tall, lean carpenter seemed to be shackled France herself.

Hanna was trembling. I put her to bed, and the carpenter brought Cognac. I wrapped her up to the chin in a large bath towel and filled the night table with all sorts of medicine and the thermometer to make it look as though she were ill. And then I rushed out to lock her door, which I had left standing open. The carpenter and his wife were ready to leave so I went down to the street to check whether it was safe for them. The gray band of the *montée* was empty. The air quivered with the chant of frogs and the rivulet whispered. That was all.

The carpenter shook hands with me, and belatedly he introduced himself, for I was no longer a foreigner, nor "one of the artist colony." We were all the same kind, helpless creatures scurrying not to be crushed by the German boot.

We made the V sign, and I watched François Mauvin and his wife Marie go down the Montée des Sarrazins. He had a knapsack and she a musette bag, the rest of their possessions they had to leave behind. It was not much, for most they had already lost when they left their Alsatian home.

I watched them walking one behind the other close to the high stone wall, Frenchmen who had become refugees inside their own country. Where were they going? Did they know? Where were the hundred thousand Jews to go?

Next day the townspeople went about with downcast eyes. Gathered in small groups, they fell silent when one of the "foreigners" passed. Everybody knew that *le pauvre* Monsieur Rosen had been taken, and *la pauvre* Madame Anna and the two girls. The people also knew that other "foreigners" had escaped capture, were hiding somewhere, but none of them wished to be told just where. Better not get involved. The previous year when their own Monsieur André was arrested, accused of *Résistance* activities, *Sûreté* men came to ask questions all over town. Of course, they did not get many answers, for the town knew what it owed its own. Not that anyone would give away the unfortunate foreigners, but to have specific information would be an unnecessary burden.

Someone going to Nice saw the train, a long train standing in the station, brimful with men, women and children. Jews. From snatches of the onlookers' talk, that person learned the train was to go across the *ligne de démarcation,* and Drancy and Auschwitz were mentioned. He told the town.

Enough doors opened to give our Jews a roof over their heads temporarily. "For a day or two until you've made arrangements."

We smiled politely, at a loss as to what arrangements we could possibly make.

The main target had been the German, Austrian and Czech Jews. The Poles, Hungarians and Romanians who had run to Ange's vineyard returned to their homes. But they felt uneasy, kept night watches, and every day someone went to Nice to gather the latest confidential news. Rumors were rampant there. It was impossible to sift what might be true from what was fantasy. What was true staggered the imagination.

Then we heard that refugees in Nice were making plans to cross the Swiss border in the darkness of night. Everybody talked about a certain path leading into the high mountains from Annecy, about a small bridge over a brooklet, about pastures sloping down to Geneva.

Eight of our Jews had to stay hidden. For how long? Weeks? Months? Years? How long would the war last? How were we to feed them without ration tickets?

We other foreigners sneaked through the streets like thieves, trying to avoid the fugitives' temporary hosts because they pressed us to free them of their charges. We ourselves could not take them in, sooner or later our houses would be searched. And in a town as small as ours, where every face was known to everybody, one could not rent a room and live there under a false name.

"Look here, *ma fille,* it was understood that it would be for a day, for a few at the most. You must make an effort, they are your friends. Certainly among you foreigners . . ." "Tonight you must move him. After all, he is sought by the authorities. And he hasn't even his bread rations." "I was looking for you. What about your friend. She's charming, *la petite* Hanna, but . . ."

Eight people! They might just as well have been a hundred. There simply was no way out.

Then we thought of the American's house. It stood empty — Barry Percy had returned to America — and Giovanna the laundress was the caretaker.

I found her in her kitchen scrubbing away on a wash-

board, her sinewy arms sudsy to the elbows. At the sight
of me she broke into wails: *"La guerra! La guerra,
miseria!* The Lord have pity on your friends." Giovanna, like a great part of our town's population, was
Italian. Their special patois made use of both languages,
though in talking to "foreigners" Giovanna restricted
herself to French. "Foreigners" also included French
refugees from the occupied part of the country. But
even Giovanna's French was liberally sprinkled with the
Italian *perchè*.

When I told her that the eight foreigners in hiding
would be on the street by night unless she gave us the
key to the Percy house, she grimaced like a deaf person.
"The house of the *americano?* Impossible, *perchè* the
americano has entrusted the house to me, *perchè* into
this hand," a sudsy index finger poked at her palm, "into
this hand the *americano* has put the key . . . *perchè*
. . . he said his heart would be at peace *perchè* Giovanna will take care of his house, *perchè* he knows
Giovanna will not let anything happen to his house."
She plunged her arms into the galvanized tub and resumed her scrubbing and kneading.

"If Percy knew about this situation he would be only
too glad to put his house at our disposal."

Vigorously she wiped her hands on the soaked apron
and rammed the white fists into her hips. "Madame
Ingrid. Every Wednesday Giovanna airs all the rooms.
Giovanna airs closets, Giovanna opens all the faucets
perchè the plumbing must not get rusty. Every other
week Giovanna turns over the mattresses, takes blankets
from chests, shakes them out, suns them, folds them
again *perchè* dust fleas and moths. If the war should be
finished tomorrow, let it be finished, let the *americano*
come back. Giovanna needs half an hour to make the

beds, that's all, *perchè* every six weeks Giovanna has washed the sheets and they smell fresh, smell good, Madame Ingrid. You must not ask for the key *perchè* no." The matter settled once and for all, Giovanna returned to the laundry.

"Giovanna, you know we can't put them up. Any day now the gendarmes will search the houses where foreigners live."

"No doubt. No, no, they must not stay with you, not safe. Not safe for one minute. And Giovanna cannot give key *perchè* Giovanna is Italian. They will say Giovanna is spy, Italian spy. The gendarmes will take Giovanna to prison. Who will air the *americano's* house? Who will shake out blankets? Eh?" Her eyes flashed triumphantly.

"Giovanna . . . I will leave. You will wash and sort of talk to yourself. You will talk about the key and where you keep it. I'll sneak back inside and steal the key. You'll be innocent."

"*Perchè* no!"

I waited. Giovanna worked at a sheet, wrung out the bulky thing with forceful lean hands, lips tightly closed.

I rolled myself a *mégot* cigarette. I needed one to pressure Giovanna. She had always been good to us, and all of us owed her for laundry. But I had to say that if she denied us the key and anything happened to the fugitives, she would be guilty of worse than spying. Instead of prison she would go to hell.

Giovanna, kneading away, seemed not to listen, but all of a sudden she dropped to her knees and, sudsy arms lifted in supplication, cried out to the Holy Virgin. The genuineness of her agony made her melodramatics heartrending, and I hated myself for battering away. "The *americano* would never forgive you. He is in the war fighting the Nazis. Maybe he's giving his life for it. Should he ever hear that you barred his house to people who could have been rescued, he would despise you. He would believe that you are a Fascist. He would not want a Fascist for a caretaker, he would take back the key."

The key in my hand, I fled from Giovanna's kitchen, hating myself, hating the war, hating the Nazis, HATING THE NAZIS!!!

In the Percy house our Jews had to speak in whispers. They had to step softly so not a sound would reach anyone passing by outside. They had to smother their coughs with a pillow. The toilet they could flush only at dawn, at the close of curfew when the gendarmes were on their way home and early risers not yet in the street. Then they had hastily to fill pails of water, since using faucets was out of the question during the day. The August sun was hot, but windows had to remain shut, and even at night they would dare open only a small back window. Only on Wednesdays when Giovanna came for the weekly airing, a routine known to the whole town, the windows were opened, and the eight went to the cellar just in case some good woman dropped in for a chat with Giovanna. After nightfall they sat in the dark, in a compact darkness, behind the shuttered windows. They could not cook. We on the outside sneaked in a pot of soup at night. This daily thin soup was all they had for the six weeks they stayed in the Percy house. None of us had much to spare for it. Each gave something, a carrot, a leek, a day's ration of bread, a potato, a bouillon cube. Of the one pound of potatoes *or* the one pound of spaghetti that was our monthly ration of starch how much could anyone spare? Flour and cereals were given to preschool children only. Our meat tickets allowed us a weekly ration the size of a luncheonette

hamburger, but more often than not the butcher shop
remained closed. The Germans needed the railroads for
purposes of their own and prohibited the transport of
produce from one *département* to the other. The people
had to make do with whatever was locally available. In
Normandy, France's dairy region, the old, rickety
bicycles of the *Résistance* couriers had to be greased
with butter, while we did not see any butter for all the
years of the war. Our area cultivated carnations for the
perfume industry, and the Germans did not permit the
flowers to be replaced with potatoes and beans, for they
needed French perfumes for their wives and sweet-
hearts. Of the grapes ripening on the hills all around us,
only a fraction reached the local market, while crates
overflowing with dew-kissed grapes were loaded on a
long train of flatcars, and all along the length of the
train large white letters repeated the heartwarming message, GIFT FROM FRANCE TO THE GERMAN PEOPLE. The
French railroad men added their personal greeting by
pissing on the grapes.

Rather than going to the market hall early in the
morning, I would sleep as late as possible, for a sleeping
stomach is peaceful. But with eight extra stomachs in the
Percy house we had to try anything, and shortly after
six A.M. I was heading downhill to the market. The
stores were still closed. Elaine, waiting for me at the
Café Littoral, had helped herself to one of the chairs
that passed the night legs up on top of the sidewalk
tables. The lineup outside the market hall was already
considerable, and the queue rapidly grew behind us.
Finally at eight the hall's big door was opened and
slowly we shuffled closer. I indulged in visions of colorful
heaps of delicate vegetables fresh from France's bounti-
ful gardens, and my senses imagined a whiff of earthy

smell, but when we reached the steps and could look inside we saw rows of empty sawbuck tables. Only one held a small pile of cabbages, and a policeman watched over the just distribution of one cabbage leaf per family. Women whose stack of ration cards proved their family was a large one were given an extra leaf or two. And when the woman ahead of us showed the ration cards of two preschool children, she was also given an extra leaf. She paid, tears rolling down her face. *"Voyons, ma belle,"* the policeman said with a wink of encouragement, and she managed a faint smile.

Elaine moved behind me to establish that we were separate parties, and we left the market hall richer by two leaves of cabbage and a ravenous hunger. Hunger and the dank market hall made us shiver. Even far from the trenches wars are cold.

It had been cold at the open-air market in Berlin in the war of my childhood. Reason tells me that we must have gone marketing also in spring and summer, but all I remember are winter mornings, the striped awnings and umbrellas of the market stalls shrouded in winter mist, the biting wind, my toes frozen, my fingers numb. Before my mind's eye I see the market women wrapped in layers and layers of clothing, and their swollen, red fingers, which emerged from knitted, fingerless gloves. They scraped away at fresh cod, and glittering scales scattered like a rain of ice chips. All the air smelled of fish and soil, for the yellow turnips, the spotted carrots, the frostbitten potatoes in wicker baskets were heavily caked with earth. It made them weigh more.

I do not remember hunger pangs, but our family was better off than most, since members of the Berlin press received Swedish relief parcels. These were so long in transit, however, that the butter in them always arrived rancid. Mama washed and kneaded the chunk of butter in salted, repeatedly changed water. Then she melted it in a saucepan and carefully scooped off the rising foam. The golden liquid was poured in a crock and cooled until it hardened. Papa would not touch the derancidified butter. But this somewhat grainy spread was the only butter we children knew, and we liked it. When Mama handed us our first slice of bread with fresh postwar butter, we all spat it out and Dalla threw up. We were of one opinion: that the new butter tasted awful.

During the six years of World War II, I had no butter of any kind. One cup of oil was our monthly ration of fat, and for a time some of it had to go into the soup for the eight in the Percy house.

It was my day to prepare that soup when there was a knock on the door. Knocks on the door always jangled our nerves, but it was just a boy, just a child. He handed me a note saying that Charon sent him, and off he ran. Charon? Charon was the police official in charge of matters concerning foreigners, but the paper I held was not the well-known tint of the *convocations* that ordered us to appear at the *commissariat de police* on such and such a day at a given time. It was a piece of white paper, folded. The two lines of printed words said:

BE AT THE CEMETERY AFTER DARK
DON'T TELL *ANYONE* ! ! !

No signature. I laughed. Charon indeed! Cemetery! Some dear friend of mine needed a good laugh. Well, I wasn't that gullible.

As the day waned, I grew uncertain. Who of my friends would make jokes of this kind just now? What if . . . but at the cemetery after dark? It was pre-posterous, reeked of a kid's hoax, of Tom Sawyer and Huckleberry Finn. I didn't know the boy, but he might be a friend of little boys who knew me. How quickly he had run off, but he had looked shy rather than mis-chievous. Most certainly I would not go.

But it kept bothering me. What if . . .

In any event the note was not from Charon. Never would Charon ask me to meet him anywhere except at his desk at the *commissariat*. The cemetery after dark. . . . Not Charon, correct Charon, unbribable Charon, who made efforts to be coolly polite so that we would not get any idea that he might swerve from the book.

What if it had to do with the eight in the Percy house? Somehow I felt it did. At this moment we could not afford to turn Charon against us, or whosoever might want to warn us or blackmail us. Go? And become the laughingstock of the town? Blackmail? Don't go? Or could it have to do with André? Some *Résistance* matter? *Merde alors,* I wish I knew!

After darkness had fallen, I was on the deserted road winding inland. Hills rising on both sides made the road very dark. And the mystery of what was waiting for me made me fearful. The slightest rustle from the deep shadows of the roadside set my heart pounding. I dug tight fists deep into the pockets of my trench coat as if my hands were all of me and I could hide there from a sudden attacker. What a fool I had been not to tell someone where I was going. What a fool! The cemetery after dark! How could I have fallen for anything so ridiculous? But the eight. . . .

A dark figure emerged from the darkness just a few feet from me, and my heart leaped into my mouth.

"Keep your voice down," Charon said.

I had never seen him out of uniform, and the Charon in shirt and cotton slacks was a new man whom I did not know at all. He glanced over his shoulder, nervously it seemed, which somewhat curbed my own fear.

"*Venez,*" he said in a whisper and ushered me into the cemetery, amidst pale gravestones, dark iron crosses, rusty wire wreaths with remnants of wilted flowers. I took note that he wasn't taller than I, slight, if wiry, and certainly strong. I made sure to keep enough distance between us so that I could kick him in the groin if necessary. So far he had given no indication that he had rape on his mind, but Frenchmen are clever, subtle. Brute force was not their way.

"*Ici,*" he said and sat down on the summer-dry grass. I sat down, too, the right space between us. I swallowed hard, but every muscle was on the alert. It was impossible to make out his face, it was all shadows. He sat with bowed head, plucking grass, saying nothing.

At last he spoke. "We did not know," he said. "We believed they were to be taken to work camps and farms to help with the harvest. Many women are alone, their men in prisoner-of-war camps. The farms need men this time of the year, need many hands, women as well. Even kids can do certain chores without coming to harm." He paused, plucked grass.

His head came up and his dark face turned to me. "We did not know that it was to be the *zone occupé* . . . Auschwitz." He pronounced it "Oshweeze."

What did he want? Absolution?

I was all in a knot and had clenched my teeth so hard they hurt.

He sighed. It sounded genuine. "Those who were taken," he said, "why didn't they go into hiding like the rest? They knew we were coming, they were dressed and packed, waiting for us to come and take them away. Why? Why, *bon Dieu!*"

The ring of distress softened me. I tried to answer his question. I wanted to make him understand, Charon, the Frenchman in shirt and slacks. Wars will not change the world for the better, but if one Charon had a change of heart, just one Charon, the world would be a little bit better. But as I listened to what I said, I found my words hopelessly inadequate. They would not reach this man. Had he ever heard about Russian pogroms, Polish ghettos? He had not seen the Jews on their knees scrubbing the pavement of Vienna's Kärtnerstrasse, not seen the young hoodlums douse them with pails of soapy water. He had not seen little Simon weep.

My words came more and more haltingly. I didn't make sense, was jumping from this to that. And I noticed that my tone of voice was angry, aggressive, all wrong. Hard as I tried, my voice grew even sharper as I felt that I was losing ground. And then I came to a stammering halt.

"*Et les autres?*" he asked softly.

That put me on my guard. This "conscience-stricken" policeman was still a policeman. Easy now, weigh each word.

"We expect orders to search," he said. "None of us at the *commissariat* will make an effort to find them. But we would have no choice if we came face to face with them. That can be avoided if you tell me where they're hiding."

The cat was out of the bag. Try again, I thought.

"Orders to search might not come to us but go to the gendarmerie. I've reason to believe that they won't give them a break."

Turn to the good police if you're up against the bad gendarmes. I hoped he did not see my smile. It thrilled me that after his almost perfect opening move, he had made a fatal blunder. Let him do the talking, it is he who wants something. In his effort to coax me into spilling the secret, he might inadvertently reveal something important for us to know.

"To be quite frank," he said, "a search order will come. It is the logical next step. The houses where foreigners live will be the first to be searched. Of course."

Good boy. Keep going.

"That no such search order has come as yet is cause for concern. Possibly the police are considered somewhat unreliable."

The good police again.

"Vichy specials might be dispatched."

Another boogeyman. The police look better by the minute.

"They might very well appear unannounced, just drop by to pick a local man to show them the way. Nonetheless, I might have ways and means to send you a warning."

. . . . .

"Whether there will be time to do something about it, that, of course, is a matter of luck. However, if we know which houses are involved, we could lead the men first to other houses and give you at least some time. You could take them into the vineyards."

. . . . .

"Look, don't fool yourself."

Did he mean they would find them anyway in the long run, therefore why not cut the agony short, get it over with?

"You don't trust me," he said.

He couldn't be that naïve! Now I have to say something, but to say I don't know where they're hiding would be too stupid. Be ambiguous. How?

"I've been aboveboard with you all these years."

Nervous laughter bubbled from my throat. To sit with a pleading policeman among shadowy gravestones and iron crosses suddenly struck me as terribly funny. I giggled like a thirteen-year-old, couldn't stop. I thought of the eight to call myself to order, but I kept at it helplessly, on the verge of tears.

"Psssst!" He was hissing at me, and I winced when he touched my hand. I quieted down finally, but my loss of self-control left me bewildered.

He gave me time to collect myself before he asked: "How do you manage to feed them? Eight people without a ration card!"

I shrugged.

"None of you has the money to buy black-market provisions. Don't think I was fooled by the ten thousand francs every one of you showed me as 'proof of means.' Whose were they?"

The ten thousand francs! He had known all along! He had known and not batted an eyelash. To admit it was to bare himself.

The day Charon was put in charge of *"les affaires des étrangers"* we knew that we were in trouble. Until then, twenty francs slipped to the official had always helped to undo a snag. But this neat, polite, soft-spoken man, without having to say so, made it unmistakably clear that he would not be bribed, would not consort in any irregularities. His calm glance spelled it out: "Your situation had better be in impeccable order." A refugee's situation, however, was rarely for long in impeccable order, because the fickle French bureaucracy would suddenly lash out at us, without rhyme or reason. It did just that when one day in the middle of the war it sent notification to all foreigners to appear at their local *commissariat de police* with "proof of means." How was it possible for them to ignore that the overwhelming majority of refugees had no means whatsoever, no bank account, no dollars hidden in drawers? And surely the dense-brained bureaucrats had to know that refugees were not allowed to accept a job. They ought to have asked themselves how it was possible we hadn't starved to death so far. Did they want to see the pennies we were paid for illicit piecework, which no Frenchman in his right mind would have accepted? Proof of means, indeed!

Yet we were frightened. What were they planning to do with us who could prove only that we were poor as church mice? Put us in a camp? Shove us off to Germany as "voluntary" workers? Word got around that ten thousand francs was the sum considered "means." TEN THOUSAND FRANCS!

Somebody's friend had a friend had a friend who was willing to entrust to us for the day the ten thousand francs he himself would present as his means at the *commissariat de police* in Nice. One of us had to be there to receive the bills as soon as he was through.

The whole lot of us were sipping Vichy water at the Café Littoral, anxiously watching the buses from Nice. The strange benefactor might have a change of heart. But then our messenger arrived, waving exuberantly, and like a flock of migrating birds we deserted the Littoral and alighted around the corner from the *commissariat*. One after the other we presented to Charon the same bills. All we could do was to let the sum vary by a few francs. And while Charon calmly counted the same bills over and over, and entered the amount into the column provided for it on the preprinted sheet, the rest of us, waiting outside, held our breath.

Charon's voice brought me back to the cemetery. "Whose money was it?" he asked. An eternity seemed to have elapsed.

"Someone in Nice," I said. "A stranger."

"I've a small vegetable garden," Charon said. "Some beans, some potatoes. I'll send something up with my son."

"The boy, was he your son?"

"My oldest."

"How many do you have?"

"Three. Madame Ingrid, I beg you to trust me. Perhaps I won't be able to help them, but if circumstances permit, I will do all I can to save them. *Voyons,* I'm a Frenchman, not a beast, not a *boche.*"

What a crazy situation! A Frenchman pleading with a German not to take him for a *boche.*

"*Voyons,* Ingrid . . ."

Everyone in town called me Madame Ingrid, the mailman, the storekeepers, but now Charon had dropped the customary "madame," addressed me as friend. Yet, I could not tell him, could not take such a risk. What if he was just a very smooth operator?

"*Hélas* . . ." he said softly and rose to his feet, brushed off his cotton slacks. "I'll do whatever is in my power. I'll be in touch with you. Should you not be home, where can a note be left safely?"

"At the right-hand corner of my door there's a loose floor tile. Under that tile."

"Check it whenever you return home."

"I will."

"You yourself, Madame Ingrid, move about with

some caution. If we don't deliver enough Jews, we will be asked, we have heard, to fill the quota with undesirable foreigners. And you, madame . . . because of Monsieur André . . . you understand . . . you're suspected of involvement with the *Résistance*. You're being watched. Avoid gendarmes. It might be wise not to sleep at home for a while."

Where would I sleep? But I acquiesced with a nod. Did they know where André was? Was he being watched? I had better warn him, post a letter first thing in the morning.

After six months of imprisonment in Fort St. Nicholas at Marseille, André was tried and sentenced to ten years for *Résistance* activity but was released on probation, a normal procedure for the *zone libre* at that time. Once he had recovered somewhat, he announced that he was going to Vichy, that he had to have a closer look at the French government that imprisoned Frenchmen for fighting France's enemy. "*Ça alors, c'est fou!*" he exclaimed unbelieving, even though he himself had been one of its victims. And that was where André was at present, in Vichy, a city crawling with Gestapo.

"*J'ai honte,*" Charon said. "I'm ashamed for France."

I was weary, couldn't think of anything better to say than: *C'est la guerre."*

"No. Even in war, a man must live with his conscience. We won't do the *boche*'s dirty work."

Hitler had called conscience a "degrading chimera."

"Should you find a blank piece of paper under that loose tile, come here," he said. "Same place, same time. A cemetery after dark is a safe meeting place. Preferably don't come by the road. Take Rue Cézanne, past Ange's house. Behind *la maison des Vignes* a path leads down, a bit overgrown at the upper end, but passable. Down here

it skirts the cemetery. Try it once in daytime to familiarize yourself with it."

"I will." .

He extended his hand. *"Amis?"*

"Friends, Charon."

He made the victory sign. *"On les aura."*

"It isn't that I don't trust you . . ."

"I understand. Believe me, I do understand." His
hand brushed my coat sleeve. "You go first. We mustn't
be seen together."

"Good night, Charon."

"Bonne nuit, belle Ingrid." His tone of voice made
"belle" synonym for "friend."

As I made my way back through the dark shadows
cast by the two hillsides, I was guided by the roofs
ahead, silvery sheets, clay roofs shining in the amazing
light cast by tiny stars far away.

I glanced back once, but could not tell whether I really
saw the vague shape of policeman Charon. It might have
been just a shrub.

Now and then something rustled by the roadside, but
I knew it was the breeze in the summer-dry grass, or
just a mouse. From the cisterns in the vineyards all
around came the rhythmic chant of the frogs, a throb-
bing that I could feel on my skin like the nearness of a
huge, pulsating heart. And for a spellbound moment it
was the heart of France.

I reached the first houses, French small-town houses
with shuttered windows. Small vegetable gardens. I wondered whether Charon lived in one of them. I passed
the bakery sitting in the curved end of the steep *montée.*
People were still sitting on dark doorsteps. *"Bon soir,*
Madame Bergère." *"Bon soir,* Madame Ingrid."

Hanna's bay window. I climbed the crooked steps to

my landing. Nobody in the Alsatians' house either. I
entered my room, went through the kitchen, and out on
my large terrace. Beyond the dark strip of shoreland
glittered the sea. From Stefan's and Martha's dark terrace came laughter. They were from Cologne. She was
Jewish, he was not. When Jews had to register, he would
not let her do it. And when other German Jews went
into hiding, he would not let her go. She must stick to
her role, go about her way as usual, he said.

The old town proper was a world by itself, and
against the outside world its inhabitants stuck together.
It was by no means a homogeneous world, for the na-
tives had little in common with the "artists." Not everybody among the "artists" was an artist, but French Im-
pressionist painters had discovered this town and made
it their own and ruled it, and ever since, anybody who
was not a native was considered an artist by the townspeople. The artist colony, like an exclusive club, did not
let anyone who was not congenial rent a room or a
house. The stringency had lessened somewhat with the
war's stream of refugees from the north. But people
who were attracted by the primitive ancient houses, and
not discouraged by the strenuous *montée,* proved to fit
in. And as unlikely as they might have seemed at first,
sooner or later they belonged.

The one exception was Erich Hillery. Hard as he
tried, he was not accepted. Even though he was constantly on the scene, he was so foreign an element that
nobody even bothered to know precisely where he lived,
or to ask how this German Jewish boy had come by the
name of Hillery. He was ignored, considered a nuisance
at the most, a stray mongrel dog who happened to be
around. One could scarcely set foot outside without
running into Hillery and then having him tag along at

one's elbow. If he found any of us at the Café Littoral, he would pull up a chair. He would climb the *montée* alongside whoever was on the way up, would be at the plaza in the afternoon. He was never asked to anyone's house. If the group he had hitched on to dropped in on someone, forever smiling Hillery would walk on, find someone else. At night he disappeared, nobody knew where to, nobody asked, nobody cared.

When at the beginning of the war, German and Austrian male refugees were interned as enemy aliens, Erich Hillery disappeared from the scene. Nobody asked after him, he was not missed.

At our gatherings at the plaza in the afternoon, we shared the letters that came from the internment camp, and one such letter mentioned Hillery. "Old diehard Hillery is busy as usual making the rounds from 'friend' to 'friend.' Who was it who called him a stray dog? He's the entire camp's dog. Only when there's mail call does he stay behind. When all of us crowd around the mail sergeant, he stands somewhere apart, that odd grin on his face. What a creepy guy."

We laughed. Hillery's permanent smile was one of the things we did not like about him. That smile was like putting a foot in the door to prevent its being closed in his face.

However, after that letter, Hillery preyed on my mind. I visualized him left behind when the others hopefully ran to mail call. Finally I sat down and wrote to him to alleviate his terrible loneliness. And the first letter was not the only one.

Then Hillery was given a medical discharge. He had only one lung. Once Hillery was back in town, I discovered that he had a friend — me. He saw to it that my friendship was no burden to me. If he knocked at my door, it was to bring me a couple of real cigarettes, or the twelve coffee beans that crowned the half pound of our monthly ersatz coffee. He would drop by to tell me "firsthand" information about matters of interest to foreigners. And if there was something I needed, or wished I had, he would run anywhere, anytime, to get it for me because one day at camp there was a letter for him at mail call. "Whatever you need, let me know. I've ways and means."

He had. He had a finger in the black market. He had contacts at the *préfecture de police* and could "fix" all sorts of difficulties. He was trafficking in foreign exchange. Other refugees also did that sort of thing for a living. As we could not make an honest living, whether one did or didn't give black-market peddling a try was almost more a question of guts than of ethics. Hillery needed money and he needed black-market provisions. He had to eat well. If his tuberculosis flared up he would die. We condemned neither him nor any of the others. Even ethics are subject to circumstance. What mattered in our life was that a person was trustworthy, that no matter what, he would not denounce others.

Unfortunately, Hillery's devotion failed to make him more appealing. My friendship was charity. His presents, his invitations to a dish of black-market ice cream, left me feeling uncomfortable, for I could not bring myself to like him.

Later, when other German Jews were in hiding, Hillery moved about as usual. Did he have no choice because he had to feed the one remaining lung, or was he confident that he would be able to "fix" it should he be picked up?

It was Hillery who told me that a great many Jews in hiding were getting ready to cross the Savoy Alps into

Switzerland by night, and that our Jews ought to do the same, for they would not survive in France. He told me that they would need forged papers for the train ride to Annecy, papers that identified them as Frenchmen. The city of Nice, he said, abounded with forgers. A false identity card cost a thousand francs, and for additional money one could buy supporting documents: birth certificates, army discharge papers, vaccination certificates, tax declarations, school graduation diplomas and whatnot. He could give me addresses to go to.

Who had a thousand francs? None of our Jews.

Hillery suggested that I find paying customers, Jews hiding in the area who could not themselves go to Nice to buy forged papers. I could be their messenger. If I brought business to a forger, he might, in due course, make identity cards for our Jews at a special price.

It proved to be amazingly easy to find customers. I mentioned to a few acquaintances that I would be available as a messenger, and before I knew it I was on the bus to Nice more often than I liked. And on my way back, the false papers burned in my shoes. These interurban buses were frequently stopped en route. Officials boarded to check parcels and pockets and finger coat seams. It happened that, cold sweat on my back, I watched other travelers ordered to step out of their shoes. On each ride, I counted the minutes until I could finally hand over the cards, be safe, still free.

Not only did I bring quite a bit of business to one of the forgers, I flirted with the ugly man and flattered him. But when the day came on which I dared appeal to him to make cards for my friends out of the goodness of his heart, he said that the extent of tragedy was too great, that there were thousands of poor devils like my friends, and were he to allow his businesslike detachment to weaken, he might just as well close up shop. "I can't afford to listen to hard luck stories, I'm only human. One thousand francs and a card is yours, no questions asked. Period."

Damn Hillery! Outside the forger's apartment I had a good cry. On my way back, the bus was flagged down by control officials. The search was specifically thorough. I was frightened, discouraged, and the risk I was running no longer had a purpose. The official took my bag, asked me to hand him my jacket. Next he might ask me to take off my shoes.

"Nervous?" He sneered and I was in tears.

The glance he gave me chilled me to the bone. All was lost. They had me! "My mother . . ." I stammered. "I won't make it to the hospital . . . I won't make it in time . . . please . . ."

He stared at me. I began to shake all over. He stared. "Your mother?"

I dropped my face into my hands, and it wasn't an act. I had gone through too many such harrowing trips. My nerves were worn thin.

Dear French gendarme, he hurried the other officials off the bus and called to the driver: *"Allez-y en vitesse! A mother is dying!"* Off we were with whatever there was in other travelers' shoes. And I swore never, not ever again, to transport forged identity cards in mine. I didn't have it in me.

Hillery said not to worry, he would find a way out. A couple of days later he was at my door. "Your problem is solved."

I let him in.

"I know some Poles. They do their forging themselves. They don't have a proper rubber stamp, but they know how to fake the imprint. All you have to do is buy card blanks and the tax stamps at the tobacconist. Don't go and buy eight at one and the same place, buy one here, one there. The seal itself is just a matter of careful drawing."

"They'll do it for us for nothing?"

"They'll show you how."

"But who'll draw the seal?"

"You'll draw it. You draw very well."

"Not the seal of *la République!* Are you out of your mind? Here, look." I displayed my identity card. *"La République,* her flowing robes, the scales, all that stuff around her. Besides, the lettering. I could never do that."

"One of them will be here tomorrow at two-thirty. You get the cards and the tax stamps and have photos, he'll bring whatever else is needed."

"Erich, no!"

"If the Poles can do it, you can do it. Since it's vital . . ."

Since it's vital. . . . No less than the seal of *la République française!* A town full of abstract painters. Who of them could draw, draw her?

The knock on my door was on schedule. I'll give him a cup of tea, let him explain, and that will be that. I hadn't found a volunteer to do the drawing.

When I opened the door, I started. The frail man's head was too big. No, it was the forehead, too high, too wide. And his ears. Thin, translucent mother-of-pearl shells that the long strands of sandy hair failed to hide. Headlong my glance plunged into his calm, very large eyes, pale gray like a misty November morning, eyes that knew how disconcerting the first look at him was. The eyes, the fine mouth, the perfect nose seemed borrowed from another head, and while they ruled the unsettling picture, they underlined the grotesqueness of this ensemble.

He remained standing there as if to give me time to recover, time to find the melancholy smile that a life-long sorrow had carved into his delicate cheeks, and that pleaded movingly for kindness.

The poor creature's hands were also beautiful but a size too large, as the hands of hunchbacks sometimes are. I asked him in and noted with relief that he was not a hunchback.

His name was a soft whisper, something like Zhizh-vizhny. He pronounced the *zh* infinitely softly, as though his name were an endearment.

His incredible, rapid French full of soft *zh*'s and roll-ing *r*'s was unintelligible to me. At first I took it for Polish. Hard as I tried to catch a word, I might just as well have tried to discover a word in the swish of rush-ing water and the rattle of rolling pebbles in a lively mountain stream.

"I'm afraid there's no one among us who can draw well enough," I said. But apparently Hillery had told him I could, for he merely smiled and went on unwrap-ping the forger's tools: hard pencils, a drawing pen, tracing paper, copy ink, and a clear imprint of the seal of *la République*.

"I couldn't . . . I can't. . . ."

"You'll learrrrrrrrrrn," he said calmly.

Since his words were mostly lost on me, I had to rely on the directions his expressive hands gave me. But pencil-tracing the seal was a taxing job, even though the lines were clearly visible through the tracing paper. The next step was to turn the paper facedown and repeat the lines with pen and copy ink on the reverse side, which resulted in a mirror image of the seal within the circle of

reversed lettering. This done, Zhizhvizhny blew on it
to dry the ink somewhat. Then he carefully put the
sketch facedown on a sheet of paper and pressed gently
with the ball of his hand and with a light index finger.
He carefully lifted the piece of tracing paper and there
it was: the seal. But both of us laughed, for the famous
lady looked like a mermaid.

"You see, I can't do it, and I gave it my best."

His pale gray eyes were compassionate, but his hand
said that I would have to practice, make as many
sketches as needed to come up with one that was usable.
Hundreds he had made, he said, to get a good one.
What was worse was hearing that each drawing could
be used to make only two good imprints. For more, one
had to make a new drawing. "What is time, what is
effort?" he said. "You give it one day, two days, three
days, as many as are needed. With such a seal you'll give
more than three days of life to the one who will be
rescued by the forged card."

Next he showed me the proper printing of the seal.
The prints mustn't come out perfect, for genuine French
seals are sloppily applied, often smudgy, and usually
pale, since the government was stingy with stamp pads,
he explained. Often only half the seal comes off.

My eyes clung to his lips to read what he was saying,
when my attention was distracted by his perfect teeth.
And suddenly there was a whole lot of them, and he was
laughing out loud.

"I'm sorry," I said. "Say that again."

He pulled from his jacket pocket an initialed silver
case and offered me a cigarette. It was an English
Player's. He smiled. I did not ask questions. The forging lesson proceeded.

We practiced printing. We dismissed *la République,*

drew mice, piggies, anything that gave us quickly something to print. It was hot, my hand stuck to the paper. I grew tired, my hand was unsteady.

Finally he was satisfied that I got the knack of it, but I was mistaken to think I could now make a cup of tea. Oh, no, he had to drill me in how to dispose of my forging tools within seconds. It would not do to be surprised at my work.

He chose the top of the high-hung water tank of my toilet for the place where I should keep the tools, and where I had to whisk them if there was a knock at my door. He gave each tool a specific place on the table and directed me always to work with the tools at precisely these designated places so that I would be able to grab them blindly and make them disappear.

"Now do it."

I put the tools at their places, sat down.

"Uncork the ink and take the pen. Draw something."

I did. "Now!" Zhizhvizhny cried, rapping the table. I grabbed the tools, pressed the cork into the ink bottle, dropped the paper, picked it up, dashed to the toilet.

"Again." Zhizhvizhny, watch in hand, was timing me.

Again, and again, and again. He frowned at my tiring. "Gathering your tools must be a reflex, needing no thought, no eyes. Even if a sudden harsh knocking unnerves you, your hands will do the motions by reflex. Therefore again, please."

I was exhausted when he let me off. We had a cup of mint tea on the terrace. Only then did he tell me to caution everyone that this kind of seal tends to smudge since copy ink doesn't ever dry completely; that they must not brush the seal in handling the cards, not plant their thumb on top of the seal.

"Such a card," I exclaimed, "they can't use."

Opening his graceful hands he calmly said: "They can. This seal is just one more risk added to the many, many risks they will take. That the seal tends to smudge is of little importance. What matters is to know that it smudges. Their safety does not depend on having the best identity card, money, and a face that doesn't look too Jewish, but on their awareness and the astute handling of their weaknesses. We are fallible." The beautiful hand brushed back the thin strands of sandy hair, passed across the too wide forehead wiping away a memory, it seemed. And he took leave with a formal bow and a Polish hand kiss.

I expected never to see him again. But I was to meet him each time I went to Nice. He would emerge from the crowd at the bus terminal. Or on Rue Massena he would walk toward me. If I stopped at a café, he would enter soon after. It was as if in the hours of tracing seals, we had traced a mysterious new circle, an invisible track on which both of us ran.

We became friends even though our friendship was like a gift we held unopened. He never spoke about himself or his past, nor did he ask about mine. I tried to piece together his past from clues such as the oval signet ring on his finger, which bore a family crest, and the worldly ease he displayed, the wide range of his knowledge, and his graceful manner. I ceased to notice his mother-of-pearl ears, and that his finely lined forehead was too high, too wide. And in time I understood better his soft sibilants and the rolling *r*'s.

I felt he was in love with me, even though he guarded his November eyes. And when he saw me to the bus his au revoir was always formal — a bow and a hand kiss that expressed only respectful devotion. Life must have taught him to love in secret to keep pain within bearable bounds.

Then came a day when Zhizhvizhny did not walk toward me, did not enter the café where I was sitting. This had to happen, after all; it was silly to have taken our chance meetings as infallible. But the next day I was back in Nice, walking down the Promenade des Anglais, the Rue Massena, looking into the cafés. Zhizhvizhny did not show.

Hillery gave me his address. Nobody answered the doorbell. Again I walked around, but nowhere did I find the strange face of my friend. Had he been forced to leave Nice suddenly? He would have dropped me a line, would have said au revoir. But nothing ever came.

Others survived because Zhizhvizhny taught me how to forge the seal of *la République*. I forged in fear, and in my dreams the bearers of my forged cards were caught because my seals were not good enough. Yet all those in the Percy house traveled safely to Annecy. And for the way on foot by night across the high mountains into Switzerland no paper was good enough.

Once they had left, I was free at last. And if, in my sleep, I frantically gathered up the forging tools and hid them on top of the water tank because someone was coming to my door, I would awaken from the nightmare to know that it was over, that I did not have to forge ever again.

Then one day André's friend Clément dropped in. His gaunt face was all smiles. He set a bottle of wine on the table and offered me a genuine cigarette.

"What are we celebrating?"

"I've sold a story."

So we celebrated. And then he came out with it. British airmen, who had parachuted into France and were in hiding, needed French identity cards to make it to the Spanish border. The man who was to make the cards for them had been rushed to the hospital. They could get another man through *Résistance* channels but there was a time squeeze. Everything was set for the airmen to be on their way, and by morning the liaison man would come for the cards. If the cards were not ready, the checkpoints along their route would have to be reorganized. "Besides, with each day they stay there's the risk that they might be discovered. You and I will have to make cards for them."

At the very thought, my throat went dry, and I stared at the photos Clément put on the table, at the young Anglo-Saxon faces. "They'll never pass for French. They look so awfully English."

"We'll make them be from Brittany. Bretons look like that. We'll do the job at my place. I'll get the card blanks and tax stamps."

That night the young faces became René Duveaux from Pont-l'Abbé, Romain Carpentier from Vannes, Pierre Ballard from Saint-Malo, Paul Villard from Saint-Brieuc. And I laughed with Clément because I was not alone.

A fortnight later a man delivered a small parcel to Clément. He said it was so crumpled because it had been passed on from hand to hand all the way from Marseille. It contained a whole pound of real coffee beans and a note: "God bless you. We'll be back."

I often wondered whether they made it home. Perhaps they still have their French identity cards, stored away in a box of war souvenirs. Henry? James? William? Andrew? I never knew your true names, only your young, so dangerously Anglo-Saxon faces.

I did not have to forge ever again. The French *Résistance,* growing in strength and efficiency, took over. The forged identity cards they supplied bore genuine rubber imprints done with seals that had been issued by the French government, and that had mysteriously disappeared from an official desk. But the identity cards provided by the *Résistance* came too late for the hundred thousand Jews caught in that August raid or soon after because they did not have the money to buy papers. They did not make it to the border; they could not move to another town and pass as Frenchmen.

Little Simon Fischbein was not the only Jewish child among my close playmates. There was Karl-Titus Schwarz. His father, a worldly, dapper gentleman, commanded respect. And Frau Schwarz most definitely did not wear a wig. They were not considered odd, and if their Jewishness was mentioned at all, it was discreetly breathed. Polite Herr Schwarz kept aloof, but Frau Schwarz was on the scene, a stately brunette whose status and authority were undisputed. As a mother she was more Prussian than any mother on the block. She upheld strict discipline and at the slightest provocation Karl-Titus would receive a resounding slap on the face. There was no trace of "Jewish mother" in her, and personally I considered her a monster. Or was this strong woman trying to slap all the Jewishness out of her only son because she did not trust civilized Germany? Was she just as fearful at heart as Frau Fischbein?

I did not like Karl-Titus. I bristled when I saw him turn into a petrified rabbit the minute his mother showed up, or when that pained look was obliterated by bleak resignation to his lot. It troubled me that his eyes never filled with tears when she slapped him, when she humiliated him in front of all of us. It would have been unbearable for me had I liked him. Occasionally I felt sorry for him, and it was out of compassion, not love, that I became engaged to him under the golden-chain laburnum by the sandbox in their small front yard. I was eight, I believe.

Karl-Titus adored me. He must have seen in me freedom personified, for whenever his eyes strayed from his Latin exercises out the window, he would see me skipping, leaping, streaking past on my scooter or bicycle. But if I was sun brightening his dull days, I was also the siren who lured him into disaster. I had the gift of evoking so tempting a picture of gold prospecting in the Grunewald one day that even browbeaten Karl-Titus faltered. But agonizingly aware that the price he had to pay for it would be banishment to his mother's "Siberia," he followed me sad-faced. For me as well that excursion had calamitous consequences. As I was getting ready, I felt the need to be handsomely girded. None of my belts were the right kind, while Dalla's new belt of rugged cowhide links was ideal for the prospector. I "borrowed" it, hiding it under my sailor's blouse until we had left our street behind us.

Only on our way home after a glorious afternoon did I notice the belt was gone. And leaving Karl-Titus to his fate, I ran back to the woods to search the pine-needle-strewn forest floor. It was hopeless. I could not tell where we passed earlier, for the landmarks I remembered belonged to vast American prairies and rocky mountain ranges.

That very evening Dalla discovered that her belt was

missing, and her eyes accused me. I felt unjustly smitten by cruel luck. I had only borrowed her belt, borrowed it for a mere couple of hours.

I helped Dalla look for it, went through all possible drawers, crawled under the beds, as if with my diligence I could atone and magically make the belt appear. That night I prayed to God, and next morning I looked in Dalla's drawer, but the belt had not come back. Such an injustice staggered me. I had only borrowed the wretched belt, borrowed it! How could such a minor wrong have such irreparable consequences? It wasn't fair!

Dalla's eyes looked at me accusingly for many years. "The belt," they kept saying. "Remember the belt."

Great adventures were written in my stars, but for each I had to pay a price. Rightly so, I was blamed for the magnificent trip to the Machnow locks, to which I was driven as if by a sacred calling. All the mothers were up in arms against me, even though it was generosity that made me take along all the children on our street.

On a previous Sunday, our grandfather had taken us to the canal locks, and to make the excursion even more interesting, he had hired a victoria. It was a sultry day, and the adults silently savored the relief-giving shade of the trees that spread a green roof above the long, straight road. I was on the jump seat facing backward and, listening to the horses' hoofbeats and the small creakings of the carriage, I watched the road slip away from under us, and time passed like nothing. It was therefore in all honesty that I told my playmates the locks weren't far.

It must have been vacation time, for we sneaked away

in the morning, small brothers or sisters on the baggage carriers of our bicycles. Only Dalla was not among us. I had not let her in on our plans, for her foresight in regard to possible dangers would have been in the way. As usual, she was on that morning engrossed in painting a flowery meadow and children dancing ring-around-a-rosy, with gentle-eyed deer and squirrels looking on. She was extraordinarily gifted, so much so that people caught their breath in amazement over her precocious mastery. I admired her enormously and considered it a special treat when she let me have a discarded sketch to color. I did not envy her the gift or the praise; what I resented was that Dalla did no wrong and was always neat. To have her constantly held up as an example, I took badly. And since our already strained relationship was recently further burdened by the belt tragedy, I could not possibly make her part of the Machnow locks adventure.

Müsi was, of course, always at my side. He never questioned the wisdom of any of my doings. For him I had the key to the wonders of the world. If his fears were always ready to surface, he trusted in me to protect him, and I did. He was the one I loved most; he was a part of myself.

Also among our troops of children were Erwin and Max, brothers living in the less elegant courtyard apartments toward the back. Some mothers had forbidden their children to associate with Erwin and Max because they used "words." Our own mother limited her disapproval to occasional sighs, for she was too democratic-minded to draw a social line. However, her face would show that *noblesse oblige* could be painful.

Skinny Gert von Havenow and his puny little sister Mousy-Mouse came along, too. Their father was a career officer. He thrashed Gert daily, either as a punishment for something Gert had done or as prophylactic therapy. And during the whippings he roared: "Never again! Not ever again!" Gert was not a likable child, but we children gave little thought to such criteria; whoever lived in the three houses on our street belonged. The treatment Gert received at home aroused little pity in us, for the somewhat fiendish grin that hardly ever left his thin, freckled face made him seem insensitive to beatings and humiliations. He had a most peculiar gait, long, slinking steps like those of a two-bit crook making his getaway. His knees were always slightly flexed as though he were keeping prepared to duck a sudden slap on the face or a hand grabbing him by the scruff of his neck.

The first part of our way, the stretch from our street to my grandparents' house, I could have done in my sleep since we walked to the Sunday family gatherings, weather permitting. On foot it took an hour.

Snickering with glee over outsmarting our parents, it seemed just minutes until we sighted the tall chestnut trees of my grandparents' street. To pass their house undetected, Müsi and I bent low over the handlebars and pedaled hard, and then burst out laughing to vent our tensions.

The next landmark was Lichterfelde East, and to get there we only had to follow the tramway tracks. But since I had no recollection of which way we had taken them, I fell silent, preoccupied. The children grew uneasy, and doubt and bad conscience stirred in them. I found the highway leading to Machnow, but my relief was short-lived, for the pastoral thoroughfare with its shade-spreading trees failed to breathe an air of peace as it had that Sunday with Grandpapa. Threats lurked in the shadows thrown upon the lonesome road. Whenever a workman on his bicycle came toward us, we would fearfully draw together, scarcely daring a glance at the man in a soft cap. Men in soft caps were the unknown, and therefore evil. One such workman, glowering at us in passing, made Mousy-Mouse burst into tears, and her high-pitched shrieks put an end to the others' self-control. They were also tired and thirsty and faltering with remorse. Except for Müsi's faithful eyes, I stood alone.

Once again I sang the praises of the locks and assured them that the clear canal waters would slake their thirst soon, for Machnow had to be around the next bend in the road.

It was not. As if bewitched, the road seemed to run on to the end of the world. The children whined for rest stops. To get them on their feet again, I had to deliver more pep talks, even though I myself wished to sit and cry. The locks had betrayed me!

The children followed, downcast, their silence accusing me. To fight my despondency I began to sing loudly.

Suddenly, there it was. "The locks!" We pushed the bicycles across the field. "A barge!" The bicycles fell with a clatter, and we ran, forgetting thirst and remorse.

"Hey, the water is rising!"

"Look, the barge is coming up!"

"There's another one waiting!"

"Yippeeeeeeee!"

The men on the barge were pulling in ropes. A capstan was screeching. Up in the lock's machine house an "old sea dog" in a watch cap was pulling levers. The lock's gate opened. And ah, the smell of the murky canal water! The smell of tar and machine oil!

Flushed and in need of a short pause, my glance leaped to the far side of the locks, to the garden restau-

rant where Grandpapa had treated us to cherry tart with
whipped cream. Grandpapa had been in a rare good
mood. Instead of disapprovingly raising his eyebrows
at the table manners of the Sunday crowd, he shook with
laughter over a woman eating her plum cake with knife
and fork, daintily lifting her little finger. But no matter
what the surroundings were, we had to observe the same
impeccable manners as if we were in one of the formal
restaurants where our grandfather took us on occasion
to familiarize us with the language of worldly menus,
the names of *haute cuisine* sauces, and wines and vin-
tages.

"Another barge coming! Two!"

Oh, wonderful world! And nobody around to tell us
what not to do.

"Eeeeeh . . . look how slimy the walls are."

An ominous shadow made us look up. The sky was
heaped with thunderclouds. A strong gust blew sand into
my eyes, and Mousy-Mouse turned into a torch of piercing shrieks.

"To my grandparents' house!" I yelled.

Driven by the threatening sky, the children pedaled
hard, looked neither right nor left. Müsi remained close
by my side.

As we approached our goal we noticed that the storm
had gone another way. Sun lay sweetly on hedges and
front lawns, and before my mind's eye hung Grandpapa's plums. His trees were not for climbing, and
Grandmama claimed the fruit for winter compotes.
However, my friends deserved my gratitude for not
breaking into mutiny.

Pondering the logistics, I viewed the two-story stucco
house from the far side of the street. I wished I could
tell whether my grandfather was at the curtained living-

room window viewing the little magnolia tree as he frequently did. To him it was a ballerina. When its bloom
came to an end, the gardener was not allowed to remove
the heap of fallen pink petals until they turned brown,
for that was the little ballerina's tutu, Grandpapa said,
and the sight of her with her tutu about her graceful
ankles pleased him.

"Listen, kids, the gate creaks. We'll have to climb
over and make a run for the side of the house." That
side held the main entrance, hiding it from prying eyes.
Into the frieze of the stone portico an inscription was
hewn in large, clear letters, admonishing the visitor:
Nütze den Tag — make use of the day. I never failed to
glance at the inscription; it commanded me to, as if it
were a voice as powerful as God's thundering THOU
SHALT NOT KILL!

Now, too, *Nütze den Tag* stared at me, and I wished
I were somewhere else, not committed to leading the
children to the plum tree. Mousy-Mouse whimpered as
we lifted and pulled and pushed her over the high fence
that enclosed the backyard. Müsi paled with fright. I
would have to think of another way of getting out. For
the moment we were safe, and I led the children through
the bushes to the small grove where the swing was and
the plum tree, and where we could not be seen from the
house. "Keep your voices down."

As if happy children would notice their voices becoming strident, as if I could keep Grandpapa on my mind.
I was ten at the most, and I loved this garden. Forgetting Grandpapa's study window, I showed my friends
the little knoll at the far end of the oval lawn, where the
stone bust of a terrier amidst a bed of vines and leafy
plants marked the spot where a little dog was buried.
Grandpapa's dog. We were not allowed to mention that

dog to him, and I wondered whether he would cry if we did. I told the children that by running off that knoll, arms spread wide, head tilted back, and eyes on the clouds, one felt as though one were flying. And to show them how, I opened my arms, tilted my head back and, as if letting myself fall into water, I raced down the slight incline. My legs ran on full speed down the gravel path and, my eyes on the sky, I delighted in the titillating dizziness of my disoriented head, when suddenly I hung suspended, hung from my grandfather's hands. We stared at each other. I scarcely dared breathe. And I did not know what to make of his eyes, of this look of stunned fascination. I hung from his hands for an everlasting moment until abruptly, without a word, without a change in his face, he put me down, turned about and hastened into the house.

Grandmama herded us inside to the bathroom. While she washed us, one after the other, she scolded us, told us in her shaky ineffectual voice that children from decent homes do not take off unchaperoned. She said we might have lost our way, might have been accosted by roughnecks, suffered heatstroke or nosebleeds, and we might have drowned in the dirty canal. The dirtiness of the water seemed worse than drowning.

Grandmama gave us a fairly good idea of what was going on at home. All the mothers were in an uproar, sure that I was the culprit. Not only did Grandmama seem to agree with them, but with wagging finger and distressed eyes she accused me of almost causing my grandfather to have a heart attack. She said she had found him at his desk staring unbelievingly at the horde of children romping on his lawn. And she said one day, when he was no more, I would be sorry for the anguish I gave him when he saw his own granddaughter in the grass, legs in the air and panties showing, as if she had lost her senses. His own grandchild not only a runaway, luring other children to the canal, but then coming here and stealing into the garden like a thief. "You heartless child!"

Not heartless, no! Not heartless! I wanted to make up to my friends for their hardship; they were tired and thirsty. Not heartless. But how to tell her? She would not understand.

At the garden table we were served refreshments, watery lemonade and leftover "Wondercake." To Grandmama, who had grown up in a puritanical home, frugality was a matter of ethics rather than of economy, and Grandpapa had failed to convert her to his view that a cultured way of life and fine foods were inseparable. The Sunday pastries for the grown-ups came from the finest shop because Grandpapa insisted on that. But since Grandmama believed that Sacher torte and petits fours were detrimental to our character development, we children always found on the table set for us in the garden her plain and exceedingly dull "Wondercake." The "Wondercake" we were served now was what we had left the previous Sunday. Therefore, it was also stale. Perhaps the cake tasted dry in my mouth because I watched uneasily Grandpapa's study window. Surely the wordless glance he had given me had not settled the matter between us. My heart sank when Grandmama stepped outside. But rather than bringing me the summons, she took us to the gate and watched us get ready to leave. She lifted Mousy-Mouse on back of Gert's bicycle and instructed her to hold on tight to big brother's jacket at all times. And she told Müsi to get off his bicycle at intersections and push it across. "And no dallying en route."

I expected to be called back into the house even at this very last minute. And when I wasn't, I could have wept with relief. From gratitude I resolved diligently to practice "Der fröhliche Landmann," the piano piece my despairing teacher had tried to teach me from time immemorial without any noticeable results. Since Grandpapa had ordered the piano lessons, not practicing was like losing my hair ribbon in the garden, a way of retaliating for "stupid little Ini." This passive resistance cost me much anxiety and humiliation, but the price must have been worth it.

On Sundays, when Grandpapa sat back with his after-dinner cigar, he would ask us to play him our latest pieces as if he were asking for an unusual favor. How I resented that these command performances were so falsely labeled.

Even though Dalla always practiced conscientiously, she would sit on the stool, nervous red blotches appearing on her neck. As to myself, all I ever had to offer was the first measures of the same old boring "Der fröhliche Landmann." DaDA . . . daDA . . . dada-dadada BLAH!!! It never failed. The wrong note would vibrate in the terrible stillness, and I would feel ten pairs of eyes on my back, accusing me of shattering the fragile peacefulness.

But as I pedaled past the suburban gardens, my heart full of thankfulness toward Grandpapa because for once he didn't cut me down to a worthless nothing, to poor, stupid little Ini, I swore to practice "Der fröhliche Landmann" for hours on end so that by next Sunday I could play it perfectly all the way through.

Envisioning the glory of that moment let me forget my sins of this day until my eye fell upon the reception committee of furious mothers lined up in front of our house. Thank God my mother was among them. Her face tense and pale, she hastened toward Müsi and me. "Get off," she snapped, "and quickly upstairs." But her hand on my arm told me that she would protect me.

The time it took to get off my bicycle, lean it against the fence, and fasten the lock, allowed me to observe what happened to Karl-Titus. Frau Schwarz slapped him right and left in the face even before he was off his bicycle, and then she dragged him by the scruff of his neck into the house, enumerating the string of punishments she had been at leisure to think up: so many additional hours of Latin cramming for the next six weeks; no dessert for six weeks; no meat for six weeks; no playing outdoors for six weeks; no playing with his tin soldiers for six weeks; no money for a ride on the merry-go-round for six weeks; dry bread for his school snack and to bed at seven o'clock.

With each new slap he received, I winced. And because of my guilt, I vowed that I would play with him and his tin soldiers six weeks hence. Tin soldiers were the only toys his mother ever gave him for Christmas or birthdays. No cuddly teddy bears for him. He owned sets and sets of infantry and cavalry together with all the accessories, cannons, trucks, wagons, Red Cross tents, and wounded men on litters. It took hours merely to set up his armies, but then they presented a surely impressive sight. Even though my mother had ingrained an aversion for war games in us, I was not insensitive to the picture this multitude of men and equipment presented and would give an occasional rainy day to them and Karl-Titus. However, I told him right away that I would not have any shooting and killing, that our playing had to restrict itself to moving companies about, loading and unloading supply trucks, and to sending out scouts who would lose their way in the woods and meet up with a wolf. But Karl-Titus lacked imagination and all of a sudden he would shout: "The enemy! To your positions, men!"

"I dare you!" I cried, shielding my troops with spread hands.

"Your men must shoot or be killed. My artillery has pinpointed your camp."

"I'm not playing war."

"War is here, you have no choice. Your soldiers must fight!"

"I won't!"

"Then your men will be killed!" He aimed a cannon. "Bang, bang!" He toppled two of my men. "They're dead."

"They're not!" I righted them.

"They are, shoot back."

"You're stupid!"

"Bang-bang-bang-bang!"

Like an angry archangel I descended upon his formations, scattering them to the four winds. "I'm not playing with you! I won't ever again! Shoot until you're blue in the face!" And I was off.

Outside, in front of the house I whirled about, skipped feverishly through our chalked hopscotch squares, climbed atop the stone post of the entrance gate and balanced there on one leg, and laughed and shrieked to show him, who sat sad-faced behind the window, what a great time I had. Served him right. It was his own fault. Yes, it was. "Hey, Erwin, try and catch me! Hey, Erwin, let's play marbles."

However, at the unhappy ending of our excursion to the Machnow locks, I vowed that six weeks hence I would give Karl-Titus and his tin soldiers another chance.

Conspicuous in the committee of angry mothers was the sole male parent, Gert von Havenow's father, riding crop in hand.

Gert, grinning stupidly, helped Mousy-Mouse off the baggage carrier. The father looked on, his face blank. When Gert moved toward him, with soft-kneed, slinking step, the father pointed the whip at the entrance door. Gert slinked inside, and the father followed with deliberately measured step.

"Come, Ini, come," my mother urged. Once we were in the safety of the mirrored elevator, she whined: "*Ach,* children . . . *ach,* terrible . . ." It was not clear to me whether she meant us or Frau Schwarz slapping Karl-Titus, but likely both. Her face had the headache look, and that made me wish with all my heart that I were a child as good as Dalla and had no inclination for excursions. By the time we reached the apartment Mama's headache look was in full bloom. Wawa had to take over. "Don't cry, children," she said. "Go to your room and play quietly. I'll bring you a cup of cocoa."

From the von Havenow's apartment, one floor below us, came Gert's high-pitched yelling: "Never again! Not ever again!" He had had his whipping and now, locked up in the toilet, he was taking it out on his teddy bear. Years later, one day in the midst of World War II, I was reminded of him, except that the Gert in soldier's uniform no longer thrashed teddy bears. The accumulated whippings he had been given he now unloaded on Jews, and "traitors," and Russian peasants, and Dutchmen, and French maquisards.

On that winter day, January 6, 1943, at the railroad station of Montluçon, I believed for a moment I saw

Gert von Havenow. Automatic rifle leveled, the German passing me moved soft-kneed and with long slinking steps. They were three Germans closing in on French-women who had thrown themselves across the tracks in front of the train that was to carry their men off to Germany. German commands were screamed across a station in turmoil, and my mind changed them to the yelling with which Gert used to accompany the beating of his teddy bear.

That day was far into the war and by then France had shaken off the stupor of defeat. Across the land Frenchmen knotted the net with which to catch the enemy. Men and women were dying for it before firing squads. Yet while boys who were never to know man-hood scratched their last message into the wall of a prison cell, someone somewhere began to circulate the myth of France's lack of moral fiber. Some said it was Berlin trying to mislead the Allies, to make them dis-count France. Some said it was to confound the French and undermine their faith in themselves. Some said London gave birth to the myth to make the Germans believe the Allies would never think of landing on French shores, but more likely in Holland. How hard the myth dies!

That winter day was already two years after André's arrest for *Résistance* activities, and six months after he left for Vichy to have a closer look at the French gov-ernment that imprisoned Frenchmen for fighting on against the enemy. And it was six weeks now that he had to run for his life, the Gestapo on his heels. And now I was traveling from the Côte d'Azur to the center of France to rejoin him at the castle of his friend Loirette, where he was hiding. We would not be to-gether for long, for André had decided to go to England

and join de Gaulle's forces. But we would be together one more time. I had to apply for a *sauf-conduit,* the permit I needed to leave the area where I was a resident, and red tape made many precious days go by. Fear that André might have to leave before I got there wore me, and I fell ill and set out on the voyage exhausted. However, a last-minute telegram from Loirette informed me that he would board my train at Vichy, and I was looking forward to having his company for the last hours of the trip.

Loirette had succeeded in having himself appointed to a high advisory position in *la Légion,* a French Nazi organization whose oath was: "I swear to fight against democracy, against Gaullist dissidence, and against Jewish leprosy." It thrilled Loirette to give fiendishly ridiculous advice, and since he was a brilliant and imaginative man, his subterfuges were brilliant. However, the main reason for his being in this post was to keep his finger on the pulse of the Vichy government without having to involve himself in deeds he abhored; to have access to top-level information, which he forwarded to the *Résistance;* to be given free access to the devil incarnate, Laval, whom he despised with all his heart. He played a delicate and most dangerous game, and frequently the tightrope he was walking threatened to snap. Then he would quickly take a leave of absence to work on his book, and eclipse himself in his castle in a remote corner of the countryside. What had made him look suspect evaporated once he was out of sight, was considered an eccentric spoof, for his insolence was too outrageous to be believed. Even though he was brilliant, he was decidedly crazy, too crazy, they thought, too disorganized, too whirly-brained to be a spy.

He was a frail, narrow-chested, toothless, almost

blind man who at first sight elicited pity rather than interest. And he had a falsetto voice. Thick eyeglasses reduced his large brown eyes to tiny beads, and shabby clothing completed the picture.

During his flight from Paris at the time of the German breakthrough, Loirette had been on foot on a country road congested with a stream of fleeing civilians. A German plane had machine-gunned the throng to clear the road for advancing German columns, and Loirette was hit in the mouth. The loss of his front teeth added a lisp to his young-boy voice. But in his poor and damaged body lived an ardent spirit, indomitable, daring, and a burning contempt for the German conquerors.

The express rolled into the station at Vichy, a station crawling with German military, *Feldgendarmerie,* and plainclothes Gestapo, whose faces gave them away as if they were in a uniform. My stomach sickened at the thought of André in this city, of the months he had moved amidst this nightmare, and of his skin-of-the-teeth escape.

Loirette! There he was, cane in hand, running alongside the train, calling my name at the top of his high, choirboy voice. To his blind eyes, my face would be a blurry disk at best, so I shouted: "Loirette! Loirette!" And like a man possessed he forged on, shoving people aside.

"Here, Loirette, here!"

He smiled vaguely in the direction of my voice, and suddenly he leaped, landing by sheer luck, it seemed, on the car's steps.

I went into the corridor and saw him stick his head into the first compartment at the far end to chirp: "Ingreede?" and push on to the next compartment, chirping away. People stared at him as if he were mad, and I struggled toward him to rescue him from ridicule. He almost ran me down. In the blind flurry of trying to steady me, he pushed my beret over my face. I had to fight his solicitous hands, which threatened rather than helped me. And outshouting his high-pitched stream of apologies, I finally made him understand that he had found me.

"Ah, *ma chère* Ingreede!" he squeaked, and the bewildered man changed into Prince Charming. The metamorphosis was uncanny. And no longer lost in a world of blurred objects, he directed a cuttingly witty remark at the all-agog onlookers, graciously acknowledging their laughter like a great clown at the end of his act.

We had to change from the express to a local at Montluçon. When the town was close we moved out into the corridor and lined up behind a German officer. Eyeing the towering back, Loirette made a derogatory sound. The officer, glancing over his shoulder down at Loirette, turned up his nose as if it were beneath him to take note of so puny a man. And Loirette, with a gasp of admiration, exclaimed at the top of his high voice: "Ah, what a superior race!"

The officer might not have let this pass had he not been distracted by "La Marseillaise," sung by a crowd outside. We could not see the station since the corridor windows faced the other way, toward empty tracks and a standing train.

"That's our train," Loirette said softly. "Board it while I see what's up. In the event that I am prevented from joining you . . . André will be at the station. He knows whom to notify of my arrest." And making a funny face, he added audibly: "Just notify my friend Pierre Laval." Flipping the silver-knobbed cane under

his arm, he took off, pushing past the officer, peeping:
"*Excusez-moi . . . excusez-moi . . .*"

At the far side of the platform stood another train,
its cars inscribed in bold white letters slapped on with
dripping brushes: LAVAL AU POTEAU! Laval up against
the wall! LA GUILLOTINE POUR PÉTAIN! The guillotine
for Pétain. NOUS SOMMES DES TRAVAILLEURS INVOLON-
TAIRES POUR L'ALLEMAGNE! We are involuntary workers for Germany! NOUS LES AURONS! We'll get them.
VICTOIRE! LIBERTÉ!

Behind the train's windows men were singing, their
clenched fists trembling above their heads. But the roar
of voices singing "La Marseillaise" came from the
street outside the station, from a throng of many thousand Frenchmen. Police were running about, *Feldgendarmerie*. Whistles shrilled, commands were shouted.
The people getting off the express into this virulent,
tense situation tried to determine with a single glance
which way to go not to get caught in it. Two German
soldiers pointed at me. Don't run, I screamed at myself,
and fright disconnected my mind. I didn't know whether
I was standing, walking or running. Another, more
canny intelligence than my conscious mind had taken
charge, had switched my senses to some sort of emer-
gency system, put them at the disposal of the all-encom-
passing sense of self-preservation. As though coming out
of a faint, I found myself on one knee on the platform
tying my shoelace, and my eye caught soldiers' boots
running past me. That was when I saw Gert von
Havenow, or rather three Gert von Havenows, automatic rifles leveled at a flock of women prostrate across
the tracks before the "volunteer" train. The three soldiers closing in on them stepped deliberately so as not to

lose their aim, stepped soft-kneed, and someone's cry sounded like Gert's childish "Never again!"

I looked on aghast. A Frenchman, passing me, whispered sharply: *"Voyons, mademoiselle, ne vous arrêtez pas!"*

He was right. Move! Move on, pretend not to see the caught men, the women on the track, the Germans' automatic rifles, and the setting for mass slaughter. To the local. Walk naturally, don't make them ask you for your identity papers — they won't pass inspection.

Ironically, I, the forger, was traveling with identity papers that would not get by even a cursory inspection. I hadn't dared travel on a French identity card, for my foreign accent would betray me. I had altered the vital statistics on my foreigner's *carte d'identité* and botched the job. The card testified that I was a Swede, a neutral. However, where originally it had said: born in Berlin, my too-hasty erasing had roughened the green cardboard and my efforts to smooth the roughness and restore the gloss with a candle had resulted in a disastrously obvious spot.

The express pulled out, freeing the way across the tracks to the local train. It was full of Germans. I found a window seat and held the one beside it for Loirette. As I met the eyes of the Frenchman opposite me, I seemed to look at a curtained window. Our glances probed, feeling out whether the other was friend or foe. And detecting the indefinable signal that said "friend," we exchanged the flicker of a smile with which the conquered shook hands.

We had three German soldiers in our compartment, and more milled in the corridor.

"Wo ist denn der Rudi gelandet?"

*"Heiner, gib mir mal gefälligst meine Zigaretten
zurück."*

"Du, der Zug ist aber anständig geheizt."

Just chitchat. I recognized the accent from the prov-
ince of Württemberg, Grandmama's. Even after spending a whole life amidst Prussians she had not lost
the gentle particularities of her hometown, Stuttgart.
Gemütlich.

The nightmare scene outside in the January haze was
still the same: the long "volunteer" train with its white,
screaming slogans. Police and Germans running this
way and that. Whistles blowing. The black sea of people
beyond the station fence. The women on the tracks. The
Gert von Havenows, their rifles leveled at them, chafing
for orders to shoot. Loirette was nowhere in sight. He
might have gone outside to the crowd.

"Fire already!" The German shout came from a window of the local train. "Let the French whores have it
in the cunt!"

One of the Germans in my compartment pushed to
the window, brushing my knee. "Pardon."

The engineer of the "volunteer" train was being
pulled from his cab. They kicked at him and beat him
with rifle butts. He tried to shield his head with his
hands, collapsed, was dragged off. Another engineer,
flanked by Germans, was escorted to the locomotive at
gunpoint. His life-span was measured by the minutes it
would take him to get up into the cab, by the steps
needed to set the train in motion.

Like a flock of sparrows taking to their wings, the
women got up to alight on the tracks a little farther
from the engine's wheels, as if they wanted to grant the
engineer another few seconds of life. The Gert von

Havenows followed in their wake and took up positions at the proper shooting distance.

The German beside me strained forward and screamed out the window: "What the hell are you waiting for? Rip their arses open!" Pale with rage he turned to his companions. "Not in all my life have I seen such incompetence." And he regained his seat and sat there, cracking his knuckles. The other two did not bother to cast a glance outside. Were such scenes boring to them by now? Were they sickened by them?

"All aboard!" The conductor's hand signal jiggled by the window. Loirette nowhere in sight. The "volunteer" train was moving now . . . very slowly. White clouds of steam billowed from the engine's wheels. The women! Get up, get up! You cannot help your men. YOU CANNOT!

The black mass of people in the station square seemed to swell. Like thick lava the crowd seemed to flow upward and over the fence. It spilled across the main platform, across the first track, in front of the locomotive and around it, and surged up against the "volunteer" train, which had stopped moving.

Our train was moving now, and there was Loirette, running! In his oddly long, narrow-cut winter coat, arms up, cane in hand, he was lightly leaping across the tracks. Dear God, he won't see that we've started up! "Loirette, stop! Stop! The train's moving!" He kept coming, head on, but must have heard me, for he swerved to fall in with the train. "Don't! Don't!" I screamed, straining out the window. And then he leaped, and I saw him with one foot on a tread, the other leg way out, flying along like something that wasn't his. A sweatered arm reached down and pulled him in.

As if applauding his rescue, a roar of voices rose, a thousand-throated burst of joy, followed by what sounded like a tremendous sigh of relief. It came from the crowd jammed around the "volunteer" train. Hundreds of hands were reaching up to the windows from which men were tumbling and jumping, more and more and more. I barely swallowed my own outcry of joy. Then a switch house slipped between, sycamores, and the station was out of my sight.

Loirette dropped in the seat beside me. *"Une cigarette, chère amie?"*

A cigarette! The magic stabilizer!

He fingered in his coat pockets for matches, tried other pockets. One of the Germans produced a lighter. Loirette gave him a wide, toothless smile, but waved his hand aside. *"Merci, mon petit, j'en ai des allumettes."*

The soldier looked baffled. He did not seem to understand French, which was for the better as he might have felt humiliated at being addressed *mon petit,* my boy. Loirette had a knack for finding the right word at the spur of the moment.

The cigarette hanging loosely from his lower lip, Loirette went through all of his pockets — his overcoat pockets, his jacket pockets, and the four small pockets of his waistcoat which, fitting tightly, made evident the frailty of his chest. And once again, leisurely, Loirette made the tour of his pockets. The Germans watched him. Their eyes hardened. It seemed to dawn on them that they were being made fools of. At the third round through his pockets, Loirette produced the matches. Surely he must have felt them on his first try.

The Germans leaped to their feet and pushed into the corridor. "Herr Leutnant, *bitte kommen Sie doch mal her."*

"They're calling their lieutenant," I told Loirette.

"Don't worry. We'll have a little fun."

"Please don't."

The lieutenant appeared. Through the window of the compartment door we could watch them talk. Their glances at Loirette were only too eloquent.

Observing the Germans from under lowered eyelids, Loirette puffed smoke rings. Why had he to provoke them!

He slipped the silver-knobbed cane into my hands. "Should it get really rough, get rid of it. It has a dagger concealed inside." He was on his feet, stepping into the corridor, giving the four strapping Germans a wide smile. They stared at him, dumbfounded. His falsetto voice a notch higher with forced friendliness, Loirette asked them: *"Où allez-vous, mes garçons?"* They did not understand, turned to their lieutenant for guidance. "Where are you headed?" Loirette translated with some pain. "Paris?" And he pronounced Paris with such an emphasis on the P that one of the Germans had to wipe his face.

"Wir gehen auf Urlaub," the lieutenant answered. "Furlough . . . home . . . *chez nous, Deutschland.*"

"Ah!" Loirette jubilated. *"Que c'est magnifique!* That's great!" And most heartily shaking hands with the startled Germans he added exuberantly: *"Bleiben Sie dort,* stay there, stay there, and *bon voyage!"* A graceful gesture of leave-taking, a slight bow, and Loirette regained his seat. He stretched out his slender legs, took the dagger cane from my hand and placed it across his knees, lit another cigarette, and drew in the smoke deeply. The brown eyes in the noncommittal face of our French traveling companion were sparkling. Loirette said to him: "They will lose the war. Since they don't understand us, how can they subjugate us?" And he nodded another bright smile toward the Germans in the corridor, who responded with naïve eagerness.

"They might not succeed in subjugating us," our companion said, "but they do succeed in killing us off."

"They try, but they won't succeed if we set our mind on our two main objectives: one . . . to fight them, two . . . to survive. To survive is as vital as beating them. Not only do they try to bleed us to death, they cart us off to Germany to leave France without men to sire children. Not only do they kill off our best, best in body as in mind, they are planning to kidnap the children of our elite, the children of our scientists and writers and artists so that France will remain without wit, without imagination, without ardor, become a nation of docile gardeners to serve the German master race. Survive! And once this war is over, go to Germany and make love to the Gretchens, and with your French blood give them a transfusion of humanism." He chuckled, but a shadow fell across his face and his gaze went over the dusky fields and lingered there, until of a sudden he returned to us to sing out in his soprano: *"Mais alors,* what a race that would produce. Their physical constitution, their diligence, their ability to organize, paired with French spirit, French logic, French humanism . . . ah, *chers amis,* what a race, what a magnificent race!"

Our three soldiers returned with somewhat vague smiles for Loirette, smiles of uncertain goodwill, it seemed, but Loirette responded with a bland stare, and their smiles fell apart. They settled down. Loirette's eyes remained on them as if they were objects, and the impersonal stare made them fidget until finally they escaped from it by closing their eyes.

Night fell. The weak, camouflaged ceiling light tinted

the dozing Germans a ghostly blue. We rolled on and on through dark landscapes unrelieved by a lighted house. The air in the compartment grew hot and stale. In a small station, I pulled down the window and took a deep breath of the chill air. The single, roofed platform was deserted. Behind it a dark house, a piece of dirt road, and then darkness thick as a wall. We rolled on.

Loirette was far away in thought. Once again I wondered what his castle might be like. I let a random assortment of castles pass before my mind's eye, but none was in keeping with his worn coat. I gave his property a high, stone-wall enclosure, made André come through its iron gate, and let him briskly walk down a dark road lined with poplars. For a fleeting moment I vividly felt the touch of his hand, but when I tried to recapture the sensation, I could not bring it back. I tried to picture him on an army cot in a British barracks, at roll call . . . but my dread kept the picture vague, unreal. If he went, I wouldn't even get letters from him, wouldn't hear him call me Grenouille until the end of the war.

Until the end of the war . . . the end of the war . . . the end of the war . . . The clatter of the wheels reverberated. We were in a tunnel. It seemed endless. The harsh sound whipped my fears, and my mind changed it to machine-gun fire. Abruptly it died. We were outside, clickety-clacking over switches. Alongside the tracks ran a board fence marked with white V's and the *croix de Lorraine*. Behind the fence, dark tenements.

"We're arriving," Loirette said.

I pushed the window down. The station, gliding toward me, seemed totally dark at first. Then a pale spot emerged, a circle of weak light, dropped by a lonely lantern upon André. No matter how weak the light, I knew it was André. What my eyes could not discern as

yet, my heart recognized. I waved, spreading my fingers
to make my white hand bigger, and André's hand shot
up.

"He's there," I said to Loirette, who replied somewhat mockingly: *"Mais oui,* the starry-eyed prince is
there." He handed me his dagger cane and took charge
of my suitcase. Climbing over baggage and German
knapsacks, we pushed toward the exit.

"Grenouille . . ." André's lean, winter-cold cheek
pressed against mine. His fingers dug into my hair. We
laughed, we were together again, his warm neck was in
my hand.

"Venez, venez donc," Loirette chirped. "Come," André said, an unsteadiness in his voice. And holding me
firmly, he picked up my suitcase with his free hand.

We crossed tracks, went through the bleak station
building, which reeked of coal smoke, urine and disin-
fectant, and stepped out onto a vast, dark square. Two
cathedral towers loomed black. Someone's footfall was
dying away in one or another dark street. Loirette
darted to bicycles chained to a lamppost, and I learned
that the tail end of the journey was a cross-country
bicycle trip.

Loirette sent a futile glance up to the dark lantern
that topped the lamppost. "Have you picked a good one
for Ingrid?" he asked. His fingers took the place of his
eyes, scurrying over the tangle of handlebars, seats and
wheels. He examined them at such close range, he appeared to be sniffing them.

How could a man that blind ride a bicycle in the
dark?

"Which one is this one?" he asked. "No rubber handles . . . but it isn't the one with the altogether rusty
handlebars, is it? No, the rusty one has a bent front fen-

der and this one doesn't. It isn't the one with the jiggly seat, is it, André? And which one is this one?"

"Let me unlock the chain," André said.

"I want Ingrid to have the best. Which one is for her?"

"The one with the rubber handles."

"The one that has five patches on the front tire?"

"Four."

"Four? Five, *mon vieux*. The one with four patches is the one that has spokes missing and a loose chain."

"No, the one with the loose chain is the yellow one."

"Yellow?"

"Well, once upon a time."

"You're confused, *cher ami,* the one with the loose chain was never yellow."

"It certainly has traces of yellow."

"Dear André, you're talking about the woman's bike it seems, the one with the loose chain, but that one has no traces of yellow, I assure you. I know my bikes."

"You're referring to the one with the new tube?"

"No. Both tubes are patched. You yourself patched the rear tire last week."

"The one I patched was the rusty one, the altogether rusty one."

"The one with the bent front fender?"

"No, the other one."

"The one that has a bell?"

"Without a bell."

"With a wooden pedal?"

"No, Fernand, it was the rusty one I patched, the good one, the lightweight one."

I could not believe my ears. How could two intelligent men engage in such a bizarre dialogue? And they were deadly serious. Little did I know that I would be partner in what André called "Loirette's bicycle game" as soon as I was sufficiently familiar with the bicycles' patches and scratches, their degree of rustiness, and their bent parts. The confusion added by a third person gave the game even more spice, it seemed. It was played daily, and there was no escape. Gathered for a chat in Loirette's study, we would waste time and nerves trying to establish which of the dozen rickety two-wheelers each of us was talking about. When I innocently asked why we didn't go to the shed, where we would have the bicycles before our eyes, Loirette gave me a furious glance, and André burst into giggles.

The bicycles were Loirette's obsession. At all times, some were kept near the station, and these were constantly switched with the ones at the castle to have the "right" ones on hand for any possible but unlikely arrivals or departures. Since each bicycle was as bad as the next, the reshuffling made no sense whatsoever. Not only did he keep *us* busy with the bicycle game, he would round up the maids' younger brother, even if he had to search for him in the fields or woods, to make him take a bicycle to the station and return with another one. No matter which bicycle the boy brought back, it was always the wrong one, and the seed for the morrow's bicycle activity was planted. What I witnessed upon my arrival was merely an introduction to the opening moves of the game.

I watched André struggle to tie my suitcase on the back of his bicycle with Loirette's solicitous, blindly fumbling hands in the way. All of a sudden I felt very tired. I asked how far it was to the castle.

"Not far," Loirette chirped. "Half an hour."

"More than that," André said. "And in the dark . . ."

More than that. . . . "I haven't sat on a bicycle for years."

"Don't worry," Loirette said. "One doesn't forget. It will come back to you in a moment."

"The road is empty after dark," André said. "And we'll take it easy."

I mounted shakily, wobbled, lost my balance, but quickly clambered back on the seat not to lose Loirette, who was halfway across the vast square already. I followed him into a street as dark as the gullet of Jonah's whale, leaving it to my imagination whether there were houses alongside or a boundless dark void. The thought of it made me sense the void, and for a moment there was nothing but the unlimited universe about me. I lost my balance, jumped off, and found good, hard stone underfoot.

"Are you all right, Grenouille?"

"It's awfully dark."

"And how! But we'll have the town behind us in a moment."

How good it was to come into the lighter night of the open fields and to have trees marking the edge of the road. But soon we turned off the road to proceed along a rutty wagon track that wound through fields shrouded with ground fog.

"Keep in the rut, *mon chou*," André advised me from behind.

I was tired. Try as I would, the bicycle had a will of its own. The front wheel jerked this way and that, skidded, ran onto the higher strip between the ruts only to drop back down hard, slamming my teeth together.

"Steer her loosely," André called to me. "Let her have her way."

Any moment I would have to tell them that I could

not go on. To get the pedals down, I had to shift my weight from side to side. Finally, my hands just dropped from the handlebars and, careening into the field, I crash-landed on lumps of moist soil. André gathered me in his arms and belatedly I admitted: "I can't go on."

"Loirette! Hey, Loirette!"

No answer.

"Fernand, wait! Fernand?"

We peered into the night. Loirette was gone, swallowed by the foggy darkness.

"We ought to have known that this would be too much for you, undernourished as you are," André said. "The miller might have lent us his wagon." Standing before me, peering down the trail, he himself was a mere wisp, as emaciated as when they released him from prison.

"Rest," he said. "Then we'll walk the last bit. It isn't far anymore." He sat down beside me, fondled my neck with cold fingers. And then we were lying in each other's hands in the wintry field, smiling into our night-dark faces.

"The smell of earth . . ." he mused. "The scent of France." And the catch in his voice told me that if he had to give his life for her, he would die for her as for a woman.

He fought the stir of emotion with strained laughter. "We've lost Loirette, haven't we? Blind as he is, unable to make out the trail, he went up and up and up into the silent fog, and he won't come back ever. La Tourelle Joliette is all ours now, and what a peaceful place it will be without him."

"You two don't get along?"

"Oh, we do, we do, but it's difficult."

"How can he ride at night at all? How can he see where he's going?"

"See? Why would he need to see? He's crazy."

"Does that help?"

"You bet it does. It's mind over matter."

"Is he really crazy? Crazy crazy?"

"Crazy as a loon. You didn't know that?"

"I don't know him that well."

"We'd better move on before you catch cold."

I had not noticed the cold.

"If it were summer," he said, "we could live in the woods, be a maquis *à deux.*" His exhilarating laughter, which I had missed so much, now played havoc with me.

We pushed the bicycles, let the wheels be guided by the ruts. The middle strip was just wide enough that, strapped together with our arms, we could walk side by side. We talked about England, but his lean hip moved under my hand.

"I'll go via Spain, Portugal," he said. "Through Spain we have to make it incognito. We're waiting for the *Résistance* to set up all the contacts. Two other guys will go with me."

"Are they at the castle?"

"No. I don't even know who they are. I don't know any specifics. Security measures. We won't be told until we meet for the final briefing."

"How long do we have?"

He shrugged. "When the contacts are set up, we'll go."

"From one moment to the other?"

"Yes. Yes, from one moment to the other. A messenger will come."

André told me that he was under orders to remain

within calling distance of the castle at all times; to pick me up at the station, he had had to ask for permission. That it had been granted was an indication that they wouldn't come for him this night. Suddenly England was a tangible threat.

"Will I learn whether you have gotten safely to England?"

"Certainly. I'll be able to send a *message personnel* over the BBC."

"What will it say?"

His arm, around me, tightened. "It will say: '*Le corbeau blanc salue la grenouille.*'" Tears came to my eyes. The lovers' names we had given each other brought home all that I was asked to give up.

"I guess there's no way of getting a letter to me," I said.

"No. You must be strong. It is necessary. It won't be for long, the end of the war is in sight. The *Résistance* is making preparations for the invasion." He believed that.

The invasion . . .

"I'll be back in no time at all to liberate France and you," André said, and my mind's eye saw blue sky dotted with thousands of parachutes.

"I *must* go, Grenouille."

"I know."

"With the Gestapo after me, I'm useless here. Changing my papers wouldn't do it, my looks are too striking, they'd recognize me at a glance. The *Résistance* won't take me for anything of consequence, they say I'd only endanger others. And I won't just sit it out in hiding. No thanks!"

"I know that."

"You'll be safe at the castle and you'll have food.

Harum-scarum Loirette can be trying but bear with him, he's a decent man and gentle at heart. Don't let his grandiose projects upset you. He won't make the castle a *Résistance* redoubt, which is one of his fantasies. By the next day he has different plans. And when he's not ridden by a pet obsession, he's brilliant and amusing and at times inspiring. You'll be more patient with him than I. You'll forgive him. You can't imagine how delighted he is at having you stay with him — he is a very lonely man. And the two boys. François couldn't wait for the day to end. I bet he won't fall asleep until he hears you arrive."

"When did they lose their mother?"

"She died in childbirth when Claude was born."

"Poor Loirette."

The trail led out to a dirt road with a brook gurgling nearby. Out of the misty darkness came Loirette's falsetto voice: *"Pour l'amour de Dieu,* where were you? Suddenly you were gone. Didn't you hear me shout?"

"We had bicycle trouble," André said calmly. "The chain."

Loirette's distress vented itself in a piercing scream.

André said: "I fixed it. I had pliers and a wrench."

"The damn bikes! They'll be my death one day. I'm chilled to the bone, I'll come down with pneumonia." He coughed tentatively.

"I'm awfully sorry, Fernand."

"It's I who should apologize, not you, the wretched bikes are mine. The very thought of having to fix a chain in the dark. What an ordeal! I'm inconsolable, *cher ami;* I beg your forgiveness."

"It wasn't that bad. You shouldn't have waited for us."

"Not waited? And let you take a wrong turn here?

Never! Rather catch pneumonia and die and let this impoverished world lose its last true knight. Ah, *chère* Ingrid, did he fill you in on his friend Fernand Loirette? This heart of mine is prepared to die for your André. And don't let this scrawny body of mine deceive you, it holds a noble soul. And this skull of mine with the thinning hair holds quite a brain, dedicated to making this world a better place. But I'll give up both should that be needed to protect your André. In the meantime I'm sacrificing precious hours, when I ought to be at my writing, to run around in search of an egg for your André. And should he ask for a bedside rug, I would not hesitate to lie at his graceful feet rather than let him do without."

He spoke with such passion that I could not say whether he was serious or clowning.

André broke in: "Ingrid knows; I've told her."

And Loirette screeched with exaltation: "Ah, *chers enfants,* life is beautiful! Life is the great adventure! *En route, en route, chevaliers!* To the castle! To the warm fires of La Tourelle Joliette!"

"It's only a minute from here," André said to me and we mounted our bicycles.

Sleek willow branches fingered a strip of leftover snow alongside the dirt road. Its pale shine guided me, when suddenly the castle stood before me, massive and black. Had we passed through a gate?

I was ushered through a stony hall into a large dining room whose sparse and modest furnishings reminded me of a monastery.

"Keep your coat on," André advised. The round iron stove was lit, but the fire it held was obviously a small one, a wartime fire. In our winter coats we repaired to the table, and a maid served piping hot *boudin,* a savory blood sausage, and there was a potato for each. The maid, in her shrunken sweater bulging with layer on layer of undergarments, looked like a *boudin* herself.

The meal was a real treat to me, but my stomach, unaccustomed to rich food, revolted. Cold sweat came to my face and I darted outside to give it all up. I let André help me upstairs, tuck me in. All I could do was smile wanly, and instead of in his arms, I fell asleep with a copper bed warmer.

I awakened in a high Empire bed that majestically dominated the random assortment of furniture: a dainty Provençal table, two rush-seat chairs like those made famous by van Gogh, a pine chest holding a faience washbowl and pitcher that had survived their original matchmates. The curtainless window was filled with thin, overcast sky and whitewashed walls reflected the gentle light of the winter morning. André's plaid robe was draped over a chair. The fine wool fabric was a lacework of moth holes, but the garment had remained precious to him since it was irreplaceable. During the weeks to come I darned the hundreds of small holes with bits of yarn of various kinds and colors; bits I had saved, and bits Loirette's maids let me have. I retrieved a length of wool yarn by unraveling the top of a sock whose foot was beyond repair. And one bit of wool thread was graciously offered me by one of the threadbare rugs.

As I contemplated the room and found it to my liking, my big toe met with the metal bed warmer, which was cold. I reached for the moth-eaten robe to take a look out the window, and had a bird's-eye view of a house deep down below, a mill whose large wooden wheel was slowly turning. Beyond stretched a valley — brown fields, and here and there a patch of trees or a square of woodland. Just fields, no farmhouse, which made me assume that the land belonged to the castle. The shallow valley might have been a small planet all its own, like Saint-Exupéry's Asteroid B-612, for beyond the wooded hills surrounding the fields there appeared to be only sky.

It puzzled me to find myself so very high up, for last night I had climbed just one flight of stairs to this bedroom. I opened the window and with a glance to right and left I took in the length of the castle and the protruding round towers at each end. Cautiously I leaned out a bit farther for a look down. Below the next row of windows was what seemed to be a high, massive foundation without doors or windows. No, it was rock. The castle was sitting on a rock and its wall was in a line with the sheer cliff, making them appear to be one continuous surface. At the bottom, the cliff tapered off at a gentler angle, and there its nakedness was covered by a bit of leaf-strewn ground curving around the rocky neck like the collar of a dress. This earthen collar was edged with a low, dry-stone wall, which turned out to be the estate's boundary line.

On a summer day before the war Loirette had acquired La Tourelle Joliette for a pittance, since the castle was a white elephant nobody wanted. After the land was sold off bit by bit, the large house was left without grounds for pleasure or privacy, without a field big enough to hold a kitchen garden, without a tract of woodland from which to cut the firewood needed to make the castle inhabitable. Even its inside walls were three feet thick, and no summer lasted long enough to warm them through to their core, where the winter chill lay dormant.

But he did not need land holdings, Loirette thought.

The rock on which his castle stood sufficed him, for nothing prevented his eye from wandering across the fields and woods around it. And they gave him as much seclusion and quiet as they would have had they been his. The quarter-acre front yard sufficed for his little François to play, for the family to sit on a sultry summer evening.

Nothing much ever bloomed there, even in peacetime, and the grass seeds he scattered never grew a lawn, because the ground was only a thin layer of soil on top of the flat rock. Some dauntless trees had made it, had grown tall and old. When they found that they could not work their way in deep for a secure hold, they spread their roots in a tightly knit web across the whole yard and claimed all the nourishment the shallow soil had to offer. By now the trees were ailing, but Loirette would not think of cutting one down to make the wartime winters more bearable. He gratefully gathered the twigs and an occasional dead branch that the trees might drop of their own accord and brought them like an offering to the tiny, voracious, potbellied stove in his study.

Split firewood was neatly stacked outside the kitchen, but never more than the predetermined number of chunks was to be removed each day. Of this ration the kitchen received the lion's share to cook the meals and to keep the two maids comfortable so that they wouldn't quit. The living-room stove received what the kitchen could spare and the room never got warm enough for us to shed our coats. Not a single chunk went to the study. The potbellied stove was the sparrow that had to make do with the crumbs Providence provided, with the twigs we gathered along our walks. The exception was one bitter day of howling wind when Loirette, in despair, smashed a chair and fed the tiny stove chair legs, rungs,

backrest and caning. Normally Loirette would not light
a fire in daytime when he tried to work on his book. And
it was a pathetic sight to see him behind the French
doors in coat and knitted cap and muffler, writing with
gloved hands.

After dinner we usually repaired to the study for a
short-lived feast of warmth. As the stove devoured
crackling twigs, we huddled close, our knees almost
touching the hot metal to let the ephemeral warmth seep
through our many-layered wraps. During this time we
discussed with passion matters of philosophy, art, ethics,
politics, war strategy, and *Résistance* tactics, constantly
switching back and forth between earnest debate and
badinage, trying to generate some heat of our own with
which to fight the cold at our backs. When the fire died,
we sat shivering pitifully, for our pores had happily
opened to the gift of warmth. The only recourse was to
dash into the winter night and briskly march back and
forth the whole length of the looming castle. I often
envied Loirette's two maids, who were cozy and warm
in the kitchen.

He would not have kept two maids except that the
sisters, Marie and Ninette, daughters of a neighboring
farmer, wouldn't have stayed one without the other.
They chose to share the same room because they were
afraid of ghosts, especially of the "Chevalier," a knight
on a black stallion who haunted the lonesome paths after
dark in search of a virgin out alone. Marie and Ninette
knew of virgins who had been snatched by him and never
seen again.

As it was winter and darkness came early, the sisters
had to be given their afternoon off together, for only
together would they dare make the few hundred yards
from their father's farm to the castle. Though they were

not young girls, it was believable they had remained
virgins from lack of opportunity. Nobody ever strayed
to this remote corner, to the small grain mill or the back-
woods farm or to the castle inhabited by a peculiar,
recluse writer. And the few men who came to visit
Loirette were not the kind to show interest in Marie and
Ninette.

Aside from the towers that blunted three corners of
the castle, two of them in back and the larger one out
front, there was a fourth, which stood by itself, away
from the building. This small, squat, windowless tower
had been the castle's dungeon in bygone days. Now
Loirette used it to store the pears from his only pear
tree on wooden planks fastened to the curving walls.
Here and there diffuse light seeped through small cracks
between the stones, thinning the darkness within. The
air was moist and fragrant with the earthen floor's
musky breath, the odor of old stone, and the sweet and
spicy emanations of pears slumbering to ripeness.

Solemnly, like a priest on his way to church, Loirette
went to "his" tower once every single day to check his
pears, make sure that no pear touched another, and to
remove those that showed spots and those too ripe to be
left there longer. And as he placed the one or two into
the small pear basket he suffered a pang of loss. He
would call us to counsel him whether they should be
eaten fresh or stewed, at dinner or after supper around
the potbellied stove. Whichever way they were finally
served, they had to be eaten with reverence and given a
loving eulogy. On occasion Loirette invited us to accompany him to the pear tower, but if we had angered him,
he would bar us from the sacred rites. Never would he
allow the "callous, insensitive, uneducated" kitchen
maids to enter the tower and touch his pears. When he

was away he preferred to let a number of them rot and give them back to the earth upon his return. However, these "callous, insensitive, uneducated" kitchen maids had full charge of his youngest son, Claude.

His two boys were so unlike one would not have taken them for brothers. Ten-year-old François was a princely child, taught polite phrases and poise, how to bow grace-fully and how to eat in a mannerly way. To him his mother had read stories about goodness, generosity and forgiveness. Four-year-old Claude was a country bump-kin who never knew a mother. The grief-stricken Loir-ette had boarded the infant with Marie and Ninette's mother, and as he could not bear the sight of the child who had killed the woman he worshiped, he rarely went to see him. Only when war made Loirette flee Paris did little Claude come to know father and brother. To-gether with Marie and Ninette he moved from the modest farm into the castle.

Loirette adored François, the son who so lavishly provided fuel for his vanity, this alert, beautiful child with a peaches-and-cream complexion, shiny blond hair, and guileless blue eyes that didn't flinch even when he was scolded. Claude was a painful thorn in Loirette's heart. Claude had the ruddy face of a village urchin, chapped hands and bruised shins, and his mop of dark hair had never been touched by a professional barber. Claude spoke the local patois, he walked like a peasant. Used to the ways of simple farm folk, it was natural he felt self-conscious in our company. When spoken to, he pulled his head between his shoulders and, with awk-ward contortions, wiped his nose on his coat sleeve. Suddenly, without being excused, he would scoot back to Marie and Ninette and to the warm familiarity of the kitchen world. Loirette threw his hands up, cried: "I implore you, Ingrid, transform this graceless creature!" I tried. Claude seemed to like me well enough, but for short spells only. My tales did not capture his imagination, and my games made him twitchy. When I put my arm around him, he slipped from my hands like a fish and was off to Marie and Ninette. I, too, preferred François, who would beam and snuggle close. And no matter what I spoke about, François's eyes would remain fastened on my face.

In spite of his love for his firstborn, Loirette corrected François incessantly, and their intercourse was formal and constrained. Several times a day, Loirette called François to him for "a talk," performances he wished us to watch approvingly. During these talks François had to stand at attention before his father, who held on to the boy's stiff arms and made weighty pronouncements beyond his comprehension. François had to respond with the line: *"Oui, mon Papa chéri."*

"François, my son, the genius of our time is Fernand Léger."

"Oui, mon Papa chéri."

"Also Céline, the bastard."

"Oui, mon Papa chéri."

"You, my beautiful son, will see the end of nationalism and other such stupidities."

"Oui, mon Papa chéri."

"Governments will be abolished and the noble at heart, the true knights, will lead the people."

"Oui, mon Papa chéri."

"The truly noble will lead the people from this sordid existence to the great, magnificent adventure. You, François, will witness the greatest revolution in the history of all mankind, the revolution of the spirit. The peoples of the world will be given new values, and the old ones they will discard like trash."

"*Oui, mon Papa chéri.*"

"Do you deeply love your Papa, *mon* François?"

"*Oui, mon Papa chéri.*"

"And is he pure and noble, your Papa, *mon* François?"

"*Oui, mon Papa chéri.*"

Loirette beamed with each new *oui, mon Papa chéri* as though it were a long-coveted acknowledgment finally won. André and I, revolted by this ridiculous parroting, itched to say what we thought of it, but watched with wonder this self-controlled child, whose features lost not for a moment their air of magnanimity and calm superiority. Never had a boy so much deserved to be called a prince.

One day I found François in his room, stretched out on the scatter rug, his fingers wandering about in the carpet's design. Noticing me, he scrambled to his feet, flushing as if he had been caught at something shameful.

"Are you traveling by boat or by train?" I asked.

His face's pink hue deepened. "Don't tell Papa. Please, don't tell Papa," he begged. His anxiety took me back to when I was eight and, in bed with the measles, traveling on the wallpaper. Suddenly Grandpapa was there, paying me a surprise visit. I hoped he had not noticed what I was doing, for certainly he would call it a nitwit's occupation. Grandpapa glanced at the untouched games and books stacked on the night table and asked what I had been doing. I squirmed and grinned stupidly, keeping my eyes away from the wallpaper, whose lilac branches had been country a moment ago, pale beaches and bluffs and beyond them meadows in an early morning mist. My bed had been a fishing trawler making its way through a gray sea, and I had felt the wind in my hair and heard the creaking of the lines and the cries of the sea gulls circling overhead. As Grandpapa's curious glance leaped to the wallpaper, I stiffened with fear that he might find there traces of my passage.

If he did, he did not comment on it. He pulled up a chair and crossed his legs, bringing the impeccable crease of his trouser leg into my field of vision. In his hand was a book bound in leather, which indicated he had taken it from the glass bookcase where he kept his most precious volumes under lock and key. And the thought that he had stood before his books wondering which one to choose for me softened the uneasiness I felt.

"I'll read you a story," he said, " 'Das Wirtshaus im Spessart' by Hauff. Do you know it?"

"Yes," I said and wished that his glance would not stray to my disheveled hair. He stroked the book, caressed its curved spine, and his fingers tenderly closed round it as though fondling a dear friend's shoulder. He gave me another glance, perhaps wondering, I thought, whether I was worthy of being read to. Then he opened the book at the silken marker.

The marvelously spine-chilling story Grandpapa read with a voice that changed with the mood of the scenes, and his face acted out the parts. He gave each character a specific, quickly identifiable manner of speech, and one of the bad men a stupid lisp.

Off and on his eyes left the printed lines to sink a meaningful glance into mine. And as though he knew the text by heart — perhaps he did — he kept on talking, and when his eyes returned to the time-yellowed paper, he found the place without faltering. He held me spell-bound, yet all the while I watched with no less fascination his hand fondling the book in one way or another. When he came to the last lines on the page, he began to caress the paper with loving strokes as if for a tender farewell. And, caressingly, his fingers would glide to the upper corner to turn the page with infinite care and smooth it down. The unyielding middle, which would not fall open altogether, he gently coaxed, and then he comforted it with a reassuringly flattened out palm. Following these loving motions, I longed for his hand to come to me. It would not. The hand he gave me when he finally rose to leave was the same as it always was, a hand reluctant to bestow tenderness, a hand that pulled back as soon as it was given.

Have I become a writer in the hope that by changing into a book Grandpapa might finally hold me in loving hands?

"I won't tell," I said to François. "I used to do the same when I was your age. I used to travel in the pattern of our wallpaper."

François's eyes filled with wonderment, and of a sudden he flew into my arms and wept. Thereafter, whenever he was alone with me, François begged to hear more about my childhood. He went about it as secretively as if the topic were taboo. And he was as avid for detail as if he never had contact with other children, could never weigh his own experiences and feelings against theirs.

I was reading when François's stare made me look up. His eyes were all plea. André was writing letters, Loirette was cutting clippings from underground newspapers, so I winked at François and quietly rose. I went outside by the side door not to stir Loirette's curiosity, for he would want to join us.

I went over the stone enclosure to avoid the gate and walked quickly down the dirt road to get out of sight. The afternoon sky had a yellow tint. The air was still but damp, and a shiver crawled down my neck. A moment later, radiant François was beside me. "Do we go for a walk?"

"Sure." Questions were already burning on his lips. "Ingrid? Your Papa . . . do you favor him? Was he handsome? Was he a noble man?" François's heart seemed to palpitate under his delicate skin.

"Well, yes, he was a fine man."

François, having made the first difficult step, exhaled audibly.

I waited.

"Ingrid . . . your Papa, did he teach you? Did you fear him? Was he a severe father? Was he easily upset?"

"No, he was a quiet man. Kind."

"My Papa is kind."

"Of course he is, François."

"He has a lot on his mind. And he worries that I might forget all I learned in Paris. He gives me exercises to do, since I can't attend school at present. I don't want to be behind after the war. He's giving me much of his time. He's shaping my mind. He's a good father."

"He loves you very much."

"He's a very erudite man. After the war he will be celebrated as one of France's greatest philosophers. I must be able to understand what Papa has written. Once his book is published, the world will change. His book says how. It will be a good world. Never again will there be war. Did your father know all about philosophy?"

"I doubt it. His special interest was gadgets: watches, stopwatches, chronometers, gauges, lighters, pedometers, speedometers and such. He had quite a collection. Gadgets were as exciting to him as philosophy is to your father."

"Did he explain the gadgets to you?"

"He did. He couldn't wait to show us his latest acquisition and how it worked. It was terribly exciting, especially for my little brother, who would beg my father to lend him a watch just for one day. Müsi promised not to look inside, just to hold it in his hand, but twenty-four hours was a long, long time for a small boy and he forgot. He would open the watch and, lost to the world he would observe the cogs. Very earnestly, and his pudgy little hands shaking with carefulness, he would take the works apart, neatly line up the little brass wheels and tiny screws to remember their proper order. When he finally reassembled the watch, invariably one small part remained as if superfluous."

"Would the watch run?"

"I don't remember. I guess not." But I remembered my mother's hue and cry on finding out. When my father, at the end of the day, was faced with the calamity, he rushed off again to a "night conference." Next day the masseuse came to restore Mama's body and soul. And the pungent aroma of her scented rubbing alcohol drifted into the hallway, giving hope for the next change of tide.

"Did your father punish Müsi?"

"No." Of course not, he was proud of his son. And when Müsi knew enough about watches and proceeded to tinker with his father's car, Papa could scarcely wait for man-to-man chats about carburetors, fuel lines, pistons and valves.

I myself did not know what to offer my father in order to lure him out of his shell and test whether he approved of me. So, I often felt unsure of myself in his gentle presence.

I felt more at ease with my difficult, emotion-tossed mother, whose thoughts and feelings were out in the open, audible and visible. If she was a changeable sea with erratic winds, I had learned to read the weather signs and how to ride out the squalls.

In later years, though, when I tried to make myself a picture of my widening world, a world that was no longer merely green mountains, open plains and winding rivers, but whirlpools of power struggles, issues, beliefs, I needed my father as a beacon.

Perhaps I went about finding him the wrong way. Perhaps my youthful aggressiveness made him shudder. Perhaps my blatant ignorance made him feel at a loss where to begin. Whatever the reason, he didn't come out from behind the haze of charming conversation: his dachshund's antics, last Sunday's regatta, a downpour on the Avus, the auto racetrack. And, suddenly, time to find him had run out, the Nazis were there and I was leaving. Across the undefinable distance between us, he said how much he would miss me.

I missed him. I missed his quiet ways, his gentle hands. I missed his knowing eyes that kept their thoughts a secret.

I saw him one more time, while I was in Yugoslavia. He came for an overnight visit to Ljuba's place. Both of us felt self-conscious, and our conversation was strained. In the five years we had not seen each other, the girl he remembered had grown into a young woman, and he must have wondered whether he still knew me. And I, who was at that moment, again and unchanged, his child, found myself up against the same old difficulty and didn't dare to ask questions, to violate his seclusion.

Ljuba entered the room to remove the tea dishes and grasped the situation with one glance. "Why don't you show your father the forest path before it gets dark." Both of us jumped at the suggestion.

The sky was still light, but among the trees it was already dusky. The dimness blurred our faces and veiled what we wanted to conceal, so that we felt less vulnerable. Or did the great forest stillness quiet our fears? Papa reached for me, for my hand, and as though we were meeting only now he asked: "How are you, Ini?" The warmth of his tone embraced me like comforting arms.

Less and less our voices seemed to be our own, the father's and the daughter's, but a single voice speaking of man's searching and of the burdens a troubled world had put on his shoulders. Night fell. The darkness was so deep we could not stroll on without giving it all our attention. We sat down, close, in the warmth of each other's nearness and the newly found trust in each other. Papa spoke of his work and how dear it had been to him throughout his life and how it felt to see it defiled. He spoke of his passion for linguistic precision and of teaching young reporters their skills. He spoke of fighting for social justice, and he ridiculed prejudice. I was surprised to find that somehow I had always known how he felt.

He spoke about the men he had known, auto racers, yachtsmen, relatives, and I realized that he loved his fellowmen and had often laughed in secret over their oddities and their stupidities, but without malice. Then he spoke of a colleague the Nazis had caught. He tried to find out which prison they had taken him to but faced an impenetrable wall. When I asked him whether it wasn't dangerous to make such inquiries, he made a contemptuous sound.

At the time the Nazis came to power, they had grabbed the big Jewish newspaper corporation within which my father had made his way from sports reporter to the board of directors. On the editorial staff, he was one of a few who were not Jews. He could have retired, but he felt that now, when his colleagues, his close friends for many years, were forced to run for their lives, he owed it to the firm to remain at his post and try as best he could to prevent the distinguished house from sinking in the Nazi morass; and were it to sink, to go down with it as a captain would with his ship.

No longer was his word all-powerful; he was merely used and knew it. But as he alone had the experience to keep the wheels turning, he made the new Nazi staff tremble before his wrath. His fits of anger reverberated all through the offices. He ripped the ticker tape off the machine and crammed the truth down their throats, called a lie a lie, called the new men nincompoops and referred to Adolf Hitler as "that paperhanger." He was not whisked off to prison — they couldn't do without him. They had to put up with "old Gustav's" ravings, which the paternoster shaft carried through the entire house, but which could, after all, not be heard by the German people outside. Let him rave.

His wrath, his frustration, was, however, more than "old Gustav" himself could take. He often fled to the printshop for a moment of peace with the old printers, many of whom had been with the firm as long as he and had known him when he was just a greenhorn. Between

him and them no words were needed. They knew how he
felt. They let tired Gustav sit among the clattering ro-
tary presses, pretending he had done so all these years.
In passing, they would ask: "How's the Avus doing,
Gustav?" To them he had always been "Gustav," even
when upstairs he became Herr Direktor. Or one and the
other would wink at him, which, like a handshake, gave
him the strength to carry on.

Then he died. He died of despising the Nazis.

His new Nazi colleagues dutifully gathered at the
funeral. His former colleagues could not attend. Some
were in prison, some in concentration camps, some dead
— shot in a prison yard, or they had themselves put an
end to their lives. Some had fled Germany, were in
France, in England, in America. His firstborn, Dalla,
was in America. Ini was in occupied France. And Müsi,
his beloved boy . . . First they had drafted him to do
his year of obligatory work for the fatherland, ditch-
digging interspersed with semimilitary drills. Then one
night, Müsi and the other boys in the work-camp barracks were aroused from sleep, handed uniforms and
rifles, and loaded on buses for an undisclosed exercise.
As the first light of morning lifted the darkness from the
fields, they were told that the goal of the outing was
Poland.

Poland?

Yes, war.

They rushed Müsi home to Berlin from the east to
attend his father's funeral. A boy in a soldier's uniform,
he stood forlorn beside the coffin, searching in vain for
a face he knew, the face of one of the Jews who had
been "uncle" to him throughout childhood.

It might well have been there, at his father's funeral,

that patient, gentle Müsi decided to run away, run from the *Heimat* that had turned into a nightmare, run from the war that was not his, run from the haunting thought that he might get orders to do something he could not bring himself to do. He would grab the first opportunity — he had to be at the front for that, any front — to step on the gas pedal of the troop carrier he was driving, floor it, and go for all the engine was worth, keep going, straight ahead and on through no-man's land, full steam until he reached enemy territory, a haven offering peace of mind.

"Are you sad?" I heard François ask. "Thinking of your Papa, has it saddened you?"

"A bit . . ." And hastily, afraid that François might ask whether Müsi was a *boche* now, I said: "We'd better go back, we've been away for quite a while."

We retraced our steps over the muddy country road. Yellow willow branches streaked the brown fields and the gray forest beyond. What a forsaken spot it was. One never encountered a soul except perhaps the miller in his wagon. Loirette liked to compare himself to Le Grande Meaulnes of Alain-Fournier's novel, and he likened his Tourelle Joliette to the mysterious Calais castle hidden amidst pathless woods, swamps and heath nobody ever ventured across unless he had lost his way. The comparison was by no means farfetched. This narrow dirt road always gave me the feeling that it led nowhere in either direction.

With a nod at the stretch of road behind us, I asked François: "Where does it go that way?"

"To St. Anne."

"A village?"

"A chapel. There's also a store, but that's boarded up. And a schoolhouse, but they closed it because of the war. To economize on coal."

"And the other way? Beyond the castle?"

"There's a slate pit, but it isn't worked now."

Because of the war . . . because the slate-pit workers were kidnapped to Germany.

I pictured a length of dirt road starting at a slate pit, passing the castle, and winding through woodland and fields to a chapel. It didn't make sense. "Does the road run on to town beyond St. Anne?"

"To town? No. It doesn't run on."

"And in the other direction?"

He looked doubtful.

"There must be a road to town. They surely didn't cart the slate over the trail we took across fields.

"There used to be a road long, long ago. Back there one can still see traces of it. The Old Road, it's called. The family who owns that land never plows up their piece of the Old Road. It's sacred to them, Papa says. It's like a historical monument. Many centuries ago it used to be a busy road. Papa says merchants came to the castle to offer their wares, and dukes and knights on horseback went back and forth. Now it's overgrown by weeds, but it's still there. I'll show you next time."

Following the vague motion of François's arm I looked across the wintry fields. One of the knights on horseback must have had a reputation as a skirt chaser and was living on as the "Chevalier" on a black stallion. And the Old Road, which served the castle in the past, had merely gone underground as had so many Frenchmen, thereby making this inaccessible neck of the woods one of the safest places in all of France, serving it even now.

Ahead, the castle was visible behind the maze of bare trees, its towers gray against the softly yellow sky. The thought struck me that a medieval knight, riding to the castle one winter afternoon, had come upon the very same sight. Neither centuries nor all the bloody wars since had altered anything here. But the thought was not comforting, it irritated me, gave new life to the feeling of being exiled. This dirt road, which we walked without fear, made me feel as though the war had slipped from my hands and was free to take a devilish turn. Not that I had ever held a rifle. But I like to think that a small wheel turned by one cog because my forging helped some British fliers return to England; because I hid a bundle of *Liberation* under my bed; because I sat by the railroad tracks jotting down the nature of freight that the Germans moved westward and eastward; because I took a secret message to someone I had never seen before and would never see again. Since the strange battle fought in conquered France depended on thousands of such minute daily contributions, the pastoral serenity here made me feel uneasy. I could not tell whether France was still making a thousand little moves a day. When André had suggested that I remain at the castle to the end of the war, how enticing safety had looked. Yet . . . Our flesh swamps us with terror so that we turn all our efforts toward its survival. But our spirit, whispering of eternity, unfolds a rainbow and fills us with a great longing for what is so beautiful. It is attainable, it says, if only you brave whatever threatens. And it persuades us to refuse a living death. With the whisperings of the body in one ear, and the whisperings of the mind in the other, we feel torn.

"Look!" François called out. "A fallen branch, a big one! I'll take it home for Papa's stove."

"Whose woods?" I asked, but I was already following François up the slight rise, which we found strewn with smaller branches as well, brought down by last night's high winds. We gathered the twigs for kindling and tied them with François's belt. And, impatient to present Loirette with our loot, we made the stretch to the castle at a run, François dragging the long limb, and I with the bundle of faggots bobbing on my shoulder. Near the gate, we burst into wild shouts. "Loirette!" "Papa!"

Loirette shot from the French doors of his study, his knitted cap askew, his face wild. "I'm coming!" he screeched. "Where are you? Answer me! Don't be afraid, answer!"

His father's incomprehensible frenzy made François answer with a quivering: "Papa . . .?" And, I, in consternation, shouted as if he were deaf rather than blind: "Here, Loirette! Here!"

It all happened so fast. Dumbfounded by the sight of zigzagging, screaming Loirette, we did not realize quickly enough that he believed us captured and crying for help. His long overcoat flapping, the frail man stormed toward us teeth bared, to rescue us from the Germans single-handedly.

André, roused by all the screaming, ran from the house, only to stop short and stare in puzzlement at Loirette, who with a jaguar's leap and a bloodcurdling scream assaulted the bundle of kindling on my shoulder. "Ouch!" he shouted. Thrown off-balance, we stumbled, clutching each other. François cried, "Papa, Papa!" And André caught us and steadied us.

Loirette's eyeglasses had flown off. Panting, he gazed at me with large, bewildered, unseeing eyes. When André handed him his glasses, he stared at the bundle of kindling that had dropped to the ground and muttered: "What a pleasant metamorphosis."

"For your stove," François said in a small, shaky voice. His father, still sorting out illusion and reality, did not grasp what he meant.

André took Loirette by the arm. "Come inside, Fernand, you've ripped your hands."

Loirette brought his hands to close range to inspect the wounds.

Shaking his head he squeaked, "An odd *boche* this one, wasn't he, François?"

"*Oui, mon Papa chéri,*" the boy replied, and tears welled in his eyes.

Dear François, your harum-scarum father, whom André had nicknamed "Hurluburlu," was a valiant knight indeed. If what he rescued us from was only a bundle of kindling, what he attacked bare-handed was an armed German, or more likely, more than just one.

But the noble knight could have been a bit easier to live with. Each day began with vows that instead of wasting precious time on household concerns, he would repair to his study and work on his book until noon. He would delegate responsibilities, asking me to plan the meals with Marie, go through the children's clothing, and hand to Ninette what needed mending. He would ask André to check the bicycle-tire patches for wear and to see how the dilapidated wooden gate might be repaired. He would ask François to keep an eye on the living-room stove, see to it that the fire didn't die or burn too lustily. And all of us had to promise to guard him against any interruption whatsoever.

Half an hour later at the most he burst from the study to run madly through the house, recall his previous orders, change the menu, make the maids weep, shoo away Claude only to call him back and frighten him with heartrending pleas for filial love, drop him the next moment and run off, storm in and out of doors becrying the frigid house, the leaf-strewn yard, the broken gate, the children's socks, cursing bicycles, the Vichy traitors, and the need to be friendly to boring farmers for an egg or a pound of potatoes. He would not be calmed, he needed such explosions. We had to endure the tirade until with a last wail: "My book is being sacrificed! I'm victimized by the kitchen! I implore you, help me!" he would drop in a chair, exhausted.

We made countless attempts to relieve him, but he did not really want to be relieved. He needed these burdens. They allowed him to desert his book, for the book that was to change the world had driven him into an impasse, and his cries of despair over household matters camouflaged the cries of the writer who could not find a way out of the deadlock. Through the French doors we could see him sit in the freezing study like a boy being punished, counting the minutes to the moment of release, unbearable minutes of mental agony. When he could no longer face his recalcitrant text and fled from the study, finding André raking the yard, me mending François's sweater, he would furiously pull the rake from André's hand, the sweater from mine as if seeing us do such chores was an insult to him. And running about bemoaning his lot, he would warm himself.

André might have been able to help him, to see where he had gone awry in his book, but Loirette's pride would not allow help. Stubbornly he professed that he had no difficulties whatsoever, that his book was all written in his mind and would be on paper were he only given half a chance to remain at this desk.

Once the storm had blown over, he felt bad about it. And trying to make amends, he would be as charming

and witty as he had been obnoxious a moment ago. Or
he would lecture us on the needs of *la douce France,* tell
us that nothing, nothing mattered but our "sacred mission." He would beg us not to squander ourselves
on household matters, to give our energies solely to
France's liberation. "I've maids, haven't I? Two!" And
elaborating on how he would transform the castle from
a retreat to a *Résistance* stronghold, he would jubilate:
"Ah, *chers amis,* with wit and ruse we will free *la
France. Nous les aurons, les boches!* To hell with kitch-
ens, children's socks and broken gates, we're engaged in
the great adventure!"

As such storms came and blew over about twice a day,
André and I were given little time to be together alone.
And when we finally retired, usually late, we were exhausted from another day with Loirette. We managed
now and then to sneak away for a walk, but our privacy
was by no means assured, for we had to remain within
calling distance. If Loirette left us alone, the cold would
soon drive us back to the house and him. A mild day was
a holiday. We would dawdle, kick pebbles, have a good
laugh over Hurluburlu's follies, marvel at the promise
of still tightly closed pussy-willow buds that spring
would come once again. We avoided talking about England or the messenger who would come one day, suddenly. And when our glances strayed to the woods
beyond the fields, we would refrain from saying that we
wished we could go there.

Not always did the walks restore us. Chilled to the
bone, and as if doing penance, we would trudge the
measured stretch to the particular tree that staked out
our limits. André fell to brooding at times, would not
notice the scattering of snow flurries, the stillness emanating from the fields. Nor would he reach for a droop-

ing willow branch to feel its sleekness in his hand. He was walking on another road, and if anyone walked with him it wasn't me, for the fields his mind's eye were seeing were British.

When he returned from the scenes of his longing, he would smile self-consciously, his eyes ask forgiveness for deserting me already. How dear his face was to me. And he was still with me. He was still with me.

Hard as he tried not to show it, having to leave me behind preyed on him. His nights were haunted by dreams in which I was teetering at the edge of a cliff or almost falling off a bridge, and he would cry out in his sleep: "Don't be afraid, my darling, I'm holding you!" His iron grip jerked me from sleep, and bewildered, I would struggle to free myself, which only made him hold on to me more frantically. When we found our bearings, we saw in the other's eyes that the fears each tried to keep to himself lay bared. We reached for each other, but our embraces could not comfort, because they were forever perhaps the last embrace.

Twice, during the time we stayed at the castle, Loirette went to Vichy to sow confusion at *la Légion,* to give them fiendish advice, and to get inside information vital for the *Résistance.* His second trip was not timed by his own choice. Several young maquisards had been arrested at Guéret, another town in the area. Loirette's scheme was to laugh at the authorities for arresting as maquisards young men who everybody knew were ordinary thieves. The ridiculed authorities would surely hasten to repair the error and imprison the young men as criminals, which was as good as having their safety assured. After a week or two in prison, the young men were to volunteer for *la Légion,* which, not being choosy, pardoned criminals in order to fill its ranks. Once the young men were enrolled, Loirette would arrange to have them transferred to another locality. He would see to it that the transfer papers never reached their destination, and the new *légionnaires* would rejoin their maquis group. This plan Loirette carried out move for move, like a game of chess.

In the calm days of his absence, André and I found La Tourelle Joliette to be an enchanted castle. Perhaps Loirette himself had known its spellbound stillness in the days when his glance had met his wife's, when they had stepped into the yard her hand in his. A happy Hurluburlu must have been an amusing and charming companion. Now all he had were memories, perhaps a sense of her presence. And still fighting the irrevocability of his loss, he ran from room to room in desperate search of some trace of her.

"A penny for your thoughts," André said. His changeable eyes were all light. The next moment a notion obliterated that purity and replaced it with a rogue's twinkle.

I wondered which words might tell him how much I loved him. And not finding any, I teased him with the line from La Fontaine that inspired me to nickname my fair André "raven." *"Bonjour, monsieur le corbeau, comme vous êtes joli, comme vous me semblez beau."* And he leaped and ruffled me up.

The morning on which the messenger came had been a restive one. Everybody was irritable. A gusty wind blew the leaves in the yard, and the rustling made me uneasy, as if forebodings were whispered through the keyholes. The house was chilly and back drafts made the living-room stove billow smoke. I had seen Loirette

storm out the gate. Hands dug deep into the pockets of
his coat, he had marched off in direction of the farm,
perhaps to warm himself in the neighbor's kitchen.
André, fidgety, had gone to the pear tower, pulling its
plank door shut.

I was shivering in one of the sagging living-room
chairs, trying to warm myself by reading Jean Giono's
descriptions of summertime Provence, when the gate
creaked. Perhaps the desperate morning had set the
mood, for I knew it was the messenger, not Loirette
returning, and was instantly on my feet and at the window. A young man. Too late my mind frantically
searched for something that would allow doubt about
the stranger. I already knew whom I was watching. His
windblown trouser legs knee-deep in hurtling leaves, his
gaze taking in the castle's facade and the big tower,
he approached the door. I heard the iron knocker. Then
I saw Marie in her shapeless skirt, in her shrunken
sweater that strained over several layers of undergarments, step outside, and strands of dark hair blowing in
her face, she pointed at the pear tower. The youth
thanked her, and just as he turned to go there the tower
door swung open and André stepped from the dark hole,
the little pear basket in his hand. He stopped short. The
wind in his light hair, he scrutinized the youth. And with
a joyous tilting back of his head, he went to him in long
strides, shook hands, beamed. "But do come inside,
cher ami," he said in a clarion voice that came clearly
through the windowpanes. And leading the way to the
house, he pranced like a tightly reined, eager colt.

I heard the front door fall shut. Then silence.

Wherever the lofty place might be where Clotho,
Lachesis and Atropos sit, weaving the threads of our

destinies, as they looked down at us at that moment, they probably dismissed the event as minor. The flick of one of their busy fingers was enough to prevent André from being propelled into the next stage of his fate. With a peremptory glance they took note of the messenger informing André that his departure for England was put off indefinitely, that important contacts had been arrested, and that setting up new ones would take considerable time.

The three sisters then picked up their shuttles and once again concentrated on their intricate weaving. Never mind André's determination to get to England. His undertakings caused no more than a momentary snarling of the thread. Try as he might, he had to bide his time. He would receive his marching orders only on the day the sisters had chosen. And the marching orders they sent him would not depend on contacts, on an underground railroad, they would not be subject to the unforeseen. Their orders would open any door to him, clear any road for him, for their marching orders would bear the seal of highest authority — of the Grim Reaper himself.

André was restless, he brooded, had no patience with Loirette's fantasies. The castle was like a prison to him now.

Loirette, pained to see André like this, offered to make the castle a *Résistance* center, or a weapons arsenal, or a redoubt, or a clandestine school for brilliant young men to be instructed in everything from the arts to strategy, to make them a cadre of valiant knights who would lead France back to greatness.

André failed to respond to the relentless, high-pitched voice that wooed him for a smile. His twitching cheek indicated that he endured it like a form of torture. His glance turned inward, he paced the floor, suddenly to run outside and frantically gather kindling, furiously split wood, rake leaves, or hammer away at the gate to make it hold together with a nail he had pulled out from some-where. One day he grabbed my hands and kneaded them in mute despair. But restlessness and moody remoteness were merely surface ripples. He was churning in his depths and would burst out. He wrote letters, rode to town to post them at the station, and henceforth he was outside morning after morning to intercept the mailman. But most days the mailman failed to show, as he had nothing to bring to our neck of the woods.

Then, one morning, André's jubilant shout made me dash outside. He was dancing by the gate, both arms up, making me hurry. Laughing, he pulled me along down the road, kept laughing instead of answering my questions. He dragged me on across the fields to the woods where we had never been, not even after we were free to go there. Under the trees, he whirled me around and then pulled a letter from his pocket. "From Auguste. I wrote five letters to him and sent them to various addresses. One finally reached him. He's in the Dauphiné, not far from Grenoble. I asked him about the *Résistance* there and about his connections to get me off to England. Listen." He unfolded a sheet of lined paper. "*Cher copain,* come any time you wish, our parlor sofa is at your disposal. I know the right people for your plans, but the mountains here are beautiful, too, and you'd have the best of company. No need to advise me of your arrival, someone will be at the house. Take an express to Valence. There you change to a local. I'm most eager to see you. Your friend, A." Laughing, André tumbled from tree to tree, hurled pinecones in the air, leaped to touch a high branch and, imitating Loirette's falsetto, screeched: "Magnificent life! The great adventure!"

My André was already off, on his way to England. It was the price I had to pay for seeing once again that burst of dazzling radiance illuminate his whole person. Laughing and hugging, we danced about, and when we noticed Loirette on the road, looking for us, we broke into uncontrollable giggles.

That night we discussed our next steps more soberly. Hard as it was on me, I agreed that André ought to go alone to the Dauphiné. Auguste's parlor sofa would not accommodate both of us. Food was too scarce for anyone to feed two extra mouths, and meals at the restaurant every day we could not afford. If all went according to André's expectations, he might be off to England in no time at all, and what would I do in a town where I had no close friends? Since I dreaded the thought of staying on alone at Loirette's as previously planned, I decided to return to the Côte d'Azur, to my many friends, to where I could feel the pulse of the war again, hear rumors, hear bomber squadrons pass at night, be misled into believing that the invasion was imminent, be hungry and free.

André reined his eagerness to be off to give us a few more days together before separating for who could tell how long. We would make them carefree, happy days, run off to the woods, be just the two of us.

Loirette begged me to stay, vowed that life would be sweet and calm. He said he loved me, told André that he had foregone the right to hold on to me, since he was deserting me. And he called him a haunted prince, an enchanting mirage, a will-o'-the-wisp, a Peter Pan. André burst into laughter, teased him. It started as banter to turn suddenly serious. With sharp and witty words they lashed out at each other as with drawn daggers. But the fighting over me was a guise to keep their true feelings from coming into the open, their accumulated resentments, their incompatibility. They chafed to strike each other down, but would not, for they were brothers-in-arms, both needed for the defense of the love they shared, *la France*. On the same tightrope, they shoved and kicked, making certain that neither would fall and be hurt. And when their cutting witticisms brought them near the point of no return, they suddenly hugged and clowned to hide their seriousness. Yet after a breathing spell they started up again, and with practice they became increasingly sharper, all the while preserving an outward attitude of courtesy. And first thing next morning they resumed their dueling.

I was wary of the air of utter peace as our last day at the castle unfolded. But not a word, not a glance would disturb it. Loirette was gentle and cheerful. He went to the mill to beg some flour and made Marie bake a loaf of bread for us to take along. Joyously, he showed us two eggs he had wheedled from the maids' father. Lovingly, he dusted the bicycles that we would ride to the station. He insisted on checking the tire patches by himself, sending André and me off so that we might have another moment alone. That night he produced two bottles of Pinot Noir that he had "liberated" at the *Légion*'s Vichy headquarters, and which he had saved for this occasion as he had known all along, he claimed, that we would not stay. We emptied the bottles around the red-hot potbellied stove, which Loirette kept feeding with the kitchen's sacred split wood. And he was so charming and so scintillatingly witty that he gave us a last night to remember.

Next day, in the afternoon, we were once again on the rutty wagon trail, André in the lead, Loirette behind me, our bulky suitcases strapped to the baggage carriers of the two knights. Loirette was talking away like a driven man, buttonholing us with incessant questions as if trying to hoard responses to feed on during the long loneliness of the days to come. He professed to be grateful for the solitude; that freed of responsibility for our safety and well-being, he would have the peace of mind needed to finish his book. He would have it wrapped up in a mere couple of weeks, and then be free to give himself fully to the *Résistance*. And elaborating once again on how he would make the castle a *Résistance* fortress, he burst into a last: *"Ah, chers amis, c'est de la vie magnifique, de la grande aventure dont je vous parle!"*

It was still daylight when we chained the bicycles to the lamppost outside the station building. André checked a tire patch for the last time. "They're all in good shape," he said and gave each bicycle seat an affectionate slap. Loirette nodded absently.

We found the station as deserted in daytime as it had been on the night of my arrival. We stood on the platform, vaguely smiling, at a loss what to say. Certainly each of us wondered whether we would meet ever again. The war had stepped from the shadows of the station and rejoined us.

Loirette's sad gaze unsettled me. "I'll write," I said.

He fingered a frayed buttonhole. His small smile said how much they would miss me, he and François. But his voice said: "Down South, the mimosas will be in bloom soon."

"Another month and spring will be here as well," I

said and made a mental note to write François asking him to pick pussy willow branches and set them on Loirette's desk for me.

"In June the castle is at its most beautiful," he said. "Would you visit us in June?" And as if afraid that I might reject the invitation, he quickly turned to André. "You'll look dashing in uniform. Too bad I won't see you."

André laughed self-consciously. Any mention of his striking looks always embarrassed him. And the trace of a blush came to his face when Loirette, gravely sincere, added: "You are a beautiful man, my friend. I envy you. Take care. It is important to survive this."

"Thanks again for everything, Fernand," André said. "You're a great guy."

Loirette quipped something but his words were lost in the clatter of the incoming train. He embraced me, and the two kissed, left cheek, right cheek, left cheek.

We pushed into the crowded train corridor. Two men standing at the window made room to let us say our farewells. A last glance at Loirette, a wave of tenderness hiding behind the last inconsequential words. He smiled a forlorn, toothless smile, fiddled with his glasses, removed them, and his large brown eyes, too myopic to really see us, glittered wetly.

The train pulled out, the solitary figure in the narrow, too long coat slipped from sight. Houses glided past, streets we had not walked, then dark fields with a scattering of trees like the fields around Loirette's Tourelle Joliette. With a sense of loss I gazed into the dusky winter sadness. Then darkness fell, coming like the blank page at the end of a book. But the story would not let us go. With an ache in our hearts, we spoke of the evenings around the potbellied stove as if they were a cherished memory. We spoke of the pear tower, the leafy yard, the disintegrating gate, and of the lonely man who professed that life was magnificent, the great adventure.

Perhaps we held on to the castle, reluctant to face that we were spending our last few hours together. The window, framing unrelieved darkness, mirrored our shadowy faces, wraiths that made me apprehensive. I offered the window to the men who had freed it for us, and we moved into their spot. The people in the crowded corridor stood almost shoulder to shoulder, so our changing places forced others to shift. Then all settled in a new pattern like stones in a kaleidoscope. I had now the view into a compartment — three Germans, the other seats vacant. A man standing near me shook his head, just a hint of a shake, and said: "You'd feel chilly in there."

André said: "Put your head on my shoulder."

No, I wanted to see him. The floor space that was mine was just about the size of my feet, but letting the train's motion shake me, I gained more room and gradually turned to face André. I found a bit of wall for my shoulder. André cradled my hands in his.

In a bleak, drafty station, we kissed good-bye, touched each other's faces with cold fingers. "Grenouille . . ." André's transparent eyes had no bottom.

"Grenouille." He drew abruptly away and walked off, light-footed, but his shoulders . . . as if he were carrying his anguish piggyback. Don't go away, André!

"Mademoiselle . . . ?"

Stiff-necked, I lifted my head, which had dropped onto a fellow traveler's shoulder.

"There's a seat for you," he said, pointing, and steered me to the vacant seat.

Morning had come, and we were halted in a station. Schoolchildren pushed through the car's corridor. Two ten-year-old boys captured the seat across from me and placed their brown satchels across their knees. Under their coats they wore the long-sleeved, black cotton smocks of French elementary-school children.

"You said Alexander the Great?" one asked the other.

"Yes. Test today."

"On Alexander?"

"Aren't you prepared?"

"Me?" Brown eyes searched the ceiling. "Alexander?"

Dear boy, he reminded me of myself, made me once again hear Grandpapa ask: "What happened at the battle of Kunersdorf?"

"Kunersdorf?" As on other Sundays, I was bent over the book depicting Frederick the Great's life.

"Yes, Kunersdorf. The picture you're looking at. What happened at the battle of Kunersdorf? Who was Frederick's enemy?"

"His enemy? Oh. Kunersdorf?"

My stupidity made Grandpapa draw in his breath sharply. Dalla shot an angry glance at me, convinced that I had given a stupid answer out of spite.

Frederick the Great, Frederick the Great, Frederick the Great! With Grandpapa's constant glorification of him, which of his qualities we were asked to worship seems to have escaped me. I did not like this king of eternal war who unfeelingly rode past the stream of people he had made homeless; who, a hard glint in his eye, watched town after town burn to the ground, Ku-

nersdorf among them. My view of him was not softened
by Grandpapa's portrayals of "our great king": Frederick spending his candle-lit evenings playing flute, his
devoted dogs at his side; Frederick sheltering Mozart;
Frederick choosing as his closest companion the greatest
mind of his time, Voltaire. That Frederick argued and
fought with Voltaire we were not told, for that was un-
suitable for children to know. In later years I puzzled
over my grandfather's veneration of Frederick. Of
course, he might have been quite critical of him without
admitting it. Possibly he dismissed Frederick's errors
because something far deeper attracted him. Indeed,
how could he not have felt a kinship with the king who,
haughty and independent, scoffed at the rules others had
to abide by, whose mind refused to be confined to what
was accepted. The Frederick who enforced harsh discipline and advocated the blessings of hard work to his
people was a brother to the man who hewed NÜTZE DEN
TAG on his portico as a constant reminder to others.

But if Frederick had Voltaire to share his arrogant
laughter with, whom did Grandpapa have? Even his
own grown sons and daughters he found unworthy of
sharing in his thoughts. With a mocking twitch of his
lip, he divulged only what he considered suitable for
them, and they were left to guess the rest like children.
Had Grandpapa shared his haughty mirth with one of
his Freemason brethren? Or had Grandpapa laughed
all alone?

Despite my abhorrence of Frederick, many a Sunday I
would lose myself in the book that depicted his life.
To confront the man I despised? Or did I hope to find
Frederick changed since last Sunday? I was incurable of
such hopes. Reading a familiar fairy tale, I would hope,

my heart pounding, that this time the imminent catastrophe would be averted, the danger thwarted, that
Snow White would refuse the apple, little brother not
drink the brook water that would change him into a
mute deer. I told myself that it was just a story, the
characters not living people, just make-believe. My mind
understood, but my heart knew otherwise.

The pictorial life of Frederick the Great was a charm-
ingly old-fashioned book. I liked the smell of its yellowed pages and the earnest, delicately colored illustra-
tions. Each picture was a scene so rich in detail that I
would frequently discover something I had not noticed
before — a face in the window of a distant house, a
rake left in a furrow, a cat up in the leaves of a tree. I
would move from page to page, from rural scene to the
candle-lit salon of Sans Souci, where Frederick, lace
ruffles falling over his wrists, was playing the flute. And
suddenly Kunersdorf! Smoldering ruins, the sky a red
glow, and in the foreground Frederick in his long battle
coat, his face grim and his pale, somewhat bulging eyes
hard, determined to fight on, *coûte que coûte*. And on the
following page a snow-rimmed, muddy road with an
endless column of exhausted people weighed down by
bundles, leading weeping children by the hand. And at
the roadside old people who cannot go any farther, and
wounded soldiers who raise pleading arms to the passing
carriage in which Frederick sits, stony faced.

"Ini is going to cry-y! Ini is going to cry-y!"

Choking on rising tears, I struck back at my cousins
with: "Stupid! Stupid!"

One of the pictures caused anguish of a different kind.
It showed Frederick squatting under the small stone
bridge over a brooklet. With fright apparent in his eyes,
his hand round his whippet's muzzle to keep the dog

from barking, Frederick was hiding from the enemy, from Maria Theresa's troops, who passed overhead. Seeing him thus, just a man alone and in fear, the king I loathed regained his humanity. As I searched the faces of the soldiers to be sure that none looked in the direction of the king, they seemed to come to life, move, march, point, turn their heads, adjust their muskets. And I grew tense at the thought that one of them might go down to the brook to quench his thirst and discover Frederick. Yet, my heart was divided. It could not forget the king who unfeelingly rode past the hands raised toward him from the roadside. And it was with a sense of burden that I finally turned the page to go on through the bitter episodes of the Seven Years' War, the Thirty Years' War, war, war, war. . . .

I am still turning pages, for the book never ended. Frederick is still around, still burns towns, still covers man's roads with throngs of fleeing people, still snatches young lads away from their plows and forces them to kill and to die. Frederick stands in rice paddies watching bamboo huts burn with eyes as hard as at Kunersdorf. Unmoved, he looks at Vietnam's small children, who, yet smaller children on their backs, run in terror not knowing where.

Since Frederick appeared to be history's champion, I closed my mind to that subject, to the endless columns of battle dates we were required to learn in school. I closed my mind to the other, countless Fredericks of German history, Frederick William, Frederick I, Frederick II, Frederick III, Frederick IV, another Frederick I, another Frederick II (the Great), and all the others. . . . How on earth did any German schoolchild keep them apart? They did though, together with the respective battle dates. They had to. Somehow I managed to stand firm. One Frederick sufficed me. And willy-nilly I knew what this one looked like. Frederick II of Prussia, the Great, was small.

In the cells of my brain reserved for history, I hung up a few pictures of man suffering and man in fear. They seem to cover what history has to tell. They proved to apply also to the history made in my own time, to Stalingrad, London in the blitz, and to the night Dresden died. Only the fires destroying these cities were bigger than those of Kunersdorf had been.

Later, I added two pictures to those I hung when a child. The first is for the wanton murder of civilians at places such as Lidice and Oradour-sur-Glane. This picture also covers My Lai. The second picture is known around the world. It shows the hill of skeletal corpses. The picture is very sharp, every detail recognizable, yet I cannot tell whether one of the faces might be Natasha's, Zhizhvizhny's, Hillery's, little Simon's, for the hollow-cheeked faces, all skull, all eye sockets, all teeth, resemble only each other and Death. Six million people took their turn on that heap. Six million — like all of Denmark, all of Saudi Arabia. If we killed all the men in Chicago and Los Angeles combined, one by one, and then all the women, and then all the children, that's what six million means. That gruesome heap is but a mere sampling.

I have moved this picture from my mind into my heart. It needed a place where it was sheltered from babbling sightseers. It should not have to listen to: "The Germans weren't the only ones." . . . "We must forget." . . . "Life goes on." . . . "Goethe, Schiller, Lessing, Heine, Bach." . . . "I am a Berliner." . . . "German toilets are clean." . . . *Gemütliches* Munich." . . .

The heap of skeletons is safe in my heart, which remembers. The very first time I looked at it, the thought came to my mind that someone on that heap had died in my stead. All he needed to slip through their fingers was a bit of luck, a few seconds allowing him to turn the next street corner, or to crawl into a thicket, or to get off a bus. And my luck might have failed at a crucial moment.

He was silenced, I am able to speak. His dying shall not be forgotten because of the countless men and women and children we are now piling up.

I don't know how they killed him, whether they gassed him or whether he simply died, life leaving him because there wasn't enough body left for life. Perhaps they told him to line up, and made him dig a mass grave, and then ordered him to jump in. If he was lucky, their bullets killed him as he jumped, and he was spared being buried alive under the weight of others on top of him; was spared choking to death on the dirt they shoveled into his mouth.

As I can hold him only in the warmth of my living heart, in the soft light of my vigil candle, as I cannot give back to him sky and summer fields and wind-rippled water, how could Germany come back to life?

The lot of the Germans does not move my heart, they get along fine without me. Two million foreign workers do their chores while they are off, back in Paris, Amsterdam, Copenhagen, and on the beaches of Normandy. Win a war, lose a war — *heute gehört uns Deutschland, morgen die ganze Welt.*

Time is running out for my pictures. They must become relics or they, together with all the history books, will perish tomorrow in the biggest fire history ever lit.

It won't matter who the aggressor was, or who fought whom, or whether this final war lasted thirty years or one day, for there won't be schoolchildren left to learn its "from . . . to."

Children taken on an outing to Frederick the Great's Sans Souci, like Dalla, Müsi and I, will lie skinless beside their Grandpapa on the paths of the royal park. Burned children and their burned Mamas will litter Fifth Avenue, the Champs Elysées, Moscow's Red Square. On the beaches of Dunkirk, which saw the most astonishing retreat in history, and on the beaches of Normandy, which saw in that dawn a sea thick with ships coming, lifeless sunbathers will lie under a cloud of putrid stench. Nobody will come to slip them into a body bag. And no one will be left to do the mop-up job. In front of the Amsterdam house where Anne Frank pleaded for her life, Dutchmen, who had survived that war, will lie dead, their clothes ripped to shreds by the force of the incredible wind. And Berliners will lie at Checkpoint Charlie, blown against a wall that divides nothing any more.

In the days following World War III no Nuremberg trials will be held because there won't be judges left to hold court, witnesses to testify, guilty to be sentenced. Alone God will be there to ponder what man has done, man whom He created in His image.

Even had school done away with history, I would still not have liked it, because from the moment one entered a Prussian school one was overcome with a sense of guilt and utter helplessness.

I failed right from the start and as ridiculous as it might seem, I had to be tutored after school in the first grade. Though Herr Wilden was a schoolteacher, he was a soft-spoken, kind man. Seated closely side by side, sharing the light that the green glass lamp dropped on the oak desk, Herr Wilden corrected his pupils' compositions while I practiced hairline upstrokes and strong downstrokes. I didn't mind filling whole pages with rows of slanted lines. I liked this small, cluttered room, being near this quiet man who did his work while I did mine. And I liked his pipe smoke, which tenderly enwrapped both of us.

But he was an oasis in a vast desert. Our other teachers were men and women grown sour and vengeful in the line of duty. All the younger teachers had apparently been killed at Verdun, together with my Uncle Ludwig. This seemed all to the better since the Republic was better served by sour teachers. They were to instill discipline and mold us into docile, obedient servants of the state. It was desirable for us to fear them, not, God forbid, to like them. If a teacher was kind, it was by default. Nor was it required of him to make his teaching inspiring. To learn was our duty, period. Our teachers' meals may have been skimpy, but they could feast on our fear of them, and we were game in season all year round. Luckily I was in their molding hands only off and on, and because of the lack of continuity, they failed to shape me into a cowering citizen. My development as a pawn was stunted. And so was my learning.

Herr Wilden could perhaps have succeeded in teaching me the multiplication tables from two to nine if a fallen horse hadn't put an end to his tutoring. At the age of six I was considered a big girl, old enough to go to the tutor by myself, even though it was winter then and dark by the time I returned home. It did not occur to my mother that I might be frightened, and she didn't know that I ran all the way, zigzagging from one side of the street to the other to avoid passing any man who might prove to be a "bad man." My nerves already on edge, I came upon the scene of an accident one day. At the intersection of Hohenzollerndamm, the tramway had rammed a horse-drawn wagon. Although the horse was not injured, it lay on the pavement, its teeth bared, its nostrils blown open, and its eyes bulging with fright. Its attempts to get up were hampered by the straining harness, the tangled reins, the wagon axle. And frenzied by its helplessness, it foiled the peoples' efforts to free it.

Sobbing, I pushed toward the horse to stroke its head, but was grabbed, pushed back. People yelled at me to be on my way. But they were too engrossed in watching, in giving advice, to pay further attention to me. The animal's fright mine, I stood rooted, staring at its terrified eyes.

At long last arms gathered me, bedding my aching chest on Wawa's bosom. And my tear-sore eyes closed against her cool neck.

Try as Mama might, she could not make me go to the tutor ever again. At the mere mention of the lessons, my mind's eye saw the terror-stricken horse, and then, by sleight-of-hand of association, myself, helplessly cornered by a "bad man."

For us children to come upon a "bad man" was an every-other-day occurrence; therefore, we saw to it that we had the company of others on our way to and from school. The "bad men" were elderly, or what looked elderly to us, and they were indistinguishable from orderly citizens going about their business. Occasionally a "bad man" would give himself away by smiling at us, tip us off to his evil intentions, for German adults rarely smiled at children. A cunning "bad man" would not smile, he would let us come close, and flipping open his coat, bare himself. Squealing, grabbing each other's hands, we would run for all we were worth.

We did not mention the "bad men" to our mothers. How could we put into words what was so unspeakably indecent? Some children even feared punishment for seeing what they saw. To tell a policeman did not occur to us. The society in which we were growing up taught us to be in awe of authority's representatives, be they policemen, teachers, or postal clerks. We had to live with our fears. Our best friends were our fast legs.

At least, we were still safe inside our houses then. Ours was guarded by a Cerberus by the name of Frau Grutz. Frau Grutz, the concierge, kept the brass knobs shining, the mirrors in the elevator glittering, the mahagony woodwork well polished, and the carpeting on the stairs immaculate. She considered those entering *her* house, stepping on *her* rugs, looking in *her* mirrors, putting their hands on *her* banisters, her personal enemies. To enter our house, outsiders had to be admitted by Frau Grutz. Adult tenants were given a key, but minors decidedly not. Only after lengthy scrutiny and after overcoming her reluctance to buzz, would Frau Grutz release the door and, her disgruntled, old-owl's face remaining in the small window of the concierge's loge, she would follow the intruder with a poisonous glance.

More than anything, Frau Grutz resented the frequent comings and goings of the tenants' ten children. But hard as she tried to terrorize us into preferring the servants' stairs to passing under her evil eye, she did not succeed. To reach the servants' stairs one had to go through a cellar pasageway full of dark nooks and shadowy corners. Only when we were many did we dare and then, to frighten off the ghosts, we would race through the cellar hollering until we burst out the back door into the large yard and the reassuring sight of its green lawns, its clusters of rhododendron, and neat signs saying "Verboten." The paved walk leading from the cellar exit to the servants' entrance door passed alongside a concrete square on which, according to the day of the week, maids beat the dust out of rugs, the ragman sent his unintelligible singsong call to the windows above, the scissors-grinder set up his wheel, or the organ-grinder's tethered monkey hopped about, picking up the coins dropped by maids from kitchen windows.

To our eyes the servants' stairs were spooky. Their dreary neatness was spooky; so were the naked lightbulbs topped by flat, enameled tin shades, the bare wooden steps, the cold walls painted halfway up with the shiny olive green considered the proper and practical embellishment for the lower classes, for schools, and for administrative buildings where lower-ranking clerks dealt with the public.

In those post–World War I years, pale and poorly dressed men frequently came to the kitchen door to beg a piece of bread. It was a matter of course that Mama, Wawa, or our maid handed the unfortunates a sandwich or a plate of hot soup, which they would eat sitting on the steps. On occasion I was charged with handing the beggar the plate, and his timid thanks and the shame in his eyes would make me swallow tears of pity. Yet when we children used the servants' stairs for one reason or another and happened upon such a beggar, our hearts would skip a beat for fear that he was a "bad man."

One day, when we ran across the weedy meadow at the far end of our goat garden, we happened upon a bum sleeping in the grass. He was a little old man. Our giggles awakened him, and all at once he had a switchblade in his hand, making us scatter, shrieking. The old man

was on his feet and after us, and we ran off, head over
heels, across the soccer field and out into the houseless
street bordering it. From a safe distance we taunted
him: "Bad man! Bad man!" His switchblade flashed in
the sun. "He's coming! Run!" We rushed down a street
that offered no refuge whatsoever. All the way to the
end of the block ran a high, unclimbable fence, and behind it lay the impenetrable green of trees and bushes
that assured the owner privacy. Panting, we dared a
glance back from the far corner. "He's coming!" We
turned the corner with a burst of speed. The old, bow-
legged man could not run as fast as we could. At
the next corner we were at leisure to call again: "Bad
man! Bad man!" And off we went, making a dash for
home.

"He's still coming!"

Indeed, the old man followed us right into our own
street, to our handsome houses with flower-planted bal-
conies. His brazenness was disconcerting. We didn't
dare lose vital seconds ringing the doorbell, waiting for
Frau Grutz's owl eyes to appear. It might take her an
eternity. "Through the cellar!"

Midway in the cellar passageway, the sound of the
cellar door made us stop dead. Aghast, we pushed into
a dark nook, clutched each other, and scarcely breathing,
listened to the slurring footfalls. Then they stopped.
He seemed to hesitate, to listen, and then shuffled on,
was coming. Flattening out against the cold wall, we
clawed each other.

His hand, clenching the knife, preceded his hunched
body. Numb with fright we stared, unable to see under
the shadow of his battered hat whether he was looking
at us. He muttered some curses and moved past us at
arm's length.

A guardian angel held us petrified until the yard door creaked, until it fell closed.

"He's out in the yard!"

We burst from the nook and out the street exit, scrambled to the entrance for *Herrschaften*. We pressed the bell button hard, holding it, peered through the oak door's cut-glass panel. Frau Grutz's surly face appeared in the small concierge window. "Frau Grutz!!!" For once the buzzer buzzed instantaneously, and we stormed inside to satiny mahogany woodwork, red carpeting, and polished brass. Frau Grutz snarled at us, but who cared.

One flight up we caught our breath. "Wow!" We grinned at each other, a trifle uncertain. Then we split up, some to one apartment door, some to another, back to our dolls and teddy bears.

Ten years later Berlin's entrances for *Herrschaften* ceased to offer protection. The "bad men," rather than being little old demented men, were strapping young fellows in snappy uniforms. And they had an "open sesame" to all doors. They bestowed power on the Frau Grutzes by elevating them to the rank of *Blockwart,* Nazi snooper. The Frau Grutzes, to whom this rise in status was a long-overdue balancing of old accounts, spied zealously on the tenants to find one they could dutifully denounce to the Gestapo. Polishing banisters was no longer a chore, merely pretext for listening at the apartment doors. Now it was the tenants' turn to bow and be polite, for the Frau Grutzes determined who should live and who should die.

In the interim years, I sat in class with the future Nazi maidens, suffering through the battle dates that bestarred our German sky. That I was not cut from heroic cloth also showed in other subjects. The countless poems and ballades we were required to memorize I was unable to learn because I cried my heart out over them. Some were to haunt me for years. One was about a sparrow alone in the winter cold, begging for a crumb outside a closed window. Another described three grenadiers who, defeated in battle, hungry, cold, and exhausted, made their sad way home. Even poems that told no sad story had me in tears. Goodness, gratitude, compassion, courage, perseverance, humility, diligence, you name it, made me weep. Time and again I came to class with a note from my mother explaining why I could not memorize the latest poem. Her note, however, would not settle the matter. The teacher ridiculed me. She ordered me to stand by the blackboard facing the class, and to the merriment of the other children, she read my mother's note in a baby voice. Worse still, she would call me a liar. She said that a child as unruly as I was, who frequently talked in class, who was disrespectful of regulations, who failed to apply herself with diligence, was certainly not the kind of child to be moved by poetry. And in bright red ink I was entered in her record book: Homework not done.

Our music teacher might have vouched for the genuineness of my tears, for they gave him a special thrill, and he delighted in making them flow. All that was needed was to make us sing "Ich hat' einen Kameraden."

He directed us to sing this song snappily, in soldierly fashion, as if the words were: "Off, friends, to war!" A German child should not notice that the beautifully simple lyrics spoke of love and of the helplessness of man at war. Even though it made me cry, I liked the song. In secret I would sing it, sing it softly and sadly, as a mourning soldier would. And at such times my warm tears brought relief. However, in class . . .

As soon as "old fatso" noticed that my lips had begun to tremble, he interrupted the class with a signal from his baton and declared: "Crybaby wants to sing solo." His hand busying about in his trouser pocket, the tall man would move down the aisle toward me with studied deliberation.

Choking on the words, I sang: *"Ich hat' einen Kameraden, einen bess'ren findst du nicht . . ."* By then I was surely in tears, sobbing on: *"Die Trommel schlug zum Streite . . . er ging an meiner Seite . . . im gleichen Schritt und Tritt."* The sharp point of the baton kept poking my chest, nudging me on. *"Eine Kugel kam geflogen . . . gilt sie mir oder gilt sie dir . . . Sie hat ihn fortgerissen . . . er liegt zu meinen Füssen als wär's ein Stück von mir."* *

When the recess bell rang my liberation, I pushed out into the hall, to the water fountain to drink avidly, to splash, to shake off humiliation and helplessness. I slid down the banister, yelled my head off, laughed like a loon, or showed off in the toilets, climbing up on top of a stall partition. If luck was against me, I was caught and sent to the principal to be hollered at.

* I had a comrade,
  Never was a better one;
  The drumbeat called us to battle —
  He walked at my side
  In step with me.
  A bullet came flying —
  For him or for me?
  It tore him away.
  He lies at my feet
  Like a part of myself.

I was freed of Prussian teachers when Elizabeth Duncan, sister of the famous Isadora, returned to Germany to reopen their dancing school, which World War I had closed. In inflation-ravaged Germany, where a single dollar was a small fortune, the Duncans, chronically short of funds, were able to run the school on a shoestring. Elizabeth leased no less than one of the *communs* of the Neue Palais, the royal palace outside of Potsdam. She and the six "Duncan girls" had scarcely moved in when I was enrolled, their first new German pupil. Frederick the Great's royal park was to be my playground, and his Sans Souci the goal of our afternoon walks. Now I could skip along the historic paths on which Grandpapa had made us walk reverently. And in Frederick's sacred glades I danced barefoot, in a skimpy veil.

The day Mama took me to the Duncan school, we made our way from the railroad station through the royal park on foot. I had just turned eight and was apprehensive of the American strangers with whom I would be left. As we walked along the weekday-quiet paths, I was overcome by a sense of great loneliness. Mama was holding my hand and she must have been speaking to me, but neither her hand nor her words offered solace. The majestic park seemed to be all sadness. The scent of fall was sad, the sound of crunching sand underfoot, a leaf soundlessly tumbling to the ground. The big fountain's jet of water seemed to fall back into the large basin like so many tears. Melancholy lay upon the wide and empty steps that rose from there, and under the large, old trees that walled in mysterious glades. Frederick's trees — awesome dark copper beeches, somber chestnut trees, enormous oaks, and now and then a birch, too delicate to lighten so much majesty. I wanted to beg Mama to take me home, let me return to the school I hated, but my plea I repeated only in my mind, for Mama seemed to be out of reach.

The landmarks Grandpapa had taken us to were Sans Souci, Frederick's Chinese tea house, his Orangerie, and the small castle, Charlottenhof. The colossal Neue Palais probably offended Grandpapa's sense of beauty. When that overpowering monstrosity came in sight, the last of any hope drained from me. The mere size of the palace was oppressive. And chilling was the bleakness of the vast drill square in front. Kings the world over surrounded their palaces with artful gardens and lovely fountains to have a pleasing view. That Prussia's kings let the fifty-eight large royal windows look across a yellow, brick-paved desert tells of their inhumanity.

At the far side of this stony expanse, and facing the palace, stood the two *communs,* two monstrosities of lesser size with a curved colonnade between them. The ladies and gentlemen in attendance at the royal household had been quartered there, and now one of them housed the Duncan dancing school.

Crossing the drill square, I thought the twin buildings were wearing Prussian spiked helmets, but getting closer I saw that the spikes were heroic figures topping each cupola. Massive stairs, curving up to a huge terrace with enormous columns, reduced me to a Thumbelina. Inside I remained just as tiny, awed by huge white marble stairs, and a ceiling as far away as the sky. And in amazement I stared at the young women greeting us, fairy-tale creatures in flowing veils and open sandals.

The only other child was ten-year-old Wilma, who took me up the curved marble stairs to show me to our room, which was the size of a royal stateroom, empty except for our two white beds, a chest of drawers, and a large table. And when I stepped to the high windows, my glance found only more emptiness — the barren drill square.

That first night, somewhat sheltered from the overwhelming space by Swiss curtains falling to both sides of my bed, I ached for the limited space of my bedroom at home; for Dalla and Müsi, with whom I had shared it. There, each time a car came down Hohenzollerndamm, its light spilled across Herr Krüger's flower nursery, throwing the pattern of the windowpanes upon our ceiling. It began distorted, as an elongated rhomboid, became an oblong, stretched into a rhomboid on the other side, and faded away. I had named this pattern of soft light and shadow my "bridge." I would lie in bed watching my bridge silently swing from one mysterious shore to the other, and imagined people moving about on it. I made myself believe that my bridge was always there, was lit up and again plunged into shadow as if by a moon behind drifting clouds. My bridge and its people kept the awesome night at bay, stood between the fathomless universe and me. And waiting for its next appearance, I would fall asleep.

Nothing emerged from the shadows of the large Duncan school ceiling. A terrible thought got hold of me that in my sleep I might drift out the royal windows, up into the big night and the great void beyond it. I forced my eyes to stay wide open, but they would not let go of the scene I had looked upon just before going to bed — the drill-ground desert, the massive, shadow-hung Neue Palais, and a moon, finding nothing it wished to touch with silver fingers, hanging above coldly aloof, its lopsided face averted.

I finally dared to stick my hand out from under the

safe blanket to unfasten the ribbons that held the Swiss curtains and draw them closed, make them overlap. As my breath warmed the fluffy tent, my mind filled it with soothing whispers.

Before this same moon waxed to fullness, the Duncan spell had transformed even the evil drill ground. At night, when Wilma and I just once more crawled out of bed to press our noses to the windowpanes, we would see indistinct figures move in the shadows of the Neue Palais, see figures flit across the silvery square. What figures? Who could tell? Crinolined ladies-in-waiting scurrying to a rendezvous with grenadiers in white breeches?

Or of a night we would tiptoe into the adjoining room, which had been put at our disposal in the event an urge to dance overcame us outside the scheduled dancing lessons. Like the other practice rooms, its walls were hung with sea-green gossamer drapes falling in soft folds from the cornices to the carpeted floor. We shed our nighties and ran about in a wide circle, flapping our arms like wings to stir up the air and make the drapes ripple and billow. Our eyes on the moon-touched waves, the night's cool breath on our bare skin, we ran round and round until we felt weightless, like flying, until sweet dizziness made us drop to the floor.

The room behind that one served as a storage room for a number of large steamer trunks filled with bolt after bolt of veil in soft pastel colors. Bits of such veil were what we wore for dancing, and since we, the little ones, had permission to help ourselves to whatever tint struck our fancy, we feasted on the boundless yardage.

Our dancing attire required no sewing. We measured two pieces of veil from shoulder to thigh, knotted them at the shoulders, and held the rest in place with a ribbon or a silk cord round the waist. Visitors to the royal park frowned with indignation when of a summer day they sighted the dozen Duncan children leaping barefoot in wispy veils in one of Frederick's serene meadows. Not for a moment did these orderly Prussians take us for elves. With good reason. No elf in its right mind would have come to Prussia.

The German climate did not permit us to wear nothing but veils all the time. However, our light blue cotton frocks, cut like Russian shirts, were just as loose and soft. The two little boys among us wore the same shirts with short pants of the same fabric, and during winter afternoons all of us embroidered the collars and wrists with earnest dedication. The Duncans did not consider embroidering an unmanly occupation. Nor did they burden us with threatening previews of the roles society demanded us to fill once we were grown men and women. The Duncan world ignored society. We easily forgot past admonishments to behave like a girl, or to take it like a man. Here we were allowed to be just children. With the same ease we dismissed other past directives and concentrated on what mattered here: the beauty of our stride, the curve of our lifted arms, graceful balance, obedient limbs. With all our heart we strove to be beautiful in body and mind, and healthy, for health, we were told, was the soil that allowed beauty to bloom. The "big girls," who were our teachers and models, took us on long walks and made us breathe deeply; and in the hours between our dancing lessons, they guided us in making beautiful things. Painting, embroidery, knotting multicolored rope, stringing pretty glass beads, were to help develop beautiful minds.

Yet our days were ordered and disciplined. First thing in the morning, we slipped into pale blue cotton jerseys and, bare-legged and barefoot, scampered down the marble stairs to gymnastics, directed by grave Dora. Morning gymnastics were sober exercises executed with precision, aimed at limbering and strengthening joints and muscles. We began with foot exercises, followed by leg exercises, back, neck and arm exercises, bending from the waist sideways, backward, forward, touching toes and up again, reach high, stretch, stretch the entire body. And then to hot oatmeal.

Gentle Erna was in charge of the mid-morning rhythmic exercises. To the soft thumpings of a tambourine we walked lightly, strode, ran, skipped, leaped, concentrating on body control while obeying the changing rhythms.

Lunch, a rest period, a walk in the park, bead stringing, and once again eager, nimble-footed children, elves in wispy veils, would scurry down the marble steps, to the dancing session this time. Now we were on our own to use our body as instrument with which to interpret the mood of a gavotte, an adagio, a polonaise, a largo, a capriccio. One child might take off in long, vigorous strides, arms spread, head tilted back, while another slowly unfolded softly curving arms.

I was happy at the Duncan school. Its earnest striving for beauty fulfilled me, and working toward mastery of my body gave me satisfaction.

The two Duncan sisters remained remote. Isadora was in Moscow, in love with the Russian poet Yessenin. I saw her only once, when in transit she stopped by the school in the dead of night. Roused from deep sleep, we exchanged nighties for veils and danced for her at three o'clock in the morning. I was too much in awe to take a good look at her; just her wide-brimmed purple velvet hat, her flowing veil and dramatic clothes made me catch my breath.

Elizabeth was not quite real either, a fairy-world creature soundlessly appearing and airily gliding down the passageway to her sanctum somewhere in the building. I could not picture her doing anything as profane as living. I imagined her sitting on silken cushions all day like a goddess in her shrine, her small face of an earnest chimpanzee transformed to beauty by the splendor of her soul.

Although we saw her for dinner, and we caught glimpses of her in flowing silk light-footedly crossing the hall on her way to teach the big girls, the day I was called to join the big girls' dancing session, I didn't dare look at the small figure seated before the soft drapes who gave her comments and spare praise in a subdued, quite matter-of-fact voice. I felt heavy, clumsy, uncertain about what I was expected to do, and the big girls, so beautiful and accomplished, concentrated on themselves. I wished that this tormenting hour would come to an end.

"Good, Ingrid," I heard Elizabeth say. Had she really said that? Her head nodded yes, her hand waved me on, and a wild rush of gladness carried me off as though I were riding a bubbling ocean wave. I barely skimmed the floor, my exalted legs lifted me powerfully in a long leap, and my fervent desire to please her made me raise my arms in the softest curve ever.

The big girls had a nimbus as well, and each of us had made one the special object of adoration. Mine was Dora, a brunette Diana, aloof and somewhat austere. She was, it seemed, harassed by the attentions of a love-struck dentist, and once I wept my heart out because I had seen her in tears over him. Dora was strict but just. Erna was gentle, Senta coquettish, and redheaded Jessica one day presented us with the most immaculate apple we had ever seen, an American Delicious.

Our strictly scheduled days passed tranquilly. Our minds on beauty whether doing our exacting exercises, painting and stringing beads round the long table, or walking through the serene park, we lived under a glass bell that protected the world the Duncans had dreamed for us.

Then the glass bell was shattered and evil hands reached for us. They were the profusely beringed hands of two Russian baronesses turned governess. The resentment over their fall in status they let out on us, as though we had brought on the Russian Revolution. If none of the big girls was present, they pinched us or hit us with their knitting needles, bullied us, humiliated us. All day long they bemoaned the splendor they had known, their Moscow salons, the fabulous receptions, maids and footmen, furs and jewelry, and they gossiped about people and events now gone. From their melancholy duets we learned that the celebrated Isadora had been at their receptions, and surely they must have been all sugar and honey or Isadora would not have asked her sister to give shelter to the unfortunate ladies. We had been happy and content playing with pretty ribbons, skipping along the royal paths, but having become these ladies' scapegoats, we grew restive and wild. On our afternoon walks, chaperoned by the baronesses, we beat hapless frogs to a pulp with willow switches. And the baronesses, so adamant about manners, looked on unconcerned.

Aside from the liberty they took of pinching us on the sneak, the baronesses, if they cared at all, had no say over our activities. As before, we painted, strung beads, and wove colored strips of shiny paper. I don't remember any hardship such as being taught the three R's, not even by the baronesses. If one of the big girls did, she must have done it so gently that it left no trace in my memory. But that also was to change.

The good citizens of Potsdam were outraged by the foreign school. Their sense of decency was offended by our dancing barefoot in the royal meadows, by the big girls showing up in Potsdam's streets in togas nonchalantly draped over the shoulders, and, lo and behold, in Greek sandals. The Potsdamers huffed and puffed. To them such garments implied anything from promiscuity to espionage.

When we little ones were taken to Potsdam once a month to spend the one-dollar pocket money Wilma received from home, Potsdam's women raised their noses and, after a thorough stare, turned away with ostentatious disapproval. What offended the Potsdamers were our "Bolshevik" coats, a gift from Isadora, loose coats of gray felt adorned with bright-colored felt appliqués and embroidery all the way down the buttonless front and on the wide sleeves. The dress considered proper for boarding-school girls was demure navy blue. However, our big-girl chaperones' smiles shielding us from the poisonous glances, we proceeded calmly to the bank to exchange Wilma's dollar for a stack of inflationary German millions, and on to the department store to spend them before they became worthless.

For the one dollar we could have bought all of Potsdam, it seemed, but all that interested us were ribbons, cocoa and sugar. We bought yards and yards of ribbon and silk cord to hold together our pieces of veil; and we bought as much cocoa and sugar as we could carry. At night we mixed them with water to a thick paste that we licked up in bed. No matter how hard we tried to spend the fortune, we always had money left. On one occasion, just to be rid of what would be worthless within a couple of days, Wilma dropped a handful of leftover bills into the shopping bag of another customer. Perhaps it was these bills that were our final undoing. An official of Potsdam's board of education paid the Duncan school a surprise visit.

We were stringing lovely beads, weaving beautiful patterns, when a grim-faced Dora entered, accompanied by the investigator. We did not need to be told that he was the enemy. It was written all over him. It was in the hard sound of his step. He glowered at us.

Half an hour later the building's great stillness was shattered by his shouts in the downstairs hall. He would put an end to our unheard-of way of life, to our foreign bohemianism, he bellowed. He would see to it that German law and order would sweep this house clean. The great oaken front door banged, and angry footsteps clattered down the regal stairs outside.

The next morning a schoolmarm arrived with orders from on high to provide us with so many hours of elementary instruction each morning. A room not vast enough for Duncan purposes was fixed up as a classroom, and our morning bead stringing and painting had to yield to reading, writing and arithmetic.

Within half an hour our teacher was tearing her hair over our multileveled and extensive ignorance. One morning a few days later, she threw up her hands and dashed out to run all over the house in search of Fräulein Duncan, only to find out that she had to ask for an audience — which she took as a lack of respect for the State.

Her appointment with Elizabeth made her come to class late next morning and in tears. That she had to talk about matters as serious as homework, spelling and multiplication tables to a woman draped in yards of thin silk, with wispy sandals on her bare feet, had so disconcerted her that she spilled it all to us. It transpired that instead of having to face an impolite and argumentative Fräulein Duncan, a manner she was accustomed to and was prepared to counter with the authority given her, she had been up against Elizabeth's Buddhistic silence and her remote, earnest eyes. For all she knew, this Fräulein Duncan didn't even understand German.

After she had collected herself, she gave us assignments and rushed out again to give her cause another chance by appealing to the school's male manager, Max Merz. Whatever happened there, we did not learn, but she returned flushed and remained fidgety.

As a last resort she turned to the baronesses. They looked down their noses at her and said all a girl needed was breeding. They said they hoped none of us would make a match so poor that we would have to manage a budget; and for what else could a girl need arithmetic?

Our teacher gasped. "The authorities ought to close this school," she said. "This school is an insult to Germany." And then she wept at her desk.

I felt sorry for her, and to please her, I made a real effort. That my diligence was short-lived was her fault, since she snuffed out my compassion. To the malassorted lot we were, she had read a story dealing with the daily life of coal miners, about which we were then to write a composition. The story had caught my imagination and I was delighted with the assignment. As I was writing my piece, I myself descended into the mine shaft at a dizzying speed, smelled the dank breath of the deep earth, heard the clanking of the miners' picks and the rattle of the lorries, and felt the gritty coal on my hands.

All aglow I handed my pages to her, certain of getting an "Excellent."

Next morning the sky fell. The pages she handed back to me were marked with a furiously written, red "Disastrous!" Unbelieving, I stared at my lines, which yesterday had throbbed with life, which had so powerfully captured the mysteriousness of the miners' world that they had brought shivers down my back.

"You evil child!" my teacher screeched.

I stared at "little hammers ping . . . ping . . ." Somehow, only every fifth word had made it to the paper. Dumbfounded I looked for blank spaces left by words that had been there yesterday, and which some black magic must have snatched away.

Wagging a threatening finger in my face, the teacher screamed: "You'll take this to Fräulein Duncan. Instantly! Let her see this! Let her see this!" And her trembling finger pointed to the door.

Crestfallen and tearful, I got to my feet, but then she revised her sentence. "To Herr Merz you will report, not to her. To him, you understand?" The poor woman, being a German, was convinced that a man would deal out a harsher punishment.

The evidence of my crime in hand, I made my way to Max Merz's door. His friendly, unsuspecting face triggered fresh tears. What would I not have done to spare him such disappointment in me. His smile died and, as though I were ill, he gently led me to one of the couches that bloomed with vividly colored throws and cushions and countless Japanese dolls.

As he listened to my confession, his face changed from concern to bafflement. And when he learned that a coal mine was the topic of our composition, he burst into peals of merry laughter. He dabbed my tears and filled my lap with his dolls, pointing out their fine features, their finely sculpted hands, details of their exquisite dress, and their intricate hairdos. And he told me about the character each of the dolls represented. He reached for a large terra-cotta vase decorated with Greek runners in flowing garments and made my finger follow the line of their legs, the folds of their garments. He dropped a thin silken throw into my hands and asked me to put my face into the cool, fluffy, mysteriously scented cloud. "The scent is sandalwood," he explained.

Not a word about my disastrous composition. He spoke about beauty — beautiful textures, colors, shapes, about beautiful bodies to be temples to house beautiful souls. He told me to keep my heart serene and to rest my eyes upon beautiful objects; to become a priestess of beauty.

Then he took me to the door. And what about my teacher?

"Bear with her without rancor," he said. He said she was a poor creature distorted beyond repair by a wrong way of life. He said to guard myself against her views; let her not disturb the tranquillity of my mind, which should be like a clear, quiet mountain pond. "Become a goddess, child. Put all your striving into becoming a goddess." His tone of voice, his smile, implied that such a goal was most natural and attainable.

With all the sincerity of my age I concentrated on becoming a goddess, on making my body a temple for a beautiful soul. I turned my eyes to beautiful things and guarded myself against teachers who were deformed beyond repair. To keep my mind as serene as a mountain pond, I dismissed the angry red marks she scrawled under my schoolwork.

I did not become a goddess, not even a dancer, but

212 / A PRIVATE TREASON

the seed the Duncans planted in my body had sprouted
and might well want to come to bloom in my next incar-
nation. What ended my unfolding was an influenza epi-
demic. It felled the war- and inflation-weakened Germans the way a violent storm ravages fields and forests.
And it did not stop at the gate of the Duncans' lovely
little garden. Frantic mothers came for their children
and so did mine. And the royal door quietly closed behind me.

Once again I wore navy blue pleated wool skirts,
striped sailor blouses, and sturdy oxfords. My glances,
rather than falling on white marble steps and Greek
columns, on veil-thin drapes that rippled softly, had to
rest on classroom walls painted an ugly green, and on
teachers whose features were marred by ill feelings.
They did not care how I set my feet and whether I
carried my head beautifully, as long as I sat straight and
showed respect. Had they known that I tried to keep my
mind as tranquil as a mountain pond, they would have
shuddered and given me a solid dressing down. Luckily
Mama's nerves did not give them time to find me out.
When Mama left for a rest cure, Grandmama saw a
unique chance to put an end to our haphazard upbringing. In came Fräulein Lotzmann. She might have been
one of the horseback riders we saw on the bridle path of
the Hohenzollerndamm mall. She was wearing a Pepita
skirt, a tailored black jacket with a bouquet of violets in
the lapel, and a white batiste blouse with a cascade of
lace-trimmed ruffles down the front. To complete the
outfit she wore a black derby low on her brow, which
made her square-jawed face even more square-jawed.
Reassuring Grandmama that she would enforce strict
discipline, she puckered her lips, which caused glances to

leap from Dalla to me, from me to Müsi, from Müsi to Dalla, finding us in agreement that it was thumbs-down on Fräulein Lotzmann. Within the next half hour we had renamed her Lotze-Kotze, *Kotze* being the German word for vomit. Our feelings must have run strong, for our vocabulary of dirty words had as yet not progressed beyond donkey, camel and pig.

We were not to attend school, since Lotze-Kotze was put in charge of our instruction. Next morning, when she bade us to bring our school books, we vanished. We climbed into the storage room above our bathroom, pulled up the ladder, and closed the small white door. When we heard Lotze-Kotze calling us, we snickered into our hands. Would Wawa help her find us, or would Wawa also reject daintily puckered lips? Lotze-Kotze kept wandering from room to room. First she tried to lure us, then she threatened to telephone Grandmama. United we stood fast. We went on rummaging in the stored-away things and unearthed a dollhouse-sized classroom with tiny wooden benches that were broken. Dalla, for once a strong ally because of the puckered lips and Lotze-Kotze's ridiculous outfit, climbed down to make a treaty with her, and to our surprise our governess yielded to our demands; no lessons. First we glued the miniature school benches, then we fabricated schoolchildren as Mama had taught us at our one and only session of arts and crafts. It was most satisfying to see Lotze-Kotze awed by our ingenuity, to have her squeal with delight and pucker her lips when we gave the little dolls shoes of sealing wax. Our glances agreed: dumb woman.

Since we managed to keep her from finding out where we disappeared each time, we negotiated other treaties, and once again I happily strung beads, wove patterns from shiny strips of colored paper, made little baskets from raffia.

Thursdays Grandmama came to check on how things were going. Somewhat uncertain of Lotze-Kotze, we listened at the door as they discussed us over coffee and cake. And Wawa, who seemed as apprehensive as we, kept drifting in to ask whether anything else was needed, to hear whether Lotze-Kotze toed the line. Lotze-Kotze did.

Then Lotze-Kotze began to receive a gentleman. She said he was her adviser with whom she had to clear up complicated matters. She asked us most sweetly to stay out of sight when the gentleman came and to keep our voices low, for her business deal would fall through should he hear children. One good deed deserved another. On the afternoons when the gentleman came, we crawled under a bed and, shut in by blankets hanging down, we told ghost stories in whispers. Wawa, I guess out of love for us, served Lotze-Kotze and the gentleman tea.

Unexpectedly, Grandmama came on a Wednesday instead of Thursday, and that put an end to Lotze-Kotze and to Mama's rest cure. We didn't shed a single tear over the loss of our comfortable arrangements since schools were closing for summer vacation anyway. And Mama enrolled Dalla and me in the Mermaid Swimming Club.

It was during this summer that Sebastian came into my life and that I fell in love for the first time, loved him with the total surrender of a child's unwary heart. I loved to be touched by his gentle hands, and my glances caressed the silky down on the backs of his fingers. When his laughing brown eyes dwelled on me, I wished I were in his arms, in his hands, as if I held a memory of our loving in a distant, veiled past, for I was still too much a child both in body and mind for such feelings.

He was a young man, twenty-four, just graduated from medical school, but that he was young, I did not notice; in the eyes of a ten-year-old a grown-up is a grown-up. He came into our street on a bright red motorcycle, getting off in front of Simon Fischbein's house. The tall, lithe man in overalls came over to us, smiling. He said that he was going to visit a friend for half an hour or so, that his Mabecco was brand-new. Of course we knew that he was going to say we should keep our fingers off it. Instead, he asked whether we would do him a favor, keep an eye on his bike. We nodded, mute with astonishment, and watched the dark-haired man walk off without once glancing back to check on us. We sat down on the curbstone and watched his motorcycle with silent concentration.

More than an hour went by before he returned. He asked us for our names and joked with us. He explained the motorcycle's buttons and levers and made the machine roar for all it was worth. And then he offered to take us for a spin around the block for having watched his new bike. He tore a piece of paper into strips and had us draw lots. Müsi drew the shortest piece and looked so disappointed that I gave him mine. However, my generosity was abetted by apprehension, for the friendly stranger's strong, dark eyebrows made me somewhat uneasy.

One by one Sebastian took the children round the block and brought them back beaming. Finally my turn came. My heart leaped into my mouth when the powerful machine flew off. He did not take me just around the block but zoomed up Hohenzollerndamm all the way to the end, then past the Grunewald tennis courts and over to the deep gardens of Hundekehle. "Fun?" he yelled over his shoulder, and the white flash of his teeth moved me strangely.

Next day Sebastian again visited his friend in Simon Fischbein's house, and afterward he let us show him our goat garden. He spun our tops, played catch with us and, hot from running and screaming, sprawled with us in the grass. He asked us what we liked best, and how we felt about this and that. Gazing into the acacia crowns, we trustingly answered his questions.

I did not go to my swimming lessons, afraid to miss Sebastian. I hung around the street waiting for him, and the day began only when his motorcycle showed up, or when he turned the street corner on foot with his long stride. "Sebastian!" Running to him on my speedy legs, I would see his laughing eyes fondly embrace me.

I no longer feared his eyebrows. They added a mysterious spice to his kindly features, and their extraordinary mobility was amusing. When he burst into laughter they leaped up high on his forehead to become exuberantly charcoaled arches. When he smiled they glistened silken. And when he pretended to be a monster, they stretched into fearsome black bars straight across his eyes. Shrieking, I would run from him, the long-legged monster in hot pursuit. And when he caught up with me, I threw myself onto the grass, and giggling, watched his hands come to grab me, waited for the sweetness of being their captive, for the moment of thrilling closeness.

Like a Pied Piper, he always had the whole lot of us in tow. Often he would lead us to the quiet streets of Dahlem to play catch on bicycles. He was better than any of us, faster, more agile. He would swerve dangerously, stop dead so abruptly that we anticipated a crash landing. Suddenly he was gone and no matter which way we turned we would not find him; then he would fly past us from behind, his feet up on the handlebars.

He would take all of us to a *Konditorei* to treat us to ice cream; take all of us to the movies to see Chaplin's *Gold Rush*. Lying under the acacia trees, he would read us Oscar Wilde's fairy tales. And when the story came to a sad part, he would reach for my hand.

Some mothers found it strange and suspicious that a young man should give so much of his time to a bunch of children. Some of us were forbidden to associate any longer with the wacky young man. But the ban was ignored. My mother invited him to visit and found that Sebastian had a good reason for his interest in us: he planned to specialize in psychology. But she didn't succeed in reassuring the other mothers, because psychology was far from being a household word.

It seemed Sebastian tired of the many children. He began to make secret dates with me, asked me to his home, took me on walks or to the quiet outdoor restaurant of Jagdschloss Grunewald where, among whirring dragonflies and whispering pines, he read to me alone, spoke to me of life, or amused me.

July, August, September, October . . . Tumbling leaves counted off the days to Sebastian's departure for America for his internship. On his last day I picked him up at his house and as so many times before, we bicycled to Dahlem, to a small park there, a spot with rhododendrons and tall pines that had become our spot. We sat down on the pine-needle-strewn ground and did not say anything for a long while. My chest was filled with a sharp ache. We would not come here any more. We would not lie here and listen to the rustle of the pines.

On this last afternoon we were lovers, even though neither our hands nor our words testified to it. Our timeless, ageless souls stepped across the gulf between child and man for a moment.

"When I come back," Sebastian said, "the years between us will not seem so many; you will be a young lady."

I don't know whether he asked me to wait for him, or whether I read it in his eyes, or unasked my heart promised it.

When Sebastian was gone, I often went to his house to look up at the fourth-floor window of his room. Or watching the door he would not come through any more, my mind's eye saw him step outside, a clamp around his trouser cuff to keep it from catching in the bicycle chain. I made him walk beside me, bicycle beside me, talk to me. I would lie in the grass, gazing into the acacia crowns, and a moving shadow would be Sebastian tiptoeing to surprise me, Sebastian come back to me.

In the letters I wrote to him, he saw me become eleven years old, twelve, thirteen, fourteen, fifteen. . . . And in each of his letters, written on Lenox Hill Hospital stationery, I found the Sebastian I loved and was waiting for.

When he finally returned, I was a "young lady," and the years between us no longer seemed so many. But there was a charming, vivacious American woman beside him, his wife.

I could not have my Sebastian, only the precious thread he had woven into the fabric of my mind. I was taught early to accept loss, for I would have to accept loss later on: love André and let him go; and love once again and lose.

When André and I separated upon leaving Loirette's castle, the time to lose was not yet. Even though it was written on the wall.

Back among oranges, mimosas, and ancient passageways, I moved into the same apartment I had before, a pleasant room, spacious kitchen, and large terrace overlooking the hillside, the shoreland and the sea. The rent was very little, but as I had owed it most of the time, I had to soften my landlady up by making her a present of the two eggs Loirette had given me.

I went to Dutch Marijke for work. Since refugees were not allowed to earn a living, the undercover work available to us was limited in kind, and one job was as ill-paid as the next. The most available was braiding and weaving raffia strips for the sandal manufacturers. Raffia sandals were the only footgear available at the time. And as they wore out fast, the manufacturers had a flourishing business. It was also most profitable. The raw material was cheap, and cheaper still was their labor, since the illegally working refugees had to accept whatever penny-ante pay was offered them. Because the braiding meant sitting in a hunched position for countless hours, the work was also backbreaking.

With an armful of raffia I went by Innocente's grocery to pick up the month's grease ration, half a cup of oil. Then I went to bring Clément greetings from André. He was still working on his movie scenario, sustained by the hope that perhaps he would sell it. He looked as though he had not eaten for a month, and I wished I had taken Loirette's loaf of bread instead of slipping it into André's baggage.

As before, I spent my days braiding, going for rations, looking for *mégots,* climbing up the *montée* in the afternoon to discuss the war with my friends at the plaza, discuss the rations and the insignificant events of the town. I wrote letters to André and waited for his. Because of censorship we had some code words: "Cousin Charles" for de Gaulle or England, my "relatives" for the Germans, "friends" for *Résistance*.

Hello Grenouille,

I've found a room. My landlords are friends. I take my meals at a small restaurant. The wine is not restricted there. You are much on my mind along with my preoccupations. Try not to worry. I'm writing at a café where I warm myself. The owners will lend me a typewriter, so I will spend much of my time here writing reviews. Have you heard from Hurluburlu? Poor man all alone in his cold castle. Here everything is magnificently organized, and it looks as if I will see Cousin Charles soon. In a few minutes I'll take a train to Grenoble to see friends, but I'll be back by tonight. It's just an hour train ride. The high school's music teacher, an old maid, has invited me for dinner tonight. It's genuine small town here, rather amusing. I'm still angry at you for putting the bread into my suitcase. You needed it more than I. I ate it sadly for had I mailed it to you it would have arrived hard as a rock. Since they aren't strict about food tickets at my bistro, I might be able to send you some grease tickets, perhaps meat tickets as well. Do you receive your meat rations now? Or is it as bad as it was? What do you find to eat? I embrace you very hard, tenderly.

Your fair raven

I always carried André's latest letter in my pocket as if by doing that I could hold him in France.

My tender Grenouille,

I've received your two letters and the package with

the mimosas. Thank you for this birthday surprise. They traveled amazingly well and are on the table before me. Please don't feel lonely. We must keep ourselves in firm hands. To keep a clear head is of the essence. If emotions get the better of us we'll be driven, and that would put an end to what we stand for. Believe me, it is as hard on me. The days are long . . . long. . . . The lethargy of waiting weighs on me. I've begun to write a novelette, I force myself to this discipline. But I'm restless, can't stay put for long. I go around as if in a dream, nothing has any reality. Just waiting. I'm holding on to our memories. At times I believe only they are meaningful, but then I tell myself that I must have a "soldier's" heart now. I must go through with my plans or I'll have regrets later on. I talk a lot to farmers, and their mentality is atrocious. Their concerns seem limited to their larders. Don't be afraid that I'll be off all of a sudden. I'll keep you informed. My congratulations to Clément for selling his story. I'm delighted for him! Tell him thanks for offering me repayment of his debt. Frankly, I had not counted on it, had marked it off. If he can repay me now, let him give the money to you. I'll manage if my reviews are accepted. I'll close now to get this letter on the seven o'clock train. A thousand caresses from your "mimosa," who's smiling at your mimosas. You've made me feel less alone on my fortieth birthday.

Your fair raven

P.S. *I still see you standing in the station in Valence. How hard is was to walk away from you.*

When I received a letter, I wondered whether the decision had perhaps come since, whether the next would be just two lines saying "I'm off," giving me no time for a last good-bye. The moment I received a letter, I answered it. Some days I wrote two letters, not to miss the

last opportunity to speak to him. So much could happen
between morning and evening, so much I wanted to say
to him before the haunting silence would set in, a silence
that would last to the end of the war. Or forever. My
dread made me feel the loss as though it were already
established fact.

Beloved Grenouille,
 *Today I received three letters, one special delivery. I
see that things are not too well. My darling, what can
I do! Auguste will come South and look you up. He'll
tell you what I can't put in letters. It's far from pastoral
here lately. It staggers my imagination. Your relatives
are monstrous! To think that at times I believed you
were exaggerating. But you were right. They defile
humanity. But they'll be made responsible for all the
tears. I shudder at the thought of what the future holds
for them. What a family! They'll pay for it, and serves
them right! I laugh about our sophisticated talks at the
castle. To see things in action is quite a different matter.
It is low and unbelievably ugly. How happy we could be,
how useful, were it not for them. More reason to get to
my goal. Your last letter brought much thrilling news.
Of course some will prove to be just rumors. Nonetheless, they give us strength, hope, if only for a few days.
We swing from hope to hope like monkeys. I would like
to answer a great many of your thoughts, but I haven't
time right now, am invited for dinner. Very important
for my stomach. I'm occupied with a thousand petty
things — see people, talk nonsense, be charming, write
reviews. They've asked for more by telegram. I'm a very
proud peacock. I'll be able to send you a small money
order. It will always help you to pay for your electricity.
To think how much money I used to squander. I have
to hold on to some as I don't know what I might need
for the trip. What a life! Among these sweet meadows*

*and gentle hills we live with a knife between our teeth.
People think only in terms of life and death. Our minds
are being twisted. One neither reasons nor acts as one
used to. Earlier I listened to the speech of Wallace, the
American vice-president. Did you? How odd to hear him
talk about "afterwards." One is so much preoccupied
with the present how can one give thought to "afterwards"? It's better we don't, for our hearts are dis-
turbed and disoriented. Everywhere one is up against
blood and heartache. The mind boggles, is of no use.
We'll see about "afterwards" when we get there, when
the barbarism is beaten. I'm suspicious of my present
thoughts. Do we think? Isn't our present reasoning
dominated by our reflexes? I'm beset by doubts about
humanitarianism, as impossible as that might sound to
you. Humanitarianism, in the light of the scene about
me, seems to be impractical. After 1918 we believed in
a "Second Peace." It was an illusion. Look where it
brought us. The wolves have profited by it. This error
must not be repeated. Mankind needs safeguards. Humanitarianism alone proves to be terribly risky. The
beast has to be caged first, his responses reconditioned.
If we fight it off and then let it go its way, it will come
again. My mind is troubled, Grenouille. I'm frightened
of my thoughts, I cherished humanitarianism. The world
will be dark without it. I try to believe that all the suffering will not have been for nothing. The millions of
crucified men will bring about some change, some human
growth, as the crucified Christ did. My darling, as you
see, not only your mind is burdened. Thank God, isolated as we are, we know at least that the universal conscience is as burdened as our own. And that conscience
will be the victor. Earlier in my letter I've said "serves
them right" regarding the penalty that will be theirs.
Now I'm bothered by it. It burst from me. These are
the blind forces their blind forces have unchained in us.
They will be the punishment for those who have un-*

leashed them. I'm shocked though to find them unleashed in myself. Alongside my "serves them right" there is a deep regret in me. It pains me to come to the realization that we won't be able to evangelize them little by little.

I couldn't finish the letter last night. I'm back at my little café. They treat me like one of the family now. If I don't show up one morning they're worried. So you see your corbeau is well protected. Grenouille, I have no word from Pierre, I'm concerned he might be in trouble. Do not call, go there, find out. Use caution! Pretend to be a customer rather than an acquaintance. Be wary of a trap!

Just now a friend dropped by to tell me there's a delay in my matters. I've a physical reaction to the word "delay." My stomach knots in the most unpleasant way. It seems they want to get me on a better train than the one they had considered. If that's all, then so be it. But the waiting is getting to me. I felt completely drained for some days. I thought I had come down with grippe. I had no temperature, no cold, merely felt terribly weary. I stayed in bed, couldn't get up enough energy to get dressed. An old lady brought me a cup of vegetable broth, and a neighbor let me have two potatoes, cooked. I'm still all nerves, but feel better today. Thanks for sending the Somerset Maugham preface. Very interesting! I embrace you most tenderly.

Your run-aground raven

P.S. Who will ever grasp what we're going through? One can tell one's children about the battles one has fought, describe an artillery barrage, men dying all around. One can tell about torture in prison, how one was beaten, but how to explain this to anyone who has not lived through it. Like an odd nightmare in which one's feet are stuck in a thick mire; like walking and walking and not getting off the mark.

P.P.S. *I missed making it to the mail train before curfew,
so I can add another line. I feel better, calmer. This
morning the sky is an incredible blue. Grenouille, we'll
get through this difficult time somehow. Step by step.
God knows what will come and when, or what won't
come. Whatever happens, know that you are always
close to my heart. Be courageous, be calm. Life isn't one
bit funny, we must muster all our strength. Be always in
touch with Pierre, with Jean, with Clément, and know
that there are still others who are also watching over
you. For reasons you well know, I can't tell you their
names, but in case you need help, they will make themselves known to you.*

*Today I'll take my bike and go in search of eggs. It's
difficult to find anything I could send you. The hardest
is to find wrapping paper and string. Always mail them
back to me. Remember our days at the castle, our lumpy
bed, my nightmares, our walks down the road. Remember all the beautiful days we had together these past
three years. Let's be together in thought. That they cannot take from us. No matter where I'll go you'll be
within me.*

Be embraced by your grave raven

On the way to the post office I ran into Breslauer, a
refugee who manufactured large wooden animals for
toddlers to ride on. He found it to his advantage to give
some work to refugees, and I had been one of his ill-paid
slaves for a time, and given the animals their coating of
high-gloss paint. The cumbersome beasts cluttered up
my apartment, and I had to live in a cloud of turpentine,
but the work was less monotonous and less backbreaking
than raffia braiding. I considered it again, but Breslauer
no longer dared risk his business permit handing out
work to refugees. However, he was looking for someone
to leave his boy with in the afternoon, someone who

could supervise his homework and keep him occupied until dinnertime. He offered very little for this service, but I accepted. I had to eat, pay my rent, electricity and gas.

After posting my letter to André, I took the bus to Nice to see André's friend Pierre. He was not home. Next day I went again. A neighbor of his saw me and told me he was out of town. "Out of town" could mean Pierre was on a trip, or in hiding, or arrested.

I was back home in time for my first afternoon with Fritzchen Breslauer, who waited for me on the steps. Under my door, I found two letters from André, both postmarked the same day. One was a regular letter, the other was a small billet glued together along its perforated edges. The two letters burning in my hand, I made efforts to get acquainted with this terribly shy boy who did not dare look me in the eyes. Absently I glanced at his list of homework. Two letters dated the same day was an ill omen. The thin billet might be just a hurried line saying "I'm off."

Keep Fritzchen busy with homework. What was it? Multiplications. A whole page full. Good. I escaped to the kitchen to read my letters. Dreading the thin note, I opened the envelope first.

Chérie Grenouille,
I could not write yesterday, had to see a movie and write a review. Then two appointments, and dinner with friends four miles out of town. Sounds hectic, yet nothing to report about that. The small-town atmosphere is tiring. I try to distract myself the best I can, see people, chat, but nothing amounts to much. I find myself scarcely listening, everything seems so unimportant, so temporary. I wish I were with you. My mind is busy with all

sorts of matters which I can't put on paper at present, which I must keep locked in my mind until later. In the meantime I go through more or less senseless motions. I traded some ration tickets for goat cheese, which I will send you. I'm able to send you some grease tickets as well. Do you have enough money to buy extra oil? Finally a letter from Pierre! He asks me to find him a chicken. God!!! Tell him it's impossible to lay hands on a chicken. Explain things to him. I'm distressed over my inability to do him this favor. I've spent a whole day going by bike all over the countryside from farm to farm, and all I came home with was one single egg, a handful of walnuts, a tiny medicine bottle full of brandy. Are you able to work on your novelette? I've picked up mine. The reviews interrupted that. Writing gives me some satisfaction. Rumors have it that something of great consequence is in the making, that it will take place soon. Holland, it seems. Everybody knows something about it, and people are electrified. It gripped me as well, even though I tell myself that it might be just another pretty bubble that will burst in a day or two. Yet one day it will be true. It must be. I would hate it if it came now, though. I want to be with Cousin Charles then. Must be! Must be! No news as far as that is concerned. How long it takes! All considered, it is due any day now. Take care of yourself, eat as well as you possibly can. Do you get your meat rations? Is the bread better? No longer moldy? Please tell me. I wish you were here, here the bread is good, but it wouldn't be sensible for you to come now. Preserve your strength, your health. I'm with you in thought a lot. One day we will be able to laugh about this insane time. Sometimes I daydream about later, what we will do. There's no limit to what we could do. Can you imagine no more hunting for food? Rid of that preoccupation, our minds will be on the great issues, free!

*I embrace you tenderly, very strongly. Your writer
still at anchor like a ship in mothballs —*

Your raven

I took a deep breath and tore off the perforated rim
of the thin note. Just two lines.

Grenouille,
*I'll see you. Leave the door unlocked. Don't tell a
soul. Tear this up.*

A.

I downed a glass of wine, reread the note many times,
tore it up. I returned to Fritzchen, attempted to check
his multiplications, but failed to concentrate on them.
Was André in flight? The Gestapo on his heels? Leave
the door unlocked. Don't tell a soul. . . . He didn't say
when. In the middle of the night? Tonight? If he was
coming by train wouldn't he have given a time? By bicycle? On some truck? Tonight?

I read to Fritzchen from Jules Verne. My lips were
reading words, my mind was with André. My eyes leaped
to the clock, wishing it would hurry so I could dismiss
the boy who sat next to me, eyes cast down, barely
breathing. I couldn't think of anything to make him comfortable. I kept reading until time was up. "See you
tomorrow, Fritzchen." Tomorrow? Who knows what
might be tomorrow.

I stretched out, covered my eyes, wishing I could reach
André by telepathy or have a vision and see whether he
was on a train, on a bicycle, or on foot. I saw nothing.

I sat up all night, straining for his light footfall
among the little sounds of the night. With the gray of
dawn, my fears were rampant.

The day stretched endlessly. I stayed home even

though I was certain that he would not come in daytime.
Don't tell a soul. . . . Everybody in town knew him, he
would be recognized at a glance, and the news would be
all over town.

By nightfall I was so exhausted I could have fallen
asleep on my feet. I picked a hard chair, but my head
dropped. I paced. I opened the camouflage drapes, the
shutters, leaned out the open window and stared at the
deserted *montée*. I returned to the chair, stared at the
door, listened to the night sounds. . . .

His touch awakened me. No, he was not in flight, he
was on his way to England, and he was hungry. All I
could offer him was a cold leek and one slice of bread.
By the light of the stars I watched him devour them. He
looked terribly thin. His hair seemed too much for so
narrow a face. It was no wider than my hand, all eyes.
Waiting for England had wasted him.

We stepped out on the terrace, to the iron railing.
André's gaze embraced the hillside's shimmering roofs,
leaped across the strip of dark shoreland to the silvery
sea. He drew me closer. I did not dare ask how soon he
would have to leave.

He spoke softly: "Have you heard that British submarines come into these waters?"

"Yes. Off Antibes, it seems."

"Also right here. They surface three miles offshore.
That's how I will leave."

The serene sea did not seem to know of war and
separations.

André rubbed his head against mine. "How about
coming with me?"

I laughed softly, happily. His words said: I love you,
I'll miss you. "You'll show me Piccadilly," I said.

"If you come maybe I will."

I laughed again, quiveringly. Why not dream?

He led me away from the railing. We sat down on the tiled floor, our backs against the wall of the house. "This is better," he said. "At night even whispers might carry." The sea glittered between the black iron bars of the railing, and the night throbbed with the chant of the frogs.

"Do you remember the official of the *Deuxième Bureau* who interrogated you after my arrest?" he asked.

"I won't forget him to the end of my days." The tiny, airless room, the barred window filled with blue December sky, with freedom, which I believed I had lost. I was pinned to the chair. The official sat so close that his knees almost touched mine. I couldn't even shift position during the hours of interrogation. He was a handsome man in his forties, trim and cold as stone. His hard, intelligent gray eyes refused to notice that I was attractive. They would not be deterred from their task. He was of a different caliber from the two police officials who interrogated me earlier that week. Not for a moment did he let my eyes escape his penetrating stare, nor would he slow the barrage of his relentless, disconcerting questions. The simplest ones were the most disconcerting. I could not tell which answer would protect André and which might give him away. How does André tie his shoelaces? Does he squat or does he rest his foot on a chair? Does he like spinach? Does he own a fishing rod? How often does he play poker? What time of the day does he prefer for writing? And again and again the question about how he tied his shoelaces. "What about him?"

"I met him. He's *Résistance* Intelligence."

"Are you sure?"

"You bet I am. He was already *Résistance* when you

were brought in. He remained in the *Deuxième Bureau* to be of service to the *Résistance,* but eventually he had to go underground."

"He didn't seem to be on our side."

"A hell of a lot was at stake, as you well know. Eight key men arrested. He was rough on you to make sure that you wouldn't falter under pressure. He had to do it for our sake."

"And had I faltered, he would have made me mysteriously disappear."

"Well, you didn't, so why conjecture?"

"How did you happen upon him? In connection with going to England?"

"One day I had the wild idea to get you to England as well. As impossible as that seemed, it wasn't. My request raised quite a stir. First I come and make big waves to get to de Gaulle in a hurry, and then I come to tell them I want my sweetheart along, and, believe it or not, my sweetheart is a German girl. You should have seen the looks I got, and I must say I felt rather foolish. But they went along. They are making great efforts to give your going some valid justification."

"What justification?"

"We'll be told in due course."

"You mean it? Really?"

"There's a good chance. You're cleared by underground Intelligence. This was essential for England to let you in. I had to put your case before quite a few men, and when I went to Grenoble to see Intelligence I was in for some real soul-searching. From the address I had been given, I was taken to another place only to be handed over to another man, who led me across half the city. Then I was put in a closed truck and driven God knows where. Sitting in the dark truck, I came to ques-

tion seriously what I was doing. And when I finally faced
that pair of sober gray eyes, I wished I could get out of
it somehow."

"Was that him?"

"Yes. Of course I didn't know it."

"What did you do?"

"I sweated. The guy handed me a brandy. I must have
looked like I needed one. He knew why I was there, since
I had to state that when I applied for the interview. He
asked me all sorts of questions concerning myself. He
knew all about me, about my imprisonment, about the
weeks in Vichy. He asked me how I could have been fool
enough to go there. He knew about Loirette, and he
knew about us. Finally he came out with it, said he knew
you, that it had been he who had interrogated you. We
had a good laugh. He's quite a guy, 'Grenouille. We
talked for hours, about the war, about the future, the
past, my life, his life, and about you. We made a date
for after the war."

"And he cleared me?"

"Of course. But that doesn't solve all your problems.
Space on the submarines is limited. It is assigned according to priority, and anybody would have priority over
you. So don't count on it too much. I considered not
telling you beforehand, but that was impractical. You
had to know to keep yourself available. You'll have to
abandon your belongings, and you can't tell anyone."

"Could I leave a note that I'm all right?"

"You could do that once we're ready to take off."

Off to England. . . . I could hardly grasp it. Me on
a British submarine? England to let me in? Me, a nobody, a German, not even Jewish? "You aren't kidding,
are you?"

"Christ!!!"

"It's too fantastic."

"It is. So is everything. We live in a weird dream. Everything is fantastic, the good as well as the bad. The fantastic has taken on the look of normality. Nothing goes as expected. For weeks and weeks I'm trying to get to England and all of a sudden I'm told I'm requested by London and will leave by submarine. I was whisked off to here. Grenouille . . . we won't be together over there. I'll be in the French forces, you'll be on your own. We would have each other's letters, but with the invasion I'd be going to France and you'd stay behind."

"You might get a weekend pass."

He laughed, his eyes were moonlit ponds. "We'd go to Hastings or some such place and stay at one of those odd boardinghouses. And we'd wander around in the fog, and then we'd have tea and biscuits, and I'd call you 'my dear frog.' "

Let us dream, we have so little else.

Late next evening there was a knock on the door. André disappeared into the kitchen, and I pushed his teacup under the bed before opening the door.

"Germaine sent me," the girl said. Germaine was the password. She told André to come to the *auberge* down by the shore. André alone. She said he had to leave right away as there was just enough time to make it before curfew.

For so long we had been prepared for the final goodbye, but this haste benumbed us, and we parted with a mute embrace.

From the terrace railing I watched André go down the *montée,* then move out of sight. In thought I followed him through the streets, pictured him making his way alongside the gardens and villas lost in the shoreland's darkness, and then along the narrow footpath. The girl had said he would not leave tonight. Gazing at the dark sea, new hope was born in me, and with it a new wait began.

Three days later, the girl came again. No, André had not left. I should come to the *auberge* in the late afternoon, go straight upstairs, and enter room number seven without knocking.

"What am I to take?"

"Nothing," she said. "He has all he needs. He wants to see you."

And I thought I was being called to a submarine ride! Or could she not tell me? Security measures?

I cleaned up my kitchen, straightened out the room, made order in my drawers, packed my writings in one carton, my photos and paintings and personal odds and ends in another, and labeled them, just in case. On a sheet of paper I wrote: "Don't worry, I am fine," and I put that in the drawer of my table. I put another note like it in my bed between the sheets. Just in case, I dressed in dark cotton slacks and a dark top, since the departure would take place at night. I also took along a black kerchief to cover my light hair. And I took along a cardigan, for in England it was colder than on the Côte d'Azur.

As I approached the isolated *auberge,* I believed I saw André behind a window, but he didn't open it, did not wave.

There was no one about the small lobby. I went up the stairs. White doors with black numbers. I opened number seven and was in André's arms.

"There's a delay." He kept his voice down. "There's still a chance that you'll come along, but we would know only at the last minute. Leave your apartment only for necessary errands, and always be home after four o'clock."

He looked pale and was exceedingly tense. We stretched out on the bed. He played with my hair but his mind was elsewhere. He seemed depressed.

"Quite a few of the cottages along the shore are German bunkers," he said. "They left them on the outside as they were, but the insides they ripped apart to make room for a thick wall of concrete." He lit a cigarette. It was an English Player's. He handed it to me and lit another for himself. "We'll be leaving in the dead of night. We'll have to creep from here to the beach, which is heavily patrolled by Germans. Just a minute or two is all we'll have to slither across the beach and get a small boat into the water. We'll have to row to a point three miles out, where the sub will surface for a moment at a designated time."

"I used to row in school, we'll spell each other."

He laughed. "You won't have to row, we won't be just the two of us. All you'd have to do is keep your nose down and your courage up. However . . . Grenouille, I've been wondering. . . . It is terribly risky. The beach . . . the *boches* would shoot. If you stayed here, I would find you alive upon my return."

"What if you don't make it across the beach? I'd rather creep with you." My wording made us laugh, and we laughed off the risks.

Then we had to say good-bye, once again perhaps for the last time. One last glance and I had to draw the door closed. From the footpath I looked back at his window, but it held only the fiery glow of the sinking sun. That night I stayed out on my terrace, eyes on the Mediterranean. I felt sure that I had been called to see André only because he was leaving in the course of the night. No doubt I wouldn't be able to see the small boat, or the submarine surfacing for a moment from the distant dark waters, but I watched as though I could protect him.

Next day I waited for the girl. She had not said that she would come to let me know that André got away safely, but wouldn't he have left a last letter for me? Nobody came.

That night I was peering at the dark shore, straining to sense whether André was there or gone, when a rustling in the terraced gardens below distracted me. Apparently someone was trying to make it home despite curfew, someone who preferred climbing up over stone walls to being caught on the *montée*. The night was dark, and the person was an indistinct shadow, yet suddenly I knew it was André. I watched him make his way uphill slowly, cautiously, and then I lost sight of him. I went to the door and saw him coming up the steps, giggling like a boy out on a lark.

"Another delay," he said. "They let me stay with you." In the kitchen he emptied his pockets: two eggs, three potatoes, a chunk of bread, a bag of genuine coffee beans, a cough-syrup bottle filled with brandy, a pack of English Player's. "Will this pay for my bed and board, Madame Grenouille?"

"For a couple of years it will do." I was in his arms, and we laughed like new lovers on their first outing alone. Just then, the day or two reprieve seemed no less than being made the gift of a whole lifetime.

Next day friends dropped by as usual and each time, André slipped behind the flowered curtain that concealed my mop and broom. When Fritzchen came, André retreated to the terrace, crawled outside on all fours not to be seen from surrounding houses.

We didn't count on another intrusion that evening, when there was a soft rapping on the door. André dashed behind the flowered curtain and I scanned the room for evidence of another person's presence. The rapping again. "Coming!" I was surprised to find Gérard at my door. He had never come to my place. Our friendly relationship had not gone beyond chance meetings along the *montée* or on the plaza. He was a Parisian refugee, a witty, flirtatious man, a charming playboy, who whiled away his too much time going to Cannes or Antibes to play tennis, or to Monte Carlo for a game of baccarat. Even now he had his tennis racket under his arm.

He slipped inside without a word of explanation and softly drew the door closed. "Where's André?" he asked.

How did he know?

"Quick, Ingrid." His handsome smile was gone.

André was already in the kitchen doorway. "Gérard!"

"André!" Gérard dashed to him, grabbed him by the shoulders. *"Mon vieux. . . .* I've bad news. The *auberge* . . . fallen. The *boches* came, there was fighting. Charles is dead, Jeanette is dead, Maurice in bad shape, Paul and Babette arrested."

André's cheek twitched spastically.

"Dear André . . ." Gérard said. And his own voice unsteady, he pleaded: "Get hold of yourself." He let go of André and swiftly turned the key in the lock, switched off the lights, ushered us into the kitchen. He stepped out on the terrace for a quick look at the surrounding houses, evaluated the drop to the garden below. "Should there be need," he said to André, "you'll go over the railing and down the hill to Brevier's house." And to me: "You and I are lovers. Go mess up the bed."

I messed up the bed and joined the two around the table in the dark kitchen. "Now get this," Gérard said to me. "You and André broke off long ago. Let's say after he was released from prison. Then you and Loirette were lovers and broke off. Since your return it was you and me. It's too short a time for you to have to know much about me."

Gérard had jettisoned his disguise, the charming playboy with a tennis racket under the arm. I did not at all know the Gérard I looked at, but knowing about him might turn into an awesome burden before this night was over.

"Any letters of André's around?"

"Yes."

"Get them."

It took me just a moment to lay hands on the bundle of letters, but I did not put them into Gérard's open hand.

"We must destroy them," he said.

"No!"

"It's necessary."

"No." I kept holding on to them.

"Grenouille . . ." André pleaded.

"They're all I have. One day they might be all I'll ever have."

"Yes," Gérard said, his hand still waiting for the letters. Finally, he hid them outside among stones, and that done we returned to the kitchen table to sit in the dark, straining our ears for sounds outside. Gérard absently fingered the big nail I had driven into the table for my raffia work, and suddenly he gave it a couple of hard whacks and jiggled it out. "This is dangerous," he said.

"I needed it for raffia braiding."

"Oh . . ." he said. "Sorry." He handed me the nail
and I put it in the cutlery drawer for safekeeping. Nails
were hard to come by. In silence, we waited, listening
into the night. Once André reached across the table and
touched Gérard's hand as if to assure himself that this
friend was still there. Gérard seemed to understand, for
he said nothing.

The deep silence held a hum. When I tried to determine from which direction it came, it disappeared. Then
I heard it again. It remained elusive, unidentifiable. I
wondered whether intense thought had a sound.

André's voice gave me a start even though he spoke
softly. "Whatever I touch takes a bad turn," he said.
"Several times everything was set for me to leave for
England when something happened, when contacts were
arrested. Now this. Gérard . . . I feel like a jinx."

Gérard grabbed André's wrists and shook him.
"Don't," he cried under his breath. "You know better!
The *boche* has us by the throat, and we're falling like
duckpins. There's not a single transmitter in all of
France they'll not beam in on sooner or later. There's no
escaping their radar trucks. Those at the *auberge* knew
that their days were numbered. They had a wary eye on
the movements of the truck that was creeping through
the area. They knew it would be just another day or two
until the *boche* jumped them. They confined your movements in order to know where to find you and get you
the hell out of the house from one moment to the next.
And they didn't send you here because of your claustro-
phobia, they threw you out because they had just about
time enough to destroy certain records and send off the
last messages to London. To let you fall with them
would have been wasting one man who was needed alive
to pick up where they had to leave off. They knew all

along that their run would be short. It does not take a
jinx, André, the *boche* has us by the throat! THEY
HAVE US BY THE THROAT, ANDRÉ!"

"Yes," André said tonelessly.

"Weep if you can. Leave the damn manliness to the
boche. He'll need it to keep laughing on the day when
he finds out that Frenchmen can shoot straight blinded
by tears."

"If I had been at the *auberge* . . . perhaps one more
gun would have made a difference."

"I know how you feel. Finding oneself alive, one
feels as though one has failed somewhere."

"Yes."

"Such feelings are a luxury we can't afford. You and I
are still sitting here only because our turn has not yet
come. But no matter how many are sacrificed, someone
will make it through. Someone will see the tricolor go up
and dance in the streets of Paris."

André laughed, "I saw myself among the liberators."

"Yes," Gérard said, "yes, of course."

How very lonely I felt with the two warriors. I could
not tell them of my relief over André's escape from
death, of my feeling of immeasurable gratitude. He was
alive! He would not have to creep across that beach.
He was safe from the German sentries. I felt ashamed
but didn't care. No heroism could cast a glow upon his
dying. I prayed to God to keep him alive. I would do
anything. I would renounce him, but not to Death. It
was not by dying that he could help the world most. His
slight body was not the stuff soldiers were made of. He
was mistaken, his place was elsewhere. If he should die,
all he had to give would be wasted.

"And where exactly does this leave me now?" André

asked. "I was under orders. Am I to wait for new orders, or am I on my own?"

"You're no longer under orders. Nonetheless, for reasons of safety, yours, ours, and the safety of the arrested, Jacquot asks that you abide by his instructions for tonight."

"Of course. What are they?"

"Unless he comes here because developments require immediate action, you're to remain in this place for the rest of the night and beat it in the morning. I, too, am to stay here for the rest of the night. We don't have to fear that those arrested might break down and confess."

"What about the chambermaid?"

"Babette is no chambermaid, she's *Résistance*. She's a Sorbonne student."

"You don't say! She never let on."

"You may be sure that Babette will most adeptly 'co-operate,' tell the Germans all she 'knows' and in such a manner that they will have no doubt as to her brain's limitations."

"Poor kid."

"Come outside, some air . . ."

Gérard had a cautious look at the *montée*. We sat down on the cool tiles, our backs against the house. It felt good to be under the sky, to sit in the gentle night breeze. We did not speak. The whispering of the rivulet was the only sound.

After another glance at his watch, Gérard said: "Tonight was to have been the night. Unless London had our message in time, the sub will surface in three minutes and fifty seconds."

We crawled to the railing and scanned the dark sea

for a conning tower. A soft sheen lay on the water even though most of the sky was overcast.

"I was with the British at Dunkirk," André said, his eyes on the water. "I was liaison officer. I grew very fond of them." That seemed to be all, but then he went on: "Thousands of men caught on that narrow strip of beach, thousands of frightened faces waiting for the slaughter, were picked out of the darkness by the flashes of artillery fire. We saw the end at hand."

"A grandiose naval operation that night," Gérard remarked.

"No. It was the British people coming for their kids. That hostile black sea was like Hades, and suddenly hundreds of small bobbing boats, as if it were the Seine on a weekend — a mirage, it seemed, a last sweet dream. I would have believed it if it had been cruisers . . . not that, not that, Gérard. Then that roar of joy. The entire beach, like a huge living beast, pushed into the water. I was swept along onto a wooden pier. A naval vessel had come alongside, and the men leaped across the wide black gulf. Some didn't make it. We heard them plead from the water below. A man grabbed me, shouted: 'Pray for me, Frenchy!' I helped him on his way with a hard push. He made it. Aboard ship he peeled off his oilcloth slicker and tossed it to me. 'Henderson is the name!' he yelled across. Henderson is the name . . . Gérard, it was like an embrace."

"Yes."

Henderson's coat, rolled in a bundle, rolled up as when Henderson tossed it, was behind the flowered curtain with my mop and broom.

"I have the coat with me," André said, "like a talisman. I believed it would get me to England."

"England," Gérard said. "She's far away, *mon* André. She's very far away."

"I've come to realize that."

"Stay in France, André."

"To do what? The *Résistance* needs dynamiters, railroad men, sabotaging factory workers."

"Wrong. We need experienced officers to train the thousands of youngsters in the mountain maquis, and with the invasion to harass the *boche* effectively. Already, reserve officers are being placed in villages all across the country. They'll stay there as in a foxhole, under orders to stay alive, to provide leadership to the people when the day comes."

"Your foxhole isn't for me," André said. "I can't take any more waiting."

How much he longed for action, longed to be the bearer of the flag. He failed to realize that bleeding for history would not assuage the anguish of his mind.

"Over there," Gérard said, "the same as here, you'd be waiting for the invasion. You'd be waiting in uniform, that's the only difference."

"Gérard, the *boche* not only has me by the throat. The blindness of hate is creeping up on me like dusk, and I dread the night that will follow. I've watched grinning murderers round up hostages at random in the street to be executed, old men, kids whose voices have scarcely changed. You read the list of their names and you can't cry out, can't do anything but walk off meekly in bitter silence. The Germans' inhumanity robs us of our humanity. I can see myself being eroded, worn away. What will I be in the end? Will I still be a man the day they finally shoot me down?"

"Don't, André, don't," Gérard said. "The *boche*

knows that he can't conquer France by killing us off, or by buying a number of pitiable souls. He knows he must destroy our spirit, and you feel his grip. I feel it. All of France feels it. We begin to doubt ourselves, and that's what they want. We can't do without you, André, de Gaulle can. We here can't spare a single man, we lose too many."

André's face, shattered with sadness, made me wish he were in England.

Gérard kept on: "Let it be France, André. Return to the Dauphiné, get in touch with the Vercors maquis."

André sat with bowed head. Then he said: "I'll stay." They embraced.

We went inside. All three of us stretched out on the bed. "Close your eyes, *mon chou*," André murmured. My hands in theirs, I fell asleep.

Grenouille,
I'm in my old room, go to the same café, the same bistro. That interlude seems like a dream, the more so since most people here don't even know that I was away. Yet I must have been away a long, long time, for I feel I have very much aged. More tomorrow.
I embrace you,
Your raven

Grenouille,
I couldn't write yesterday, I stayed overnight in the mountains. How I wished you could have come with me to see our friends. It was an overwhelming experience. And the landscape! Towering cliffs, deep ravines, and impenetrable brush. It was a rough way up, pushing my bicycle all the way. Now and again I was stopped, but I had been announced and the reception was incredibly warm, intoxicating. They showed me around and we had

long talks deep into the night. The greater was my dis-
appointment that I won't be able to stay with them right
now. I'll have to stay where I am for the time being.
Foxhole, remember? I'll be writing reviews at my little
café while waiting. No way out. I committed myself. I
try to be calm.

Your disappointed raven

Grenouille chérie,
  Under no circumstances must you get so upset if you
haven't a letter from me for a few days. Should any-
thing disastrous happen to me, A. would let you know.
You must be harder, you must preserve your strength.
We're not near the end of the road yet. We must be fit
in order to cope with whatever comes. I was ill. I came
down with a case of jaundice and was sick as a dog for
some days. I'm better now but washed out. Nerves, I
guess, too much heartache, too much disappointment.
The little energy I have goes to finding something I'm
allowed to eat. Boiled potatoes. Forgive me for adding
to your burdens, but you'd guess. We must accept this
situation as a challenge. We must not let it get us down.
I wish I were a soldier, able to act, but the "test of fire"
I must pass is enduring this endless waiting, forever
waiting for something that might never come. The same
is your share. We have no choice. We must accept the
challenge or it will destroy us . . .

  Must accept the challenge. . . . The words made
me feel sand between my teeth, the North Sea island's
forever drifting sand. Old reflexes snapped to attention as if once again answering to the "Viking"
school's roll call.
  "Hardiness . . ."
  "Here!"
  "Fortitude . . ."

"Here!"
"Valor . . ."
"Here!"
"Chivalry . . ."
"Here!"
"Self-control . . ."
"Here!"
"Endurance . . ."
"Here!"
"Welcoming any challenge . . ."
"Here!"

André's remonstration stung me as though I were still in boarding school and had once again failed to live up to what a true Viking should be.

I was thirteen when my mother saw the need to find a school more compatible with my temperament than the ones available in Berlin, which developed in me nothing but vigorous passive resistance. She found this North Sea island school whose efforts went into shaping boys and girls into "magnificent Vikings." I was eager for the adventurous life the school's brochure promised. However, becoming a Viking proved to be a very strenuous task. We were told we were the "elite" and had to take on the responsibility of becoming "the leaders of tomorrow." Therefore we had to be pure of heart and mind, noble, magnanimous, chivalrous, generous, proud. Pride was to be a moat between us and doing any wrong, giving in to weakness of any kind, or shirking responsibility. I often wished I did not have to be quite so magnificent.

The bare, windswept Frisian island washed by the morose, gray North Sea fit the "Viking spirit" well. Hearts less hardy than ours, though, might have fallen victim to melancholia. The island was lean and white,

and the wind was her mate. Not a single tree adorned
her. Trees could not take the incessant wind, found no
hold in the loose, forever drifting sand. What might
have been called land was only about a hundred yards
wide, and sandy as well. Only beach grass grew of its
own accord. The rest was a row of white dunes running
the length of the island like a spine. Beyond them
stretched a very wide, windswept beach, swept clean
of all dry sand. The dunes held a whisper, as if
haunted by the spirit of men lost at sea. The whisper
was the fine, dry sand constantly trickling down the
white slopes, and sand drifting, and sand falling like a
constant drizzle. Drifting, drifting, it scoured our souls.

A true Viking accepted uncomplaining the sand between his teeth, sand in his hair, sand in his shoes, sand
in his bed, sand in all of his belongings. At early-morning gymnastics on the beach, or playing hockey, the
drifting sand stung our bare limbs, the harsh glare
blinded us, the wind carried the ball astray, but to a
true Viking that was just another challenge. We had to
be tough sailors who thought nothing of it when a sudden fog made us run aground on a shoal, and we had to
wait there until the next high tide. We were expected
to welcome hunger pangs and the clammy cold as a
chance to test our fortitude. A true Viking had to
volunteer eagerly for unpleasant tasks and hard man-
ual labor, for digging ditches and building dikes. Never
would he assume that exhaustion, an icy wind, or a
scorching sun might be reason to quit before time was
up. To shirk and falter was beneath a Viking, and so
was kissing in the dunes. But just as the real Vikings
must have done, we did kiss, if guiltily, in the night-
pale valleys of the whispering dunes.

Nor were we immune to the dark moods of our

touchy age. But as moaning and moping were unworthy of a Viking, we invented mad-walking, which was then officially sanctioned and respected. When I was in the grip of Weltschmerz, or when my Viking worth was doubted, I hated the school from the bottom of my heart, and mad-walking was the only cure. Fists dug deep into my coat pockets, head pulled between the shoulders, torment written all over my face, I would take off with long, dramatic steps toward the beach. The wind in my hair, I would walk on and on along the water's edge, in the thunder of the surf, my loneliness echoed by the still dunes and the somber sea.

Eventually, the great, lonesome sea and the endless, lonesome beach would cut my troubles down to size. Suddenly my pain was gone, as if washed out of me by lungs full of strong salt air. In its place there was a great longing for the limitedness of a house, for my roommates' voices, for being with the others and feeling the school around me; with long eager strides I would head back, a purified Viking willing to strive on toward magnificence.

Our educators were diehard mavericks who refused to teach elsewhere. They found the Viking school a haven from conformity and from rules and regulations. As the school's premise was that good teaching depended on the quality of thought rather than on the breadth of ground covered, each teacher taught only what he liked best. This made our curriculum somewhat restricted, yet of high quality. Our German teacher assumed that we would read Goethe, Schiller, and Lessing on our own sometime in our life. His favorite was Shakespeare and that was what he taught. Yes, Shakespeare. History was confined to the French Renaissance. Mathematics and Physics was mathematics and physics not because this was the teacher's subject but his passion. As his other passion was revolution, he stirred us up to be against something, to revolt against whatever we could find to revolt against. And the school calmly looked on. He was just another wind blowing across the Viking sea, and the more winds we learned to sail under, the better.

Our biology teacher was a gentle, totally introverted researcher. He was scarcely aware of the school or of us in the classroom. As he spent all of his free time dissecting a seal or fish, he walked about in a cloud of formaldehyde, the only hardship he subjected us to. In his class we fooled around, conversed, and read Edgar Wallace mysteries. And he, murmuring as if to himself, chalked countless amoebas lovingly on the blackboard. His drawings were so beautiful that we hated to wash them off. And they have remained unfaded in my memory. We could go to his room any time, day or night, and ask him to explain once again Mendel's law of inheritance. Often one or the other did that just for sport. Without a word he would put down his dissecting knives, or patiently get up from bed, to cover whole pages with generations of beautifully drawn, gentle-faced mice, so many black, so many white. And when we had enough of it, he would, with a faraway glance, gently nod. We loved him.

Music was Bach. Our music teacher was a concert pianist and composer who, vacationing on the island, had visited the school and fallen victim to the Viking spirit. As the school realized that a man of his stature could not be reduced to merely teaching so minor a subject as music, he was given free hand to put as much music into our days as he wished. Since he considered Bach the music best suited for young minds, Bach was integrated into the Viking spirit. Bach began and ended our days. The school orchestra, ably taught and sternly drilled, performed Bach concertos, and the choir sang Bach cantatas. We were impregnated with Bach and did not resist in the least, as we had not heard of Bach being dull. We hummed Bach in the shower, whistled Bach while the action was at the other end of the hockey field, and on walks we sang Brandenburg Concertos with a text improvised on the spur of the moment. A Bach hallelujah was a "hit song" to us.

Outsiders could not understand that Bach, Shakespeare and Vikingism were all of the same cloth. And our peers of the outside world looked down their noses at us, which let us look down our noses at them and tighten our Viking lines.

What was hard was to be an isolated Viking home on vacation. In Berlin I felt clumsy in my Viking sweaters. If I exchanged them for more citified dress, I felt disguised and ill at ease. I looked in awe at Dalla's cosmetic jars, her permanent waves and blue eyelashes, but I did not give them a try, not I, a Viking. I had no choice but to suffer, believing that my straight, salt-water-bleached Viking hair was unattractive. The city girls' dainty hands made me hide mine, which had carted heavy loads of sand, built dikes, cut sod, scrubbed the boat, fastened lines, braced against a powerful wind. They were good Viking hands, strong and skillful and not squeamish, but in Berlin they did not score.

Nor did my purity and noble mind score with Berlin's cynical youth. And their sophistication stumped me, made me feel like a babe in the woods. I knew nothing of what they talked about. Theirs was a foreign world. I knew nothing of politics, of government and parties, Reichstag delegates, elections, economics, or foreign affairs. I turned sixteen without ever having read a newspaper. And had I tried, I wouldn't have understood one word. Finally the Chicken Boy took me in hand.

When I bumped into the Chicken Boy on a Berlin street during summer vacation I was delighted by the mere sight of another North Sea bleached head. The Chicken Boy was not a Viking, just a lad hired by the school to take care of the chickens, which was not heroic enough a task to be given to us. On that day the Chicken Boy was on the way to an exhibit, and as I had no particular goal of my own, I fell in with him. The exhibit, sponsored by the League of Human Rights, showed photos of men beaten bloody, hanged, or shot for political reasons. Harrowed, I stared at bloody flesh that had once been a human face, at eyes long past comprehension, at blood-streaked limbs, backs criss-crossed with welts, at lifeless bodies hanging from ropes or slumped to the ground in prison yards. The captions told me that the mutilated bodies had been Communists, Socialists, Spartacists, anarchists. I did not ask the Chicken Boy what that was. I was afraid to be called stupid. Trying to hide my horror, I moved on to the picture of a stately woman with earnest eyes, wearing an elaborate, old-fashioned dress like one that Grandmama wore in an old picture. This woman was neither bloody nor dead. The caption read: "Rosa Luxemburg in her lifetime." What? Rosa Luxemburg? That was Rosa Luxemburg? My mind raced back to my Rosa and the Rettloff boys. The next picture showed the funeral of murdered Rosa Luxemburg. I told the Chicken Boy that I wanted to leave.

I did not care to go and meet his friends, but I was so shaken that I did not know which way to turn. We took a tramway. I scanned the numb-faced passengers, wondering whether they knew that people were being murdered and beaten bloody. By whom? Why? Because of their convictions? I tried to formulate my grandfather's convictions, but all that came to my mind was: one doesn't count money in the presence of others; aristocracy is of the mind; books must be handled reverently; a child has no opinions. . . .

I followed the Chicken Boy into a vacation-empty school and up silent stairs. In a classroom, boys and girls seated around a long table were heatedly arguing. They spoke with assurance and passion, but what it was about I couldn't tell. A boy who needed a haircut rose tremblingly, calling those at the far end of the table *Panzerkreuzerpazifisten,* battleship pacifists. The others responded with: "Muscovite." A young man pleaded for moderation, referred to the common enemy, but was not heeded. Insults, incomprehensible to me, were shouted, and suddenly half of them marched out, heads high, lips set.

A girl cried out: "No!" and burst into tears. Feeling like an eavesdropper, I hid behind the Chicken Boy. Those who had stayed listened to the receding footfalls of the others, and then they stared at the empty chairs. I felt as though I had strayed into a house where someone had just died.

Softly and sadly the gathered mourners began to speak of those who left. They had been misled by warmongers, they agreed, by black reaction. Of all the words they used I understood only "world peace." They were for world peace, and so was I. All was well.

The meeting was adjourned, and the Chicken Boy introduced me. I shook hands with Bernhard, Hans,

Richard, Dorothea, Liese, Gerda, Paul, Max, Heiner, Waldemar. Bernhard said to me that we must all close ranks, overlook minor differences of opinion. I nodded yes not to have to admit that I did not know what it was all about. Bernhard asked me whether I had any schooling. I told him about the island school, and the others scattered, stifling giggles. Bernhard called them to order and, very kindly, said: "I meant political schooling. Surely you can tell me whether you are an idealist or a materialist." Thank God, I knew that. "An idealist," I said firmly, and even Bernhard burst into merry laughter. Poor, stupid little Ini!

Bernhard invited me for next Sunday to their tent colony on the shore of the Müggelsee. Dorothea would take me. He handed me a booklet and with a friendly nod said: "Read that."

I did not get very far into the *Communist Manifesto*. For all I understood, it could have been written in a foreign language.

I looked up "Communist" in the dictionary: "A person who endorses or supports the Communist philosophy; one who supports the Commune of Paris 1871." That did not help.

On Sunday morning I met Dorothea at the train station. She was weighed down by a bulging knapsack. To my great relief she did not mention the *Communist Manifesto* nor *Panzerkreuzerpazifisten,* but was very much interested in hearing about my Viking school. Then she told me about the tent colony, that the young people there came from families on relief. I wondered what relief and eviction meant.

She said that she herself lacked nothing, that her father was a university professor. But since she had access to wealthy people, she collected clothing and food for the others at the tent colony. Of course she could not bring enough, but others did the same.

"How many are you at the colony?"

"It varies. A hundred, a hundred and fifty."

"My God!"

"The time they spend at the colony is perhaps their only chance to escape TB — the sun and swimming in the lake."

I had once been to the Müggelsee with my father, to attend a regatta. That day it had been so crowded with folding boats, canoes, rowboats, and other small craft that one could barely see the lake. We had trouble getting out into open water, which that day, because of the regatta, was prohibited to the general public. Water police, blowing their whistles, had to open a channel for our press motorboat.

The train ride was followed by a hike through the woods. Dorothea walked bent forward, holding on to the straps of the heavy knapsack. It was a hot day, and her face glistened with sweat. I offered to take turns but she would not hear of it, I was a guest. She trudged on in silence, her gaze fixed on the ground.

Only when I heard the voices did I see the countless gray tents that blended with the gray beach, the gray forest floor, and the gray tree trunks. Here and there red flags hung limply from branches. Then we were stepping over gray blankets, sandy towels, Primus cookers, canteens, potato sacks, and baskets of onions and carrots; and along our way I shook countless sandy hands. Bernhard, long legged in faded shorts, a red bandanna on his head, greeted Dorothea with a firm, comradely handshake, but I saw in their eyes that they were in love.

"Tea water is almost boiling," he said. "I give you one minute for a quick swim."

"I'm dying for one," Dorothea said, at once peeling off her garments. And then she stood there stark naked, deeply tanned except for her white breasts and white behind. "Come on," she said. "Nobody looks. You're not among bourgeois here." She stepped into faded shorts and tied a piece of polka-dotted fabric around her chest. I changed hastily, just a few feet from Bernhard, who, eyes cast down, busied himself with the Primus cooker.

The lake water was tepid and clouded, the beach was gray, the tea was served in banged-up aluminum cups, and I was among strangers, yet something in their faces or in their ways made them seem akin to us Vikings.

"Come, idealist," Bernhard said. "Let's go for a walk."

Meandering through the woods, Bernhard told me what eviction meant. He explained how a family with a row of children lived in a *Schrebergarten* hut. Werner, one of the group he was part of, could not go out after two in the afternoon because he shared one pair of shoes with his brother. Everyone in Lisa's family had TB. Since she was all right so far, they would try to keep her at the colony throughout the summer. Bernhard told me of fathers who, crushed by hopelessness, got drunk every night and became violent. And he said that many of the youngsters knew only meals consisting of potatoes and a cup of coffee, on Sundays perhaps gravy. He mentioned the staggering sums that went into armament, and how little it would cost in comparison to provide everyone with a pair of shoes and a pork chop for dinner.

We returned to the lakeside; a whiff of onions and

celery tugged at my stomach. Groups of young people
sat around steaming pots precariously balanced on the
small Primus cookers. Our group was gathered, earnestly watching Werner stir the soup with a stick.

"Smells delicious," Bernhard said.

"Man, that's a soup today," said Werner. "Everything but the kitchen sink is in it, even bacon rind."

"Do we have a plate for our guest?"

"Man, do we!" Werner beamed. "How does this
look to you? I scoured it with sand, shines like sterling
silver." He was holding up a bent but shining aluminum
plate, the name WERNER scratched into it in large thin
letters. "I'll eat out of the frying pan," he added.

I ate Werner's soup with a guiltily ravenous appetite. I even accepted a share of the second helping —
two remaining potatoes justly divided into six parts.
When I volunteered to do the dishes, they thought I
would not know how to cope with the lake facilities, but
proudly I showed them that a Viking was no sissy.
Werner clapped my shoulder: "You're okay," he said.
"I like you." And a little later he presented me with a
red sleeve band, a souvenir of a Communist demonstration.

At dusk they lit bonfires and everybody gathered to
sing. I didn't know most of their songs, but I sang
along without words. In between came folk songs that
were sung by Vikings as well. I wished I could stay overnight, but I had to be home. Late that night Bernhard
and Werner took me to the railroad station. Arms interlocked, we crossed the pitch-dark forest, walked
through the summer night scented with pine.

The station was deserted, the waiting train empty. I
leaned out the window and smiled at Werner and Bernhard, who were slapping mosquitoes. Bernhard still

wore the red bandanna. Perhaps he had chosen a red
one to dare the world, to tell it where he stood. But
at the Müggelsee, where he could take a breather from
inequity, the reason for the red bandanna was possibly
that it was becoming to him.

The train began to move. Bernhard's hand reached
up. "So long, idealist." I almost cried. My other hand
met Werner's. "What is your shoe size?" I asked.
They had to let go of my hands. "My what?" "Your
shoe size," I shouted. "Thir-ty nine!" And he spread
nine fingers. The two barefoot, long-legged boys in
faded shorts, waving and slapping mosquitoes, were
slipping from sight. I do not know what happened to
them, whether they died in Hitler's prisons or died for
him in Russia. Some days later I returned to my Viking
school, to Bach cantatas and Shakespeare, to the bracing
surf of the North Sea and platters laden with sliced
roast and vegetables.

A year passed. Then I left the Viking island. To
soften the impact of a switch of school short of graduation, my mother enrolled me in the only progressive
school Berlin had to offer, an experimental one deep
in the worker district of Neukölln. Each morning I went
by subway to the opposite end of Berlin, to a world so
different from mine and so puzzling that I might have
been Alice fallen down the rabbit hole. My classmates talked in mystifying abbreviations, KPD, SPD,
NSDAP, AGITPROP, USSR. They were restless, always rushing somewhere as if saying: "I'm late, I'm
late, for a very important date." They skipped classes
to distribute handbills in the street, and they were excused from gym to line up at a soup kitchen. They had
no winter coats, and during the ten o'clock break they
discussed committee decisions. All my classmates were

258 / A PRIVATE TREASON

Communists. My political ignorance staggered them, but they treated me kindly, as though I were a wondrous foreign bird. They came to like me and took pity on me. "We'll teach you," they said. "Come with us." They were going to a mass meeting of Red Berlin at the *Sportpalast* where I used to cheer the Canadian ice hockey team and Sonja Henie from first-row press seats. A whole block from the *Sportpalast* the crowd was so thick that it moved toward the entrance shuffling slowly. My classmates put their arms around me to protect me from the line of vicious Nazi hecklers, and they kept a watchful eye on the nervously prancing police horses.

The great arena inside was packed, and the rising rows of seats were black with people all the way up to where huge red flags were hung. The din was deafening. Declarations and petitions were being circulated, and we signed them, one for peace, one for free milk, one against evictions, one against armament. My classmates patiently explained each. The thunderous singing of the "Internationale" opened the meeting. And thunderous applause greeted the first speaker. Berlin in want and anger roared, surged with outrage, cried out for justice, and burst into laughter over the jokes. A huge choir sang a solemn antiwar song. The audience stood up, the men removed their caps, and I, moved to the quick, filled my heart with billowing red flags.

Red Berlin hastily taught me its ABC. Time was too short for thorough instruction. Some slogans, some vague notions were the little raft on which I had to sail the rough waters. In the mist, my blinking beacon was "world peace," and I trusted that there was a shore somewhere.

I finished school, left home to enter medical school

at a small southern town. Nazis marched, singing their threatening songs. I joined the Red Student Group, but I was still only an idealist, and in this year in which German democracy would die, they had no time to bother with someone like me. "Look," they said, "you mean well, but . . ." Suddenly I stood all alone, not knowing where I might belong. And where could I have belonged, odd mixture that I was of Grandpapa's maxims, Duncan ideals, Viking virtues, and longings for a Müggelsee world-brotherhood? I sadly hoped time would tell. But time was running out.

On a dreary, wintry day, some weeks before the Nazis seized power, I walked for one last time in a demonstration. But it was scarcely a demonstration. It was a wake.

I was going home to my furnished room from afternoon lectures. A morose, misty dusk was settling in the quiet, small-town streets when an odd sound made me glance over my shoulder. The sound was the footfall of a column of men and women, coming my way. The marchers were silent, and they carried their red flags horizontally, like in a funeral march. They seemed to know that this march was their last, that rather than demonstrators they were already victims. The next time, they would be on the way to the moors, carrying spades, or circling in a prison yard. Out of respect for them, and defiant toward those who would beat them bloody, I fell in step alongside. The few pedestrians barely looked, already fearful, or self-conscious because of the role they would play tomorrow. Darkness fell. Weak street lanterns dropped circles of pale light on the gloomy street corners, in puddles. Then we moved into the light spilling from the ground-floor windows of a school building. The heads of small children appeared and little hands waved. Nuns fluttered to the window, peered out, and black-sleeved arms hurriedly pulled billowing white drapes. The marchers halted and with one voice burst into song, as though they wanted the children to remember that someone had cried out before Germany died.

Then the marchers dispersed. A man and his wife walked silently alongside me. When our ways parted, they shook hands with me. "Good night," he said, "and good luck, comrade." His voice, unexpectedly resonant and spirited, said that he was ready for the challenge the morrow would bring.

Grenouille, chérie,

No letter for three days. Are you worse? Has the doctor seen you again? Do you have enough to eat? Please write, I'm worrying.

I embrace you with great tenderness.

Your raven

Grenouille,

I've decided that you must come here. To me. You'll get well. I've mailed off some apples. I will send more as soon as you return the wrapping paper and string. And the box, even if it is crushed. I'll glue it. Let me know by return mail whether you want to come. I've already asked some people about rooms. It seems to be difficult, but I'll find something for us, if not in town then in the countryside. We'll have to live modestly, make do on what I have. No raffia work here, or anything else for you to augment our resources. Would you cook for us or would that be too much for you? Do you feel any better? I'm worrying. The truth is that I can no longer do without you. I myself will fall ill from wanting you near me. God, I want it so much. I'm a little scared that for some reason you might say no. You've given me no

*reason for such fears but I'm all nerves. It was stupid to
have waited so long. Waited for what? Waiting, waiting,
waiting! It held me in its clutches. I met a friend in the
street, and what did he say? "Aah, here comes a happy
man!" I wanted to punch him. Six months of waiting, of
frustration, of loneliness, of longing, and he says: "Here
comes a happy man." How callous people are, how
blind. What happiness did he see? There isn't a grain
of happiness in me, only a tremendous sustained effort to
keep myself in hand. But if you come. . . . Did the
thought of it make me look radiant? True, the moment
I made the decision I experienced a deep relief, like
throwing off a crushing burden I carried for too long.
My darling. Answer the minute you get this. Take your
letter to the post office or have somebody take it to
speed it on its way. All the hills of the Dauphiné embrace you tenderly. I want my loving to be what cures
you.*

*Your vain, impatient, and please remember rather
handsome raven*

It seemed to be too late. Events precipitated. Sicily
fell, and the Allies crossed the Strait of Messina. Free
French forces took Corsica. Italy surrendered. The Germans occupied the major Italian cities and made the Italian troops stranded in France prisoners. Surely before
I could get to André he would receive orders for action.
Hadn't he been asked to lie low and wait for precisely
this moment? Still, I hurried down the *montée* to post
my letter.

Everybody was in the street. The invasion was imminent, people said. Someone had learned that the Free
French on Corsica would cross by night and land on our
shore by morning. Everybody had heard that thousands
of British paratroopers had been dropped in the Mari-
time Alps. They were coming, guided by maquisards, to

give cover to the invading troops. I hurried on as though I could run all the way to André. I did not want to hear what the people said, did not want to know that now it was too late.

The main road seemed in motion, everybody was running. I heard shouts: "To the station!" After quickly posting my letter, I followed the crowd. The wide station square was packed with people standing in silence. A long train sat in the small station, crammed with Italian prisoners. Germans with their backs to us lined the platform at convenient shooting distance from the cars. They stood motionless, like statues.

The hot September sun was beating down on the train. The prisoners asked for water, timidly at first, then demanding it, quoting the Geneva convention. The Germans stood as though hewn from stone. The prisoners cried out in outrage, in despair, and finally they pleaded for mercy. But the Germans did not hear, and their unflinching eyes did not see the hands stretch from the train windows.

The townspeople grew restless. Scattered outcries rose but bounced off the Germans' backs. Muttering, the crowd drew together, and then a number of people broke away on the run. The runners returned carrying pails, pitchers, saucepans, and the crowd opened to let them through. A whistle shrilled, a command was barked. Every second German snappily turned about-face and clutched his rifle, ready to bar the people from approaching the train. *"Zurück,"* they shouted. *"Marsch, zurück."*

The Italians, pushing into the windows, cried: *"Acqua! Avete pièta!"*

The people fell back, stood wavering, eyeing the German rifles.

"Acqua! Acqua!"

"Salauds!" The old woman's screech quivered above the sea of angry faces, and the next moment the people forged ahead in a solid mass.

Rifles took aim. *"Zurück! Zurück!"*

"Voyons, copains, allons-y!" A man's white-sleeved arm rose like a battle flag as the people burst forward. They scattered, trying to make it to the train in jack-rabbit runs. The Germans struck out, hitting heads, kicking shins, jamming rifle butts into bellies. They knocked away pails and pots despite tightly gripping hands, and water and coffee spilled in the dust. None-theless, a French canteen here and an enamel pot there made it, and was immediately grabbed. The French were hungry themselves, and fruit was scarce and dear, but in their anger, they forgot how long they had stood in line for it. Peaches and tomatoes came flying from the rear, clearing German helmets, and within seconds the dusty train was dripping with smashed fruit. Prisoners hung out the windows to retrieve some of the precious moisture, and those behind them strained, calling to the French people: *"Compadri! Compadri! La Madonna vi benedicà!"* And the French answered: *"On les aura! On les aura!"*

The line of German soldiers was in total disarray, all of them striking out at pails and pitchers, heads and backs and running legs, screaming: *"Schweinehunde! Sauhuren!"* And they licked lips parched dry by hate, by the hot sun and dust of France, and by their great loneliness.

Grenouille,
I might have an apartment, room and kitchen at a farmhouse, separate entrance. I will know tomorrow.

The farm couple seems somewhat mistrustful. They
wanted to think it over. The house stands amidst fields,
about ten minutes from a small village, four miles from
town. I have my bicycle. Reserve a seat on the first train
possible. If we don't get this place, we'll find another.
Don't delay for any reason! Things are coming to a
head at an incredible speed. You must be with me. I'm
crazy with joy. I can't hide my happiness, and friends
tease me. I don't mind.

 I crush you in my arms,

        Your corbeau

Waves of bomber squadrons passed overhead that
night, and next day all train traffic was suspended. André wired: "Don't delay." After a few days the trains
ran again. Clément rushed to Nice to get a seat reserva-
tion for me. But in the night Royal Air Force planes
bombed the Viaduct d'Anthéor, and trains were again
suspended for a day, even though the BBC announced
that the damage done to the viaduct was negligible.
Clément advised against leaving for fear the RAF might
try a daylight bombing raid to hit the narrow target.
Next morning he took me to the train. The passengers
were restive, wondering whether the train would leave.
The conductor, weary of questions, just shrugged his
shoulders. I could not believe that I would be with André by night. Something would happen, the train would
not leave, the viaduct would be destroyed, or something
else would keep us apart.

The train left late. It rolled out of the station too
slowly, as if uncertain. My traveling companions sat
listening for the sound of distant explosions. Would it
carry that far in daytime? In its uncertain manner, the
train made it to Antibes, to Juan les Pins, to Cannes.
There it stood. It seemed this was as far as it would go.

A man poured me a jigger of Cognac from a hip flask,
nodded encouragingly. People gathered on the station
platform and stared at the train. Passengers called out
asking about the viaduct. No, the viaduct had not been
attacked again. The passengers regained their seats,
waited in silence.

Finally the train set into motion. The people began
to talk, discussed once again the viaduct bombing and
the likelihood of a daytime attack. One man said that it
was practically impossible to hit the narrow viaduct
from the air. And, after scanning the faces, he added
that the *Résistance* should dynamite it. The others gave
no sign of what they thought about that, except for the
man who had given me Cognac. He said that nobody
could get near the viaduct, that the Germans guarded
it from below and from surrounding cliffs. He smiled
at the other man, and their glances interlocked. The
others watched closely this meeting of glances, but their
expressions remained uncommitted.

We reached Saint-Raphaël, pink houses, bougainvillea-
hung stone walls, grape arbors, stone steps, small cafés
dozing in the sun. Everybody pushed into the corridor
to watch the approach to Fréjus, to the viaduct. Everybody scanned the serene sky.

"There it is — the viaduct."

"Can you see any damage?"

"No . . . no, nothing."

The train was creeping. Someone gave me a turn to
look out the window. Deep down below, foaming waves
churned around the red rock. I could not see any Germans. Then we were on the viaduct. The train slowed
down even more, as though tiptoeing. Once we were
across, the train picked up momentum.

At Toulon a plump little woman in a fluffy dress was

taken off the train by *Feldgendarmerie*. Crying and vili-
fying the Germans, she was dragged into the station
building. The train stood. The platform was deserted
except for a *Feldgendarmerie* soldier with chain-draped
chest who guarded the door behind which the woman
had disappeared. Finally the door opened and she reappeared, still sobbing and cursing. They pushed her
into our car, and the train pulled out. The weeping
woman grabbed me by the wrist and dragged me along
to the toilet. There she told me that she was going to a
wedding at Avignon, and not to crease her good dress,
she had lifted the ample skirt and sat on a newspaper.
It seemed she had perspired in the summer heat, and the
newspaper ink had transferred itself to her thighs. Lean-
ing out the window at the viaduct, she had exposed her
printed thighs to the eyes of a German, who had her
taken off the train. Behind that guarded door, they had
forced her to back up against a mirror, skirt lifted, so
they could read what was printed on her backside. And
with German thoroughness they stamped her buttocks
and thighs with: "Passed inspection — German *Feldgendarmerie*."

The small space of the toilet scarcely accommodated
the two of us. Of necessity we stood pressed together,
and I was engulfed by a cloud of Provençal scents —
garlic, thyme, basil, laurel. Once I had succeeded in calming her, she almost made the tiny room burst with her
full-throated Mediterranean laughter. Then she turned
to business. Out of her handbag came a sliver of soap
and a small bottle of cologne, with which I was to wash
off the latest news and the Germans' rubber stamp. Lack
of space would not allow her to bend over, or me to bend
over her. The door had to be opened. A man in the

corridor volunteered to stand guard, and the delicate operation was undertaken and successfully completed. She compensated me with a black market can of sardines and garlic-scented kisses. Exhausted, I went back to my seat and fell asleep, sleepily accepting another kiss at Avignon.

I awakened ravenously hungry and devoured the piece of dry bread that was that day's ration. My friend handed me another jigger of Cognac to wash it down with. "It puts color in your face," he said, and reaching for my hand he added, "Come, let's try the dining car, I'm hungry." His name was Emile Doderet, if that was his name, if it wasn't a nom de guerre, a name borrowed because his own had become hazardous. The poor meal the dining car had to offer and his friendly company helped pass the time to Valence, where I changed trains. Emile Doderet helped me with my suitcase and, shaking hands, said: "The very best of luck." If the words did not say very much, I knew what he meant. Even though we had not confided in each other, we sensed that we were of like mind. Circumstance had sharpened our sense of recognition.

The local train for Grenoble was crowded with workmen, but I found a seat. A young man hoisted my suitcase to the baggage net and pushed it in among black canteens. In less than an hour I would be with André. I couldn't quite grasp it.

The train did not leave on time. Ten minutes passed, fifteen, twenty. . . . A nameless fear crept over me. Just nerves, I told myself, just fatigue, trains are late. The fear grew. The stationmaster on the platform was fiddling with his whistle. He stood there quite dully, looking as though he knew what the delay was about, knew that everything was under control. Just an ordinary delay. Yet that fear dried my throat. I swallowed. It didn't help. I won't get to André.

By the time I was scheduled to arrive, the train was still standing in the Valence station. The conductor came and punched tickets. He answered my question with an unconcerned shrug. The workers looked at me. One asked: "You're not from here?"

"From the *côte,*" I said.

They nodded as if that explained my ignorance, but that was all. Perhaps the delay was usual, a delay that had become schedule. The others looked only bored and tired, resigned. My eyes, wandering over the black canteens, sent unfortunate signals to my stomach.

Darkness fell. The camouflaged ceiling light went on, tinting faces blue. One pair of eyes after the other closed. Perhaps the workers knew that we would not leave at all. Unable to make it home they were allowed to sleep on the train.

My hands hurt. I must have held them tightly clenched for some time. I stuck them into my coat pockets. A cold draft made me shiver. We were moving! We moved out of the station, clattered over switches. Bleak houses glided by, smoke-blackened brick, camouflaged windows. The train rolled to a stop. Then it went on, dawdled along through the lightless night, halted. It surprised me that we had reached the first stop, Romans. Two of the men nodded good-night, got off, two others pushed their canteens into the baggage net and took the seats. The train dawdled on. I peered through the window, but the blackness held only the dimly blue faces of my companions.

Another stop, Saint-Paul. A flock of workers got off, a breath of chill air got on. Five minutes later another stop. This was a real milk train. I could not see any station platform. One of the men pushed the window down, leaned out. Another asked: "Is it them?"

"No," he said. "Unless they're on the other side." He stepped over legs into the corridor. I leaned out of the window to get some fresh air. We were halted among fields. No station platform in sight. The air smelled of coal smoke. The signal ahead of the locomotive was green. Why were we standing? At once I tasted the familiar fear that gives us a head start at moments when freedom and capture might lie in balance. My glance swept down the train, checked for Germans; my mind suggested a dash into the fields, into the thick darkness there. But I saw no Germans, and the train began to move.

It began to rain. Slanted lines of pale blue drops streaked the windowpane. My glance returned to the black canteens. They would be empty.

The rain, heavy now, splattered on the station platform of Saint-Hilaire. Workers getting off covered their heads with their jackets and hurried away into the night. A man with an umbrella ran to the locomotive, seemed to give a message to the engineer. Then he returned on the run to jump on a bicycle, laughing, jiggling the umbrella at us. We were moving again. I pictured André on such a small, rain-drenched station — unless he had given up, for the train was hours late. I did not even know the name of the village near which he had found a room and a kitchen, only the name of the farmers, Ferron.

The locomotive cried out, three short piercing shrieks, and the train came to a grinding stop. At once everybody was on their feet, pushing into the corridor, letting down the windows. And suddenly everybody was talking, joking, laughing. A robust old man with a thick mop of gray hair offered me a spot at the window. *"Venez, mademoiselle,* have a look out there — that's the maquisards from the Vercors. They'll blow up the tracks as soon as we have passed. They do it every night so that the *boche* can't move his stuff during the night. By the time the damage is repaired, it's time to bring us back to the factories."

Out there a group of drenched men was standing in the soggy field, only their legs lit up by the dim light of the lanterns they carried.

"The *boches* delay our train in the hope that the maquisards will give up waiting; or that they will blow up the tracks before we've passed. The *boches* believe that if we get stranded midway, we'll vent our anger on the maquisards. *Hélas,* the *boches* will never learn." I felt a hand expertly passing over my hip, but the old man's guilty smile was disarming. Besides, I did not want to miss the questions called from the train windows to the men outside: "How do you cook your beans up there at Vassieux-en-Vercors?"

"A la croix de Lorraine!" was the answer, and a white hand made the V sign.

"How long to liberation?"

"First minute after doomsday."

"Is it true that you have German prisoners on the Vercors?"

"No, they're voluntary workers."

"Who's your commander up there?"

"De Gaulle, *mon vieux,* de Gaulle."

"What if the *boches* cart us off to Germany?"

"Not a chance, Philippe Bourdet, not a chance. It's we who control the rails."

"How come you know my name?"

"Simple. Each of you is related to one or another of us."

I felt a rush of exhilaration at seeing how unafraid these men were.

The train began to move. The old man pushed to the window shouting: "Say *bonsoir* to Armand Sauvage, *mes garçons!* Armand Sauvage!" And from the figures slipping away a young voice answered: *"Bien sûr, Papa, bien sûr!"*

The man's heavy hand slipped to my shoulder, but this time it was a father's hand wanting to feel a young shoulder like his son's. Down the length of the train people were straining out the windows, making the V sign. Cold raindrops hit my hand. I was flying, free as a bird. And the train was flying, the car careening. The locomotive kept whistling in short, joyous shrieks as if telling the land that all was well, that it was bringing the husbands home. I'm coming, André!

Another stop. I smiled at a wet bench. Men got off laughing, waving good-night, running off to their homes somewhere in the wet darkness.

"Next stop is yours," the man facing me said. He reached for my suitcase and carried it to the exit door. I pressed my face to the windowpane. A switch hut flew by, a crossing gate, then three-story houses with shuttered windows. The train braked, jerked to a halt. I was running toward the lonely figure in Henderson's foul-weather gear. "André!"

"Grenouille!" Our kiss was doused by a splash of water from the brim of his hat. We stood in the pouring rain looking at each other, laughing. His dear face, that fine, mysteriously illuminated face. No man was as movingly beautiful as he.

Outside the train station waited a *gazogène*-driven car

with driver. Sputtering and burping it took us through deserted streets, then down a wet, straight road fenced in by darkness. And saying this and that in anticipation of home, we kept kneading each other's hands.

"This is the village," André said, but before I had turned to look, we were already leaving it, were already on the path to the Ferrons' farm, to that enchanted year that was a farewell gift. But as we were spared the knowledge of how short a time we had, we filled this year with the small tasks of day-to-day living and with the glances and touches of lovers at peace.

We called our part of the Ferron farmhouse "Bear Castle" because the kitchen had much in common with a bear cave. It must have been a larder originally, and then its stone walls were a desirable feature, for it stayed cold even in summer. Lacking windows, it was also dark unless we kept the door open, which we did even in winter when the path was white with snow. The cold outside seemed not worse than the dank cold inside. In one of the kitchen's stony corners sat a quarter-round sink, and above it, way up near the ceiling, there was a narrow, stained-glass window that could not be opened; nor did it let light in. In another dark corner stood a low wood-burning stove that we could light only for cooking our meals, since we had to economize on stove wood. We did our chores wearing coats and wool caps the greater part of the year, and I often wished I could do the dishes wearing mittens. The sink had a drain but no faucet. We had to draw our water at the pump in the barnyard at the far side of the house. When André went to refill the tall tin pitchers, he slipped into a pair of clogs that we kept by the door, for the Ferrons' barnyard was muddy most of the year, and in summer carpeted with horse, cow, and chicken manure. We spent as little time as possible in our cold, bleak kitchen, and when it was time to prepare dinner, André always joined me, not to let me suffer alone. He would take his English grammar to the pine table and brush up on his English, conjugate aloud irregular verbs. When he tired, he fabricated dialogues using English idioms translated word for word into French, and our laughter warmed us.

Outside the kitchen, alongside the path, flowed the Dnieper, a brooklet three feet wide. It proudly accepted the name of the great Russian stream that prominently figured in the news communiqués at the time, a milestone marking the German retreat. I washed our laundry in the Dnieper, mostly with the brook bed's sand, for our monthly soap ration scarcely stretched even for our personal use. In winter, the cold water sometimes made me shed secret tears. André hollered for relief as he took the icy pieces of laundry to the wash line on the run, and hanging them, he would hop from one foot to the other and blow on his hands. But the cold of the Dnieper water was only the cold of winter and could be relieved with a cup of hot tisane, mint or linden blossom, in the warmth of our cozy room. And the warmth of living let us laugh off hardship.

In contrast to the inhospitable kitchen our large upstairs room was sunny and cheerful, and warm even in the worst of winter. Steep stairs led to it through a trapdoor, and when that was shut we felt as if in a world all our own.

The room's two windows were strategically placed. One looked south across the fields and meadows through which the path wound to the village, whose church tower showed above the trees of the Place de l'Eglise. We could see anybody coming from the village as soon as he was alongside the cemetery wall, and by next fall, when Vlassov's troops were let loose on a raping rampage to punish the villages for supporting the Vercors maquis, neighbor Cott's girls and I took turns keeping watch at that window around the clock, ready to run into the hills should they come. However, our village was spared.

The west window, sitting above our kitchen door, allowed us to check on who was coming from the opposite direction, mostly Cott's cow going to her pasture in the morning and returning for milking in the afternoon. However, this window also looked at the hills where the British dropped weapons by night to waiting maquisards.

In our eyes the room was a two-room apartment with bath, even though it lacked partition walls. The corner between the trap door and the Dnieper-side window, holding a small pine table with faience bowl and water pitcher, was the bathroom. To sponge-bathe ourselves limb by limb, we had to leave the trapdoor down or else we ran the danger of stepping into the stair hole. Along the inside wall stood our handsome Empire bed and a fine old chest. The rest of the room was a study and living room. Our two desks faced each other so that each could glance out the south window, and to permit us an occasional exchange of smiles. As pleasing as the furnishings were, the most cherished piece was the ugly, sawdust-burning stove we had had built from two oil drums. It stood in the very center of the room with a plume of black stovepipe fifteen feet long. Filled in the morning, with the sawdust well packed down, it would glow away all day and all night until next morning, leaving not more than a handful of ashes to be cleaned out. The design was of Russian origin, handed on to us by an old Englishman who lived in the village. He also constructed a tobacco slicer that was surreptitiously handed around.

The Dauphiné is tobacco-growing country, but in France tobacco is government controlled and any unlicensed selling of it, in whatever form, is prohibited by law. During the war, government officials went to the tobacco growers in the spring to count the sprouting tobacco leaves, and came harvest time, government eyes watched while the leaves were hung to dry. The day the dried leaves were collected, the farmers were given their share, but for their personal use only. They were as niggardly with their leaves as they were with sharing an egg or a rabbit, and they had the law for an excuse.

One had to give much time and apply much diplomacy to acquire anything outside the official rations. To win a farmer over required many hours courting him, discussing the war, the weather, the *ravitaillement,* fondling his children. Eventually we would come home with an egg one day, with a couple of potatoes another, and few and far between, a scrawny chicken. If the loot was a tobacco leaf, we had to hide it under our clothes to be safe from the gendarme's vigilant eyes. André would go to the old Englishman for the tobacco slicer and bring it home in the uncertain light of dusk. The cumbersome thing had to be artfully wrapped in a coat so that the bundle would not arouse suspicion. No gendarme in his right mind would have believed that it was a sausage slicer, since nobody ever had enough sausage worth slicing. I would nervously peer out the south window until I saw André safe on the field path.

Everybody took pride in their tobacco curing, and among friends we exchanged technical secrets. Some left the soaked and tightly wrapped tobacco leaf in the warmth of a dung heap for three weeks. We used more conservative methods, mostly because we could rarely wait three weeks. Our "tobacco nights" always had a festive air. Transforming a brittle brown leaf into lovely, curling strands of tobacco was an exhilarating process. The presoaked leaf, tightly rolled up, was squeezed into the wooden channel of the slicer, and while thin disk after thin disk peeled from my slicing knife, André pushed against the diminishing leaf with a piece of wood to keep it from going slack. The round tobacco slices we carefully transferred to a sheet of newspaper and then gently tossed them with loving fingers to make the disks fall apart and become brown tobacco curls. Before leaving them to dry we sprinkled them with droplets of thinned honey to make "Lucky Strikes." May the Lucky Strike manufacturers forgive us our presumption, for the truth is that our tobacco was pitch black and poisonously strong, needing a period of adjustment for a smoker not to choke on it.

To have a farmer for landlord gave us little advantage. Louis Ferron's field was the size of an American farmer's kitchen garden. His livestock consisted of one horse, one cow, one sow, some rabbits, and a flock of chickens and guinea hens. And he, like the other farmers, poured out hard luck stories the moment we looked as though we might ask for an egg. The war, it seemed, enervated guinea hens, saddened chickens, felled rabbits; and moping cows refused to give milk. Once in a while, usually on a Sunday, the Ferron cow's spirits lifted and she gave an extra cup of milk. Sometimes, when André made efforts to charm Madame Ferron, the rabbits showed signs of recovery and Madame would sacrifice one for us.

The Ferrons were not used to sharing; they were a

childless couple. They lived for each other, for the cow that gave them milk, for the horse that plowed their field, and for the chickens and rabbits that gave them their meat. And out of fear of having to give of that, they refrained from socializing with their neighbors. Madame Ferron might have chosen differently, as she was a lively, intelligent person, quite bored with her phlegmatic husband. She always welcomed us when we dropped into their kitchen at night. And for the life we brought into their twosome solitude, she compensated us with roasted chestnuts and sometimes with a glass of Monsieur's home-distilled eau-de-vie. She was avid for André's thoughts on the war, while Monsieur preferred not to hear them. To know too much was dangerous. Once our talk went beyond the safe topics of the difficulties of alimentation, or the faraway Russian front, Monsieur would retreat behind clouds of pipe smoke, or leave the kitchen to attend to something in the barn. It was not a great loss, for we had many friends, and especially with Mademoiselle Anne, or with the family of the postmistress, Madame Giraux, we did not have to weigh our words.

Mademoiselle Anne was the authorities' sole representative, since the village was too small to have a *commissariat de police* or a gendarmerie. All it had was the *mairie,* the town hall. Mademoiselle Anne was the mayor's girl Friday, but as he wasn't a man of courage, he preferred to keep aloof from the difficulties and touchy situations of wartime, and so left Mademoiselle Anne in complete charge of *mairie* affairs. He himself stayed at home tending to his flowers, or peeling chestnuts for his wife. Whenever Anne had turned to him at a moment of crisis, he offered her scarcely more than his distress. Finally, Anne decided to spare him such upset.

She was a long, thin bean pole, as flat in front as in back. Above her grave black eyes sat strong black eyebrows, and she wore her straight hair gathered in a modest knot at the nape of her neck. She was very devout. Without fail she attended the six A.M. mass as well as the vesper service, and it was not unusual to see her sitting in a pew at other times of the day.

Lately, however, when going to church, she did not humble herself before God or put before Him her rather minor sins. These she saved for the father confessor, not to go to him empty-handed. She went to church to review in the Lord's presence actions planned by the *Résistance* that demanded her cooperation or active participation. When the fate of France first called on her to make a choice between obeying the decrees of the authority in power or being with the *Résistance,* she had had no doubt where her place was. As she had always been a conscientious public servant, she decided that within the powers of her office, and with God standing by to free her from fear, she would dedicate herself to protecting the men and women within her realm from hunger, capture, and death. Principles of duty and obedience, which had lost their validity with the turn the war took, she set calmly aside. Her conscience at peace, and her heart in God's hands, she applied herself to her tasks of resistance unobtrusively and quietly, as though they were all in a routine day's work.

When I first arrived, I had to go to the *mairie* to be registered. The normal procedure was that such a registration was forwarded to the *préfecture de police* of the *département.* The *préfecture* would then send for my dossier at the *préfecture* whence I had come. But since I was now living on forged identity papers, there would be no file corresponding to my data, and I would be in grave trouble. Even though André assured me that I could trust Mademoiselle Anne, I dreaded going to her. Yet I had to register; my presence was known, and ration cards depended on being registered.

My heart sank as we stepped into the *mairie*. Just the smell of bureaucracy jangled my nerves, and Mademoiselle Anne's austere face was not reassuring. I wished I could run. But her stern eyes upon me, I stammered, giving away my precarious situation. The eyes calmly waited until the truth was out: my papers were forged, I was not who they said I was, I was a refugee. I withheld the information that I was a German refugee, since I could not add that I was Jewish, which would have made my situation perfectly clear to anyone. But being a non-Jewish German refugee brought countless questions to people's minds.

Nodding gravely, and without inquiring who and what I was, Mademoiselle Anne entered my false data on a form and handed back my identity papers. Not a hint on her thin face whether my registration would remain with her, or whether she had to forward it to Grenoble. And I couldn't ask. It never occurred to her that I might doubt her doing what was morally right.

We were to meet Mademoiselle Anne frequently at the Giraux house, where we went almost every evening to listen to the BBC and talk. Or Anne would go with us into the woods on a Sunday to gather mushrooms. Yet she never asked who I really was or of what nationality, nor was that question in her eyes. It seemed not to matter to her. I was one more human being God had put under her protection.

Madame Giraux, Mademoiselle Anne's best friend, was the village postmistress. She was an energetic, down-to-earth woman who kept her soft plumpness neatly

packaged in a laced corset, and who preferred to spend
her spare time in the kitchen rather than going to church.
Their kitchen was blessed. To make up for the lack of
sugar, many local farmers had acquired bees. But when
the bees proved to be troublesome, they turned to gentle
Monsieur Giraux, who was never stung. He cared for
their bees, and they compensated him with farm prod-
ucts. Madame Giraux's eyes always filled with boundless
tenderness when she looked at her husband — whom she
would have defended tooth and nail had the need arisen.

Her tiny post office and her home sat under the same
roof, facing the *mairie,* across the village's main street.
She had only to step in the doorway and whistle to let
Anne know that something of importance had come up.
And since the post office doubled as a *Résistance* drop,
Madame Giraux had firsthand information of the latest
parachute drops, maquis sabotage, and arrests made in
the area. Whenever a casserole needed her attention,
she would drop the bars of the small postal window and
hang up a sign saying "Kitchen." Local people would
have known where to find her, but she did not want a
maquisard unfamiliar with her habits, or the bearer of
a clandestine message, to have to ask around.

One day Madame Giraux handed to a maquisard the
accumulated postal receipts, for the *Résistance,* rather
than the Vichy puppet government, had a just claim to
what belonged to France. While this transaction was
taking place, Anne was out in the street to detain with
friendly chatter anyone headed for the post office. Once
she saw the young man come out and take off on his
bicycle, she entered the post office for the follow-up.
She found her friend "in tears," and Madame Giraux
spent some time moaning and lamenting to allow the
maquisard to make his getaway. Finally she "pulled

herself together" and told Anne of the "assault." Anne
reached for the official telephone and, her voice hys-
terically strident, reported the "assault" to the gendarmerie. By now, she knew, the maquisard and his bicycle had been picked up by a truck that was well on
its way to safety. In due course the gendarmes arrived.
They could not do much except jot down the details of
the "assault," which paralleled other such assaults. And
sipping the glass of eau-de-vie offered them, they tried
to quiet the two "frightened" and "distraught" women,
two public servants whose records were without blemish.

Since the Germans needed men to fill the gaps in the
labor force at home, they ordered a census that would
provide them with information for the selection of "voluntary" workers. Lists were to be prepared in triplicate
registering all men, their present occupation, skills, and
age. It was Mademoiselle Anne's duty to fill out these
census lists for the village. She spread the big sheets
across several large tables in an upstairs room in the
mairie, and henceforth she was seen there, bent over,
filling in long columns. Even at night one could see light
in the window of that room, for she had to work late to
transfer to the duplicate and triplicate sheets the data
she had gathered in the course of the day. Everybody
was witness to her diligence.

The men had no choice but to come and be counted.
Only those registered would receive next month's food
ration tickets, so they looked on helplessly as Anne
entered their particulars. For each man she had a grave
nod and the advice to trust in God. Since they knew how
sincerely she meant that, they kept to themselves their
doubts regarding God's power when He was up against
the Germans.

When the date for the closing of the census approached, many a man wondered whether the time had not come for him to take to the maquis, or at least to sleep elsewhere than at home.

The night following the last day of census taking, Mademoiselle Anne sat up even later than usual. Many had put off coming to the last day, and she was busy filling in duplicate and triplicate sheets.

The village was asleep by the time she finally gathered the lists and arranged them in alphabetical order. Her painstaking handwriting made the sheets look like models of calligraphy. That, too, belonged to the picture of the conscientious clerk, which she had knowingly upheld.

She folded the sheets neatly and stuck them into a large manila envelope, which she addressed to the *préfecture de police* at Grenoble. Had somebody seen the light at the *mairie* and dropped in, he would have seen the bulging envelope addressed and sealed. However, nobody dropped in, and she did not really need such a witness.

She picked up the envelope and gazed at it gravely, for in her hands she held the men of her village and the surrounding farms. The census envelope pressed to her bony chest, she stepped to the window and opened it. First she scanned the dark, deserted street in both directions, then she lifted her eyes to the night sky where God, though invisible to her, was looking down at her and the envelope. She felt that He gave her a nod, even though it was not to seek His approval that she had lifted her eyes. God knew that looking up at the sky was the agreed-upon signal to tell Claire Giraux that she was done and unhampered. In answer, the door across the street opened, and Claire let out the cat.

Anne shut the window, stepped to the big potbellied stove, and stoked the fire until bright tongues of flames shot up. She ripped the envelope open. She deftly tore the census sheets in half and then in quarters before she fed them piece by piece to the lusty fire. With the poker she stirred up the blackened paper, making sure that it was consumed to the last flake.

Meanwhile, across the street, Madame Giraux in nightgown watched the minute hand of her kitchen clock. "Now," she said to herself. She slipped into her robe, and dashed into the post office to call the gendarmerie. Breathlessly, she reported that a truck looking like a maquis truck had pulled up in front of the *mairie,* that dear Anne was up there alone, still working on the census lists. Her voice suddenly rising with agitation, she described what was supposedly taking place just then. "They're coming out! Four of them! They've got rifles! They're getting on the truck! One is holding a large manila envelope! My husband is running after them! There's Anne now, thank God she looks all right! She, too, is running after them, but they're driving off. They're heading for the *route nationale!*"

The gendarme at the other end said that a detachment would be sent out immediately to intercept them; that she should take care of poor Mademoiselle Anne; that they would come by in the morning to take down the particulars for the official report. She hung up. Calmly she called the *mairie* and let it ring once. Across the street the lights were switched off. Anne appeared, a thin shadow crossing the street.

"Done," Anne said.

"Albert has coffee ready."

Had the gendarmes changed their minds and come by

that night, they would have found them as they expected, Monsieur and Madame Giraux comforting Mademoiselle Anne.

One morning we awakened to a surprising quiet and
a great brightness, even though the sky was a morose
gray. Snow! It must have snowed all night; the path to
the village was gone. We dashed downstairs, pulled the
door open, and a high sill of snow remained in the doorway. André reached down, made a snowball, and flung
it at one of Monsieur Cott's apple trees across the
Dnieper. *"Que c'est merveilleux!"* he exclaimed with
chattering teeth. We were still young enough to lick at
fresh snow, to laugh out loud because we felt like it, and
to hop outside in pajamas and war-worn slippers to
build a snowman. Shivering, we hurried upstairs to get
dressed, but first I crawled back into bed, giving André
priority at the washbowl. From my warm loge I watched
his graceful poses as he performed his morning ballet
of sponging himself down, bending this way, bending
that way, lifting one knee, then the other.

He turned and saw me smiling. "A penny for your
thoughts."

I answered with: *"Bonjour, monsieur le corbeau,
comme vous êtes joli, comme vous me semblez
beau . . ."* And he came running to pull the blanket
over my head.

In the barn we found a battered and broken sled,
which the Ferrons let us have. As we needed some nails
to fix it, we snitched them from the barn walls, pulling
them from nonvital places. Then we tested the sled on
the nearest hillside until we were wet and cold and had
to retreat to our sawdust stove. Waiting for our clothes

to dry, we spoke of childhood winters and of Christmas. I described the crisp, brown, succulent Christmas goose that had been a tradition at home, and goose on our mind, we trudged uphill that same day to pay a visit to a mountain farmer whom we had courted for considerable time. It was a long trek and our footprints were the only marks in the fresh snow. However, we could look forward to a sled ride home.

We made a cheerful entry in the farmhouse kitchen. I presented Madame with a colorful, empty cookie tin, and she was delighted beyond expectation. Monsieur looked on, his misgivings written all over his face. While Madame roasted chestnuts, I drew pictures for their little girl, and André let the boy ride on his knee. *"Sur mon cheval-e gris . . . hop, hop, hop, je vais à Paris. Sur mon cheval-e brun . . . hop, hop, hop, je vais à Melun."* As a precautionary measure, Monsieur began to chant the sad song of chickens that fail to lay eggs, and rabbits that mysteriously die. It was as bad a moment as any when we finally mentioned the goose of our dreams. This was worse than what Monsieur had feared. He had to reach for the eau-de-vie bottle. André adroitly softened the tragic moment with war talk, and Monsieur rallied. André spoke of this war's first Christmas, and I moved from there to Christmas at home which, we had implied, was Alsace. When suppertime neared and we were still around, Monsieur faltered. It was a gray goose he brought, and its size made me wonder whether it wasn't half chicken. However, we would have six weeks to fatten it up.

The protesting bird was lifted into our knapsack, but we allowed it to stick out its long neck. However, when André hoisted it to his shoulders, the goose honked and bit him in the ear. Wincing, André laughed off this goosey prank not to cause Monsieur to change his mind.

We had to walk quite a stretch through the snow-lit night before the road turned downhill. The goose was peaceful, now and then softly honking. It seemed to like the gentle rocking. Once we took to the sled, the goose honked louder, with exhilaration it seemed, rather than protest. But the ride was not at all smooth going, and every so often we had to walk another stretch. Finally came a long and speedy run. Our eyes tearing and blinded, we flew downhill, hoping for the best, when the goose, which perhaps had had its fill of blistering wind, stuck its beak down André's collar and, finding it warm there, sunk it down as far as its long neck would go. I heard André yelp. The next moment a load of cold snow pushed into my mouth and another down my back. Since two of the Ferron barn's precious nails now were somewhere in the snowbank, we had to make the rest of the way on foot, I with the goose, André with the sled on his back and carrying one of the runners in his hand. We arrived at the cold Bear Castle kitchen long past suppertime with three stomachs hollowed out by the great outdoors.

The goose was housed in the corner cabinet under the kitchen sink, a space perfect for the bird to put on fat, Madame Ferron instructed us. The cabinet doors were adorned with a circle of drill holes for ventilation. And since these holes were the exact size to accommodate a goose's eye, an eye henceforth stared at us throughout our meals.

Our goose proved to be a sociable bird. When we were in the kitchen it would drum with its beak on the cabinet doors with the power of a pneumatic drill. We wondered what the goose wanted, and by trial and error we discovered what stopped the infernal racket —

reciting poetry. André knew by heart long ballades as well as some monologues from classical drama. I, who had failed to learn my poems in school, knew at best a first line. I tried to substitute prose, but the goose wanted rhythm. I had to improvise, create special goose poetry to have some peace while doing dishes or peeling potatoes.

> *Goose, caboose, kalinkanoose,*
> *Ibi sera kasalari,*
> *Juxta posa albatroose,*
> *Mili cetra aspergasi.*

The goose approved.

When André placed the English grammar under the kitchen's dreary bulb and settled down to evening studies, one cabinet-doorhole, filled with an eye, looked on in breathless expectancy. Forsake, forsook, forsaken; slay, slew, slain; eat, ate, eaten . . . was poetry to our goose.

The idea of fattening up a goose in wartime, which I feared would be regarded as an outrageous extravagance, made French eyes shine. To my surprise we were slapped on the shoulder and encouraged as though we were their favorites competing in the *Tour de France*. Our goose made village news. People we had never spoken to stopped us in the street to give us advice, and cagey farmers who would have pleaded disaster had we asked for a cup of cornmeal for ourselves voluntarily offered a whole jarful for our goose. Fattening a goose, it seemed, belonged to the realm of art, not alimentation.

The instructions we got put a damper on my enthusiasm. Force-feeding sounded as cruel as water torture, and I was ready to let the poor beast remain as scrawny as it was. I would have to stuff cornmeal balls down the goose's throat, force them down by massaging its long neck, keep feeding it even if it gagged. That, no, never! But our goose was no longer a private matter. We were watched.

Neighbor Cott standing by, I prepared for the first time the prescribed ration of cornmeal balls, lining them up on the kitchen table in neat rows. I wished neighbor Cott would leave, he seemed too eager to violate a reluctant goose's throat and to stuff its stomach to the point of vomiting. He helped me get the goose out of its cabinet and put the astonished bird on a chair. While he was showing me how to hold it to have a firm grip on it, the goose saw the balls. Its beak shot forward, grabbed a ball, and with a sensual curving of its neck, the ball went down. And out went the beak for the next ball, and the next, and the next, to the very last, followed by a clatter of its beak and a contented honk-honk. *"Hélas, la guerre,"* said neighbor Cott, patting the goose pityingly. Apparently he informed the neighborhood of the goose's war appetite, for we received more unsolicited donations of cornmeal. We ourselves had a cornmeal supper in addition to generously increasing the goose's ration. The goose never put me in the position of having to force-feed it. It eagerly hopped on its chair and gobbled down any amount of cornmeal balls I offered it.

We grew very fond of our goose. Unprotestingly we accepted its pneumatic-drill drummings and hurried to give it its poetry. Nor did we mind eating our own meals under the beady stare filling one of the cabinet-door holes.

However, the goose's days were numbered. One crisp

December morning it waddled behind us to the barn, honking happily, then honking haughtily at Monsieur Ferron, who was to twist its neck in our behalf.

For a last time we stroked our goose's head. It responded with an affectionate honk and a flutter of wings, which we interpreted as a last request for a few lines of poetry. Disregarding the cynical Monsieur Ferron, André gave it the best he had:

> *If music be the food of love, play on!*
> *Give me excess of it, that, surfeiting,*
> *The appetite may sicken, and so die.*
> *That strain again! It had a dying fall;*
> *O, it came over my ear like the sweet sound*
> *That breathes upon a bank of violets,*
> *Stealing and giving odour! Enough! no more!*
> *'Tis not so sweet now as it was before.*

"*Bon Dieu!* What's that?" cried Monsieur Ferron.

"Shakespeare," André said dryly. "*Twelfth Night, Scene 1.*"

"What?"

André took me by the hand. Even though smirking, Monsieur Ferron kept his promise to wait with the killing until we were out of sight.

The plucked bird, hanging from its yellow feet, swaying in the frosty air, was startlingly scrawny. But if its chest looked like that of a consumptive, the orange beak held a peaceful grin, as if the goose's last vision had been rows and rows of cornmeal balls neatly lined up on the kitchen table.

It took time for us to adjust to the eyeless holes of the sink cabinet doors, to peeling potatoes without reciting, to homecomings that failed to explode with joy-

ous drummings. Goose, caboose, kalinkanoose . . . it
hadn't even been succulent.

The Germans offered some distraction. They had
made only very rare appearances, except for an occasional staff car speeding through the treacherous maquis-
controlled countryside as though the devil were after it.
They had preferred to show their muscle in Grenoble,
where they had the upper hand, but now they came to do
some quick killing also in our town, blew in, machine-
gunned, and were off again.

People moved about guardedly, and we stayed away
from town, waiting to see whether more of the same was
coming. Then we heard that great amounts of fresh
cauliflower were offered at the market square, and that
was too tempting. We mounted our bicycle and rode to
town. While I lined up at the market, André went to
gather news. There was such a wealth of cauliflower
that I was given two without argument. And with a
snow-white cauliflower under each arm I went to rejoin
him. I was on the narrow main street when suddenly
the crowd there dispersed like fall leaves blown into
doorways by a freak gust. I stared at four Germans,
whose leveled weapons seemed to be pointing straight
at me. Two others, walking backwards, covered their
rear. Somebody grabbed my arm and pulled me into a
doorway. "Upstairs, quickly," the man said. At the
next landing he knocked at a door. A woman opened.
"Monsieur?"

"Les boches," he said, and she let us in. We watched
the Germans through her shuttered window. They
looked frightened. Their rifles moved with their glances
from one side of the street to the other, and up the
housefronts. They acted as if they were the attacked
rather than the attackers. It puzzled us. The whole

town seemed to hold its breath, and the Germans' foot-fall sounded very loud in the eerie silence. Then they halted, and the four who had been in the lead moving backwards, they returned whence they came. At once people trickled from doorways, gathered in groups, pointed down the street.

I took my cauliflowers and went to look for André. I found him in front of his little café. He said a freight train loaded with sugar and flour for Germany had been halted in the station by red signals. When the signal did not change, the German soldiers guarding the train had gone to look for the stationmaster, but they found the station deserted, the telephone dead. They ventured into town to confront the invisible foe but found only deserted streets and a deadly silence. Suspecting a trap, they slunk back to the train. There they took up positions on top of the boxcars, their weapons aimed in all directions.

Surely they expected that Grenoble would wonder where the train was and, finding the telephone dead, would come to their rescue. But by the time night fell, they were still sitting on their perches.

Come morning the train was still there, but its guards were gone. Rumor had it that the maquis had captured them in the course of the night. Then the train was seen leaving, not in the direction of Grenoble but back toward Valence. And the man in the caboose was a Frenchman.

When we went to town to hear the latest, people said the train had never even reached Saint-Hilaire. But how could the maquisards have taken a whole train off the tracks and made it disappear?

One day later, our village store distributed an extra ration of sugar and flour, courtesy of the Vercors maquis.

Early one January day German infantry was seen leaving Grenoble. People living along the road watched to determine which route they were taking and alerted the villages farther down the road. An hour later the entire Isère valley knew that the Germans were headed for the Vercors. Germans and maquisards clashed. Then the maquisards vanished in the dense, almost impenetrable brush of the Vercors, into its caves and gorges. The Germans burned down the hamlet of Baraques-en-Vercors, picked up their dead and wounded, and marched back to Grenoble.

Icicles were dripping away. André and I were sitting on top of our dwindling woodpile outside the kitchen, our faces lifted toward the sun. Its warmth seeped into our sweaters. André mumbled: "Just like St. Moritz."

Civilian males had to guard the railway tracks at night against sabotage. Armed with broomsticks, each man had to walk back and forth along his hundred feet of track, and before retracing his steps he had to make contact with the next man. Still, night after night the tracks were dynamited somewhere, and guards were found lying lined up on the embankment, their hands tied, but supplied with wine or eau-de-vie to keep them warm. The guards were given whistles but still they were found "overpowered."

André, too, had to take his turn. He always strapped the feather comforter to the baggage carrier. He wanted to be comfortable, in case. He also took along a deck of cards and a chunk or two of firewood, his contribution to the little stove in the switchman's hut.

In the morning, I would watch the field path, fearful

that the inspectors had finally gotten wise to the deception of bound hands, or had found the guards in the hut playing belote.

In March and then again in April, the Germans made attempts to penetrate the Vercors. They arrived in greater force, but the maquisards had planted explosives under bridges and at tunnel exits. And German tanks were ineffective, for they could not maneuver on the narrow roads hewn into the rock, with a cliff a hundred feet high at the one side and a drop as steep at the other. Once again the Germans moved back to Grenoble.

Much more frequently now came the small British plane that dropped weapons to one or another hill pasture at night. It even came several nights in a row.

The Vercors mountains, with their tremendous cliffs and deep ravines, were too rugged for safe drops. Precious canisters would have fallen to inaccessible spots and would have had to remain there, irretrievable. Therefore, drops were made in the gentler hills of the Isère valley, onto one or another heath staked out with flares by the maquisards. They would take the precious gifts to Vercors headquarters by truck, sometimes with gendarmes in hot pursuit. But in time it was to be no longer clear whether the pursuit was in earnest or was a sham. The gendarmes had had time to think, and as the number of maquisards in the Vercors grew to four thousand, even gendarmes had younger brothers up there, or cousins, or childhood friends. One night a number of arms canisters were dropped by mistake to a field in the valley and picked up by gendarmes. But then we heard that they had handed the canisters over to the

maquisards. To cover themselves, they had the maquisards stage a "surprise attack" on the gendarmerie late
at night.

Today I am scarcely awakened by a sound as faint as
the hum of a small Lysander plane. Then we were, perhaps because our hearts were listening for it. It was a
sound so faint at first that we often thought our anxious-
ness had fooled us, or that it had been the far-off barking of a dog. We would sit up and strain our ears, and,
sure enough, suddenly we would hear it, faintly, like
the hum of an insect. At once we would be at the window, searching the night. We tried to guess from the
lonesome drone which field the plane was circling, and
we searched the dark hills for a glimmer of flares. We
never saw any. Patches of forest shielded them. But
listening to the plane's melody, we learned to know what
it was doing, whether it was still looking for the flare-
fringed heath or whether it had found it and was going
into the low overflight for the drop. We certainly knew
when this was accomplished, for as though with a cry of
relief, the plane would give all it had to regain altitude
quickly. And we would strain out the window, make the
victory sign toward the invisible plane until its fading
drone assured us that it was safely off.

One such small plane mistakenly circled our meadows,
came down so low that it buzzed our roof with a thundering roar. André grabbed an armful of sheets and
towels, ran outside, and hastily laid out a big NO on
Ferron's field. The plane came again, terribly low and
straight at André, who madly pointed toward the hills
that were the usual drop zone. The pilot understood.
With a last roaring dip of thank you, he swerved off,
and soon the familiar tune told us that he had finally
found his target.

The Germans were nervous that spring, resorting to greater terror and harsher reprisals. Yet railroad tracks were blown up as before, locomotives broke down, essential tools were misplaced in factories, information was forwarded to London, and the maquis kidnapped the gendarmes. The newspaper said the maquis surprised the gendarmes asleep in their barracks. The grapevine said the shooting had been a farce to make it look as if the gendarmes had put up resistance. It had been done to protect their families against reprisal. We happened to spend that night in town, staying with friends, and the column of tarpaulin-covered maquis trucks passed right under our windows. But the darkness in the narrow street made it impossible to see whose trucks they were and we took them for German. Shooting started, but down in the street a man began to sing a French lullaby, calmly, soothingly. And when the trucks returned, that shadowy man was picked up. Words were exchanged which, even though indistinguishable to us, had a French ring to them.

It was a dangerous spring. People moved about with great caution, on guard against German traps. But it was spring nonetheless, and neighbor Cott seeded his field, moving along the brown furrows with a measured, dancelike step, dipping into the bulging apron that he held gathered, and scattering the seed with a wide, generous movement of the arm.

May came. André and I went into the blooming meadows and painted water colors of the hills with their veil of first green — the last spring green André was to see.

June came. The Dauphiné was at its sweetest. Nights were balmy, and we would linger in the open window long after the Lysander had left.

June 6. Dewy grass and a silken sky. "Today is Martha's birthday," I said. André smiled, buttoned his shirt, brushed his hair, turned on our antediluvian radio. The usual crackle and screeches, then a voice: "We repeat . . . This morning at daybreak Allied forces landed on Normandy beachheads . . ." Joy tore through us like a sharp pain, bringing tears. André frantically turned knobs to catch the phrases that wilted and faded out. Over and over we listened to whatever words we caught of the repeated bulletin: "This morning at daybreak Allied forces landed . . . Allied forces landed . . ." All the waiting through endless years, all the hope, all the absurd rumors found their justification in this grave voice announcing: "Allied forces landed . . ." No matter which station we tuned in, it was the same: "Allied forces landed . . ." We got an underground transmitter that shouted: "The Allies have come!"

Madame Ferron sailed into our arms. Monsieur remained cautiously calm. We bicycled to the jubilant village, laughed and wept with friends, embraced strangers. Madame Giraux's closed postal window held a sign saying "Invasion." The Giraux kitchen was crowded with people listening insatiably to the forever-repeated communiqué. And Mademoiselle Anne went to church to thank God on behalf of everybody.

In the course of the day the communiqués changed, reporting bitter fighting, heavy casualties. Until late that night, long past curfew, we sat around the Giraux radio, listening in silence, praying for the men on the flaming beaches.

A couple of days later we rode to the village, both on the same bicycle for a last time. We stopped at the post office. Madame Giraux dropped the bars of the postal window to press André to her heart. And at the *mairie,* Mademoiselle Anne blessed him.

The way to the *route nationale* we made on foot, walking slowly, André guiding the bicycle with one hand. The sky was blue, the fields were in bloom, and the tremendous cliffs of the Vercors, rising from the Isère valley, were bathed in sun. It seemed the land knew that liberation was close at hand.

On a day as clear as this, one could see the lighter patches of high heath, and I thought how easy it would be to imagine André walking there. He would not be so far, not unreachable, as he would have been had he gone to England.

But when we reached the main road and turned to each other, I knew with a sharp, irrefutable clarity that of all the last good-byes, this was the final one. He gave me a puzzled look and took me in his arms. "But the war is over, Grenouille! The Nazis are finished."

I must not waste precious seconds, seconds that had to take the place of an entire life. I needed them to engrave the beloved face in my heart, his radiant, finely chiseled face with its volatile lines of sadness.

A last hug. André mounted the bicycle. Exuberantly, he shouted to the fields: *"Nous les aurons!"* and he took off to his death.

He glanced over his shoulder again and again, waved. His arm stretching high, he jiggled his hand. He tilted his head back, and I knew he was laughing with the joy of life.

He moved away farther and farther, waving once again. Then he kept his eyes on the Vercors mountains.

A messenger brought me a letter.

Darling Grenouille,

I wish you were here. It is much more exciting than I ever dreamed it would be. I'm with the same kind of people I used to be with at Dunkirk, have the same job. They are eight. I have a room of my own in a house and am very comfortable. The farmers are magnificent. They give us all they can spare and then some. I'm very, very busy, very exhilarated. I hope to see you soon for a visit.

Loving embraces,
Your raven

July 14 — In the morning forty-eight American bombers accompanied by fighter planes filled the sky above the Vercors. In their first overflight they put the French flag in the air: a thousand parachutes, blue, white and red. During subsequent flights more and more of such colored parachutes opened, thousands of them, bringing rifles and ammunition for the maquis. But barely had the Allied planes turned homeward when German bombers and Messerschmitts appeared. We were all out on the village street, watching. We heard the detonations. Flags of smoke rose from the mountains and were dispersed by the wind. Finally the planes flew off. One Messerschmitt came our way. We stood looking at it, when suddenly it dived, nosing straight for us. The next moment it roared overhead, spitting fire. The string of bullets hitting the roofs alongside sounded like the clatter of running feet. It happened so fast that nobody ducked. We stood gaping. Then the plane was gone. Someone said: *"Ça alors . . ."*

July 15

My meadow frog,
I wished I could have been with you for your birth-

day, but I'm sure you saw all the planes that came to say
"Happy birthday, Grenouille." Of course, then the
others came, and they kept us busy all day. One village
burned the whole night. Remember when we used to
jump out of bed for our little plane? The last three
nights I watched that close up, got to bed only by 4 A.M.
It is unbelievably exciting. I've received your letters.
Please be so good and make a package of the following:
my riding breeches; my boot brush; one pair of shoe
trees. Give the parcel to Madame G. It will be picked
up. Do you have enough money? I'm thinking of you
and our bear cave. I embrace you strongly. Happy
birthday!

Your raven

I went to see a doctor. He thought I might be preg-
nant but he would have to wait for the results of a
laboratory test.

July 17

Grenouille,
   All is well. I'm a genuine mountain bear. I am glad to
hear that you are in good spirits. Maybe I'll be able to
see you soon. Everything is terribly exciting. Give my
thanks to our good friends G. Tell them the eau-de-vie
is excellent. I embrace you,

A.

July 19

My grand Grenouille,
   I'm on my bed resting, as I was once again up until
4 A.M. I've received your letters and am glad that all is
well. Please send me a cigarette-rolling gadget, I've lost
mine. Thanks, my Grenouille. What I'm doing was
worth all the waiting. Have you finished your story? Do
you see our friends? Have you been out painting? I'm

laughing at myself for having taken my box of water colors along. The very thought that I might have one minute to spare! I wish I had your camera. We'll see later. I'm trying to come down for forty-eight hours. I want to embrace you. The maps we bought are on the walls of my room.

Soon more,
A.

The laboratory report was positive. I was so happy, I embraced the doctor and sang all the way home. But when I entered our Bear Castle, a cold hand touched me: I was given this child because André would be killed.

I pushed the thought from me. It was stupid. Why should something so terrible happen now? Should I tell André in a letter? Or wait until he came?

I took my note to Madame Giraux for forwarding.

Early next morning, the Germans moved two divisions out of Grenoble for their final assault on the Vercors. Tanks crawled up the mountain roads. Germans with mountaineering equipment climbed the sheer cliffs. The maquisards blasted roads, tunnels, made bridges tumble into ravines and gorges, but it was two divisions armed to the teeth against four thousand maquisards armed with hand grenades and rifles. The Vercors command asked the Allies for airborne support.

On the morning of July 21, the maquisards heard the drone of planes above the low-hanging clouds, and maquisards as well as civilians streamed to the newly cleared airstrip at Vassieux-en-Vercors. Laughing and shouting they pointed at shadows showing between the drifting clouds. The first planes zoomed down. The people shielded their faces against the prop wash and then froze, unbelieving. The soldiers pouring from planes and gliders were German *Waffen* SS.

Even though the Germans strung a tight cordon around the Vercors mountains, news of the massacre came through with the very few who managed to escape. Others who had tried were fished out of the Isère River riddled with bullets. One who made it came to the Bear Castle to bring me a verbal message from André: "I'm all right. One of these days soon I'll be with you." The young man said that André went down to the valley at the far side of the mountain; that it would be some time before he could safely come.

In the meantime, Americans had landed on the Côte d'Azur. Breathlessly we listened to the communiqués of their advance up the Rhone valley. The communiqués were guarded, hinted at difficulties, strong German resistance. Rumors were rampant and, contrary to the official reports, word of mouth had it that the Americans were coming up the Route Napoleon, cleared for them by maquisards, and might reach us any day.

The towns and villages in the Dauphiné changed hands from one hour to the next, were liberated by *Résistance* forces, then recaptured by the Germans. Small open trucks with ragged young men who rode standing sped through town. The men carried rifles and on their sleeves they wore makeshift FFI armbands, French Forces of the Interior. On occasion they stopped at a café, poured down a glass of wine, and were off again to rescue another town in flames. Daily I went to town, always hoping to get a glimpse of André in one of these trucks.

One day news hit the town that the Americans were

just a few miles away. Within minutes every house was flagged, and the streets were black with people waiting for the liberators. A group of maquisards from a region far south of us rode into town, looked at the flags in amazement, and took off again. Five minutes later an FFI truck raced down the main street, the men shouting that the Germans were coming. The people disappeared, the flags came down, and window shutters closed. But neither Germans nor Americans came that day.

August 22d. I was resting when I heard Madame Ferron outside shouting and clapping her hands. The piglets had escaped. They were running around in the field, Madame Ferron after them. Her efforts to shoo the fast and cunning piglets back to the barn were quite futile. Nor did my help bring any results. While I was running about, luring and shooing, I heard a distant hum like that of passing planes. I vaguely wondered why the sound neither increased nor faded, but I was too preoccupied to make deductions. Then, all of a sudden, it struck me that the sound was coming from the *route nationale,* that in the hum there was a rattle and a clatter, that it was not planes, but vehicles. The Americans!

The realization left me literally speechless. I waved to Madame Ferron, but she took it to be part of the chase. My legs still functioned. I ran to the house, grabbed the bicycle friends had lent me, and pedaled down the field path for all I was worth.

The village was as lifeless as if disaster had struck it. Doors stood open. Not even a dog was in sight. The hum was now a distinct rumble and clanking. I rode on. I was so excited my hands trembled and my feet slipped off the pedals. The stretch to the highway seemed endless.

Then I saw it. It looked like a huge, ponderously moving snake. Sherman tanks as big as houses, bumper to bumper with carrier trucks, cannons, jeeps . . . a huge dust-gray snake creeping with an infernal clanking and roar. Then I was one among the people shouting, waving, weeping, touching hands hanging down the sides of the trucks, American hands. The hands were limp from shaking French hands for countless miles, from Saint-Tropez to Draguignan, to Pertuis, to Forcalquier, to Sisteron, to Veynes, to Die, to Saint-Lattier, and still more hands, an unending line, and more to come before they got to Grenoble. The GIs' hands could no longer clasp, nor the arms reach, but they were there to be clutched, pressed, held for a moment.

Someone called out: *"Voyez donc leur dents magnifiques!"* And all eyes, wide with awe, focused on the rows of perfect white teeth passing by like an everlasting advertisement for toothpaste.

Forever anew the crowd surged against the trucks. *"Vive l'Amérique!"* And no end in sight to the tanks, the jeeps, the guns. GIs, smiles fixed on their faces from having to smile for too many miles, just nodded to the unending line of Frenchmen. And from all the different vehicles rained the liberators' riches: cigarettes and instant coffee and egg powder and Spam and toilet paper and O'Henrys and Hershey bars and crackers and toothpaste and sugar.

A soldier jumped from a truck, ran into the crowd, hugged an old woman, saying: "Hello, Ma." And the crowd, roaring with delight, lifted him off his feet and carried him back to his truck, lifted him to the hands of his buddies.

304 A PRIVATE TREASON

The convoy had been passing for hours and still it came, on and on. Our own hands grew limp, but with new zest we forged against the vehicles to touch one more American hand, to say "hello." And weary soldiers found still another box of K rations, a can of Spam, another handful of cigarettes.

"Vive l'Amérique! Victoire! Liberté!"

"Yes," GIs nodded, "yes," smiling the longest smile of their life.

Had a soldier asked for tomatoes? Baskets full arrived and tomatoes were handed to eagerly reaching hands, to jeeps, to command cars. Tomatoes were skillfully aimed at the tiny windows high up on the huge tanks. One splashed all over the face of a man, and thanking the people with a wide grin, he licked off what his tongue could reach.

Daylight began to fade. An officer standing in a jeep called to the people to step back, that the convoy would pick up speed now. The crowd moved back into the field shouting. *"Victoire! Vive l'Amérique!"*

Once the convoy started to go faster, the rattle and clatter of steel drowned our shouts. Night fell and the deep darkness of war obliterated white teeth and GI hands.

We began to sing. Against the deafening noise of tank treads rose our *". . . le jour de gloire est arrivé . . ."* When we reached the last line of the anthem, we started all over again so that the Americans, who could no longer see us, would know that we were still there. As the night wore on, and the convoy was still passing, the older people took the very young home. The rest of us, huddled together against the chill of the late-summer haze, kept on singing. We sang "Sonny Boy," and "It's a Long Long Way to Tipperary," and again and again "La Marseillaise." We stayed in the field all night, so that with the first light of morning *les Américains* would find us at their side. I wished André were with me. But the Germans were still between this field and the valley where I believed him to be.

For the next few days American soldiers were all over town, trading cigarettes and Hershey bars for fresh French bread and tomatoes. Everybody knew Curly, a tall young Texan, who had enlisted the entire town to find him a wife. Every morning I went to town hoping that one of the FFI trucks would bring André.

I picked up the bicycle at André's café and set out for home. The sinking sun's glow was tinting the fields, even the granite-paved *route nationale*.

André will come. The message had said "I'm all right."

One night I will wake up and dash to the window, and there he will be, coming down the path.

Jean Giraux saw me and waved at me to stop. "Ma wants you to drop by," he said.

I found a maquisard with Madame and Monsieur Giraux. They asked me to sit down and reached for another glass. The man said he was from the Vercors. He said he had been with André. In a group of eight they had made their way down. Just short of reaching the village of Sassenage, their goal, he himself had left the group to look in on relatives who had a farm nearby.

He said that from the wooded hillside he was climbing, he had seen the others continue down a path. Ahead was a small bridge, and beyond it the roofs of Sassenage. He saw them suddenly stop and reach for their rifles, but already he heard the machine gun and saw the

German by the bridge. None of them fell into German hands alive. They were spared that, he said.

I felt a hand on my shoulder, but I was alone in a vast, dark landscape. The darkness was strange, not the darkness of night. It allowed me to see far, but everything, near or far, was shadowy. Before me lay a wide black river, and from the distant shore came the sound of faint voices — my friends, I knew, but I could not understand what they were calling. The river grew darker and darker and finally dissolved in the darkness of the endless landscape. The voices were gone, leaving me in a stillness bare of any sound. I was running this way and that searching for André, straining not to miss his weak voice. But the dead stillness held no voice, and the vast darkness where trees and hills had seemed to be before was now endless, flat, empty ground.

I was sitting in the stillness of our room, cutting up André's fine woolen undershirts to make little clothes for our child. Above in the attic mice were rolling nuts and corncobs. Fall leaves whispered outside, and walnuts dropped to the path with a hard thud.

I was not alone. André was in the breath of our room.

I would awaken at night and see him standing by the stove in his light whipcord breeches and gray tweed jacket. Then he would fade out against the window overlooking the Dnieper.

Some nights I found myself on the path with André. We would walk a piece of the way together until he turned his sad, still face to me and I knew that now we had to part.

I would wake up in my bed, feeling strangely certain that, indeed, I had been on the path a moment ago.

A quarter of a century has passed since. Our son is a man. And that hope-filled war is history now. Other wars have followed.

Another man has walked by my side, another hand's touch was dear to me, and together we watched our son and André's grow up, watched with fear in our hearts, for a war was waiting for them, Vietnam. They were spared, but a hundred thousand other sons were not. And now, when I watch my two small grandsons at play on a New England hillside, I look beyond the years, wondering for whose "honor," for whose thirst for power they will be asked to give their lives away.

Looking at their faces asleep among Smokey Bears, rabbits and pandas, I wonder what their fate will be, no longer threatened only by war after war but by dead soil and poisoned water. Will they know heretofore unknown want and suffering? Rock their children to death with tales of past meadows? Or might they be the new man passing over the threshold of a new world? At moments, such a world seems to be moving closer with no less dizzying speed than catastrophe. What we are doing is long obsolete, no longer works, is ridiculous. Not only the young, even I, who was born into the old world, can see that. Surely, here will be a world in which nations live in peace to cherish and tend man's Earth. But Mankind will scarcely bring about the change because it has matured. It will because it has to.

I tiptoe from the children's room, go outside to the

lawn, and move away from the windows' shine into deeper darkness. I sit down on a rock. Stillness falls like a blessed rain. Behind me, the forest stands black and mighty. Foliage is whispering. The air has a spicy smell. The little lights of man, one here, one there, on a hill across the valley, speak softly.

I look up into the sky, at thousands of stars crowding. I look for Mars, whose landscapes we now know.

The vast night weighs lightly on my shoulders, replenishes me as though it were God's consoling hand.